Critical praise for this book

'The impacts of colonisation on indigenous peoples are often considered in an historical context. In contrast, this book provides sound evidence of the consequences that international forces can have in contemporary times. Makere Stewart-Harawira has undertaken a thorough and scholarly examination of indigeneity in a global environment and has made a valuable and major contribution to the indigenous literature.' – Professor Mason Durie, Assistant Vice-Chancellor (Maori), Massey University, New Zealand

'This book is a timely and welcome addition to the critical literature emerging as a response to globalization. It is an impressive piece of work – huge in scope, intellectually challenging and ambitious in its aims.' – Professor Michael Peters, Research Professor of Education, University of Glasgow, Scotland

'In this timely and important book, Stewart-Harawira provides a wide-ranging critique of globalization from an interdisciplinary perspective. But this is not all. This book also develops a sophisticated analysis of the impact of globalization on indigenous peoples, and more radically, what indigenous epistemological perspectives can offer in return to the theories and practices of globalization.' – Professor Stephen May, University of Waikato, New Zealand

'This is a magnificent work.' – Professor Carl Urion, Emeritus Professor of Anthropology, University of Alberta, Canada

'Given the global impact of neoliberalism on indigenous cultures, and on those cultures in all parts of the globe who lack power and resources, it is important to understand what effects such policies have, and what strategies of resistance are possible. This book enables such an understanding. It is at once both an in-depth investigation into the processes of globalization, and an assessment of the effects on indigenous peoples. Utilizing Hardt and Negri's important concept of a "return to empire", Stewart-Harawira traces the rise of a new bio-power of surveillance and control in the interests of global domination. This book is essential reading for those wanting an introduction to a complex area of study, and for specialists as well.' – Professor Mark Olssen, Department of Political, International and Policy Studies, University of Surrey

'This is an outstanding contribution to the debate on globalization, knowledge and societies. Stewart-Harawira's grasp of the complex changes taking place which affect indigenous peoples today is second to none. This kind of critical analysis provides a basis for informed social action.' – Professor Susan Robertson, University of Bristol, UK, Editor of *Globalisation, Societies and Education*

About this book

Developed during a time of dramatic global upheavals and transformations, *The New Imperial Order* is concerned with the political economy of world order and the ontologies of being upon which the emergent global order is predicated. Positioned from a Maori perspective and contextualized within the international political and juridical framework, this book examines the political and juridical ontologies that shaped the development of international law and the world order of nation states. In engaging with these issues across macro and micro levels, the book identifies the nation state and new forms of regionalism as sites for the reshaping of the global politico/economic order and the re-emergence of Empire. Stewart-Harawira also tracks the role of education and the reconstruction of sovereign indigenous nations into dependent populations in the development of world order, and the profound impact of indigenous peoples' proactive global and local responses in the reshaping of international law.

In this work, the problematics of globalization are made visible through the privatization of services, the restructuring and commodification of knowledge and the creation of new categories of the dispossessed. Overarching these issues is a new form of global domination in which the connecting roles of militarism and the economy, and the increase in technologies of surveillance and control have acquired overt significance. In the first chapter of the book, the author identifies ontological and cosmological principles that are shared by many indigenous peoples as key signifiers of an alternative framework for socio/politico/economic order. In the final chapter she draws these principles together within the context of the fragmentation and integration which characterize the globalizing process, and proffers them as central to the revisioning of a transformed global order.

About the author

Makere Stewart-Harawira is an Assistant Professor in Educational Policy Studies at the University of Alberta where she teaches in the Indigenous Peoples Graduate Education programme. She previously taught in the School of Education at the University of Auckland and in the Graduate Programme of Te Whare Wananga o Awanuiarangi, a Maori tribal university in Whakatane, New Zealand. Makere's current research interests are indigenous ontologies, global citizenship, and new formations of global governance. Makere is of Maori and Scots descent. Her tribal affiliation is Waitaha.

The New Imperial Order

Indigenous Responses to Globalization

Makere Stewart-Harawira

Zed Books
LONDON & NEW YORK

Huia Publishers
WELLINGTON

The New Imperial Order: Indigenous Responses to Globalization
was first published in 2005

in New Zealand and Australia by
Huia Publishers, POB 17335, Karori, Wellington, Aotearoa-New Zealand

www.huia.co.nz

and in the rest of the world by
Zed Books Ltd, 7 Cynthia Street, London N1 9JF, UK and
Room 400, 175 Fifth Avenue, New York, NY 10010, USA

www.zedbooks.co.uk

Cover designed by Andrew Corbett
Set in 11/12½ pt Bembo
by Long House, Cumbria, UK
Printed and bound in Malta by Gutenberg Ltd

Distributed exclusively in the USA by Palgrave Macmillan, a division of
St Martin's Press, LLC, 175 Fifth Avenue, New York, NY 10010

A catalogue record for this book
is available from the British Library

US Cataloging-in-Publication Data
is available from the Library of Congress

ISBN: Aotearoa-New Zealand
1 86969 160 1 Pb

ISBN: rest of the world
1 84277 528 6 Hb
1 84277 529 4 Pb

CONTENTS

✹

ACKNOWLEDGEMENTS

❈

There are many to be thanked for their contribution to the writing of this book. In the first instance, Nga Pae o Te Maramatanga, of the University of Auckland Centre of Research Excellence, for financial support through a fellowship that enabled the work to be completed. Particular thanks go to my doctoral supervisors Professors Michael Peters and Graham Smith for their ongoing encouragement, to the students of Te Whare Wananga o Awanuiarangi, to my colleagues at the University of Auckland and Te Whare Wananga o Awanuiarangi and others who gave important assistance. For his patient reading and helpful comments, I thank Professor Stephen May as well as my special friend and colleague Dr Maxine Stephenson, whose generosity, as well as her dedication to her students, has always been outstanding. Particular thanks also go to Walter McIntosh whose valuable support included editing, web searches, and fact checking. The work of eco-philosopher Dr Henryk Skolimowski had a profound impact on my thinking and I thank him for his generosity in sharing it with me. Most importantly, this book would never have made it to publication without the patience and support of my editor, Anna Hardman of Zed Books, to whom I owe an immense debt of gratitude.

I will be forever grateful to my friend, teacher and mentor Errol Cheal and my dear friend Patricia O'Connor for their unconditional love and support. To my long-suffering extended family and especially to my sisters Robin and Kathryn, my family Bill and Laurrell, Tracey, Carl, Daryn and Deirdre, Shahna, and Liam, and my precious grandchildren Mark, Tessa, Isis, Nathan and Kate – my love and my thanks – for absolutely everything.

For Billy, Tracey, Carl, Daryn, Shahna and Liam

Abbreviations

AIDS	Auto-Immune Deficiency Syndrome
APEC	Asia–Pacific Economic Cooperation
CBD	Convention on Biological Diversity
CDI	Centre for Defence Information
CFR	Council for Foreign Relations
CHR	Commission on Human Rights
CIA	Central Intelligence Agency
DSU	dispute settlement system
GATS	General Agreement on Trade in Services
GATT	General Agreement on Tariffs and Trade
GNP	gross national product
HTVL	Human T-cell lymphoma virus
HUGO	Human Genome Organization
IBRD	International Bank for Reconstruction and Development
ICCPR	International Covenant on Civil and Political Rights
ICESCR	International Covenant on Economic, Social and Cultural Rights
ICJ	International Court of Justice
ILO	International Labour Organization
IPR	intellectual property right
ITO	International Trade Organization
KWNS	Keynesian welfare national states
LOTIS	Liberalization of Trade in Services
MAI	Multilateral Agreement on Investment
MFN	most-favoured nation
MNC	multinational corporation
NAFTA	North American Free Trade Association

NATO	North Atlantic Treaty Organization
NIEO	New International Economic Order
NT	national treatment
OECD	Organization for Economic Cooperation and Development
OIC	Overseas Investment Commission (New Zealand)
OPEC	Organization of Petroleum-Exporting Countries
PCR	polymerase chain reaction
PNAC	Project for a New American Century
RAFI	Rural Advancement Foundation
SWA	South West Africa
TRIMS	Trade Related Investment Measures
TRIPS	Trade Related Intellectual Property Rights
UN	United Nations
UNCHR	United Nations Commission on Human Rights
UNCTAD	United Nations Conference on Trade and Development
UNEP	United Nations Environmental Programme
UNESCO	United Nations Educational, Scientific and Cultural Organization
WCIP	World Council of Indigenous Peoples
WEF	World Economic Forum
WGIP	Working Group on Indigenous Populations
WTO	World Trade Organization

FOREWORD

MICHAEL A. PETERS

In this book Makere Stewart-Harawira presents us with a sprawling world-historical narrative, an in-depth investigation of the processes of globalization and the emerging global order, of their combined impact on indigenous peoples and of the invention of new forms of resistance to the structures of neo-imperialism. This book is a well-informed argument that draws upon a series of expert and inter-related literatures in world politics, indigenous philosophy and international law at its intersection with the contemporary discourses of human and property rights. It is written out of a deeply held commitment to social justice and the beliefs of an indigenous political philosophy that speaks to 'existence' and 'being', and it calls for a 'new political ontology of global order' informed by indigenous world views and values.

There is no doubt in my mind that this book – the result of some seven years of research based upon doctoral study – is both a timely and a welcome addition to the critical literature emerging as a response to globalization: it is original in its outlook and comprehensive in its argument; it elucidates many important issues of current world order and their implications for indigenous peoples; it is strongly critical, drawing upon extant political and philosophical theory; and, perhaps most importantly, it is written in an accessible style. In short, it is an impressive piece of work based on advanced scholarship and research.

This is also an ambitious book that provides notes towards an indigenous global ontology by focusing on the nature of knowledge, existence, and relationships, which is a massive undertaking. Yet Stewart-Harawira provides enough of a sketch to ground her analysis of globalization. She also examines questions of sovereignty, the problem of government, self-determination, and the subjugation of indigenous populations, exploring the shape of the liberal international order with the establishment of the United Nations, the development of the Bretton Woods institutions and the new international economic order, and decolonization in the post-war period. At the heart of her account is the question of state sovereignty and indigenous self-determination, which she investigates by studying the contested sites of human rights law, the concept of self-determination in international law, and international engagement by indigenous peoples.

Stewart-Harawira is not afraid of the 'big picture' as she investigates the emergence of neoliberalism, the reconstitution of democracy, the reassertion of the Bretton Woods financial and economic discipline in the structural adjustment policies of the 1980s and 1990s and the construction of a global economic order.

One theme that figures prominently in her analysis is 'the return of empire'. As she writes in her Introduction:

> Of enormous significance in the current context, the connecting roles of militarism and the economy and the increase in technologies of surveillance and control have become key elements of a new form of biopower and the exercise of global domination. In this regard, the re-emergence of the 'just war' doctrine and the racialized rhetoric of global terrorism have become dominating metaphors for a postmodern imperialism.

Stewart-Harawira provides contrasting perspectives on the return to empire – among them, those of Robert Cooper (a one-time policy adviser to Tony Blair) and of Hardt and Negri in their celebrated book *Empire* – and she concludes by looking at 'globalization from below', detailing forms of resistance and transformation, and the development of a framework for a new eco-humanism that embodies indigenous world views. This is an informative account, huge in scope and intellectually challenging and ambitious in its aims. Yet it achieves the 'big picture' necessary for understanding complex world politics and for locating questions of indigenous resistance and transformation.

Stewart-Harawira draws on a wide range of critical traditions, from the Gramscian-inspired political economy of Robert Cox and the philosophical hermeneutics of Hans-Georg Gadamer to the indigenous theoretical approach known as *Kaupapa* Maori, which, as she acknowledges, 'develops the emancipatory goal of critical theory within a specific context' of development. *Kaupapa* Maori theory was developed in Aotearoa-New Zealand by Maori scholars such as Graham Smith on the basis of both the Maori experience of decolonization and Maori identity and engagement in the research process. As such, it also represents Stewart-Harawira's own academic research and teaching background, her own standpoint perspective, and her spiritual outlook.

This book, like others that question the hegemony of American empire and the structural oppressions and increasing inequalities built into processes of world 'free trade' and globalization, makes the case for renewal and for hope of an alternative and essentially more just world order based on the values of indigenous peoples. As Makere Stewart-Harawira herself comments:

> far from irrelevant in the modern world, traditional indigenous social, political and cosmological ontologies are profoundly important to the development of transformative alternative frameworks for global order and new ways of being.

This hope is not just a pious one driven by flights of fancy: it is informed by the political and economic rights and hard-won compensatory gains in resources that indigenous peoples have struggled for and some have successfully achieved in their own territories; it is underwritten by some successful strategic international developments at the United Nations and in other world indigenous forums for the recognition of indigenous rights as they apply not only to the peoples themselves but also to their knowledge base, their material and symbolic cultural resources, and their skills and understandings of their environment. Perhaps even more importantly – and here ecological arguments really kick in – at the intellectual and ethical levels there is increasing recognition that it is no accident that traditional and indigenous cultures have survived for many thousands of years. While it is easy to romanticize these claims, it is also imperative that we look afresh at a global self-understanding that minimally includes bringing to world consciousness the necessity for protecting and enhancing our linguistic, cultural, biological and ecological diversity as part of the global biota bequeathed to us and to our children's children.

University of Glasgow

INTRODUCTION

Te Ao Hurihuri
te ao huri ai ki tona tauranga:
te ao rapu;
ko te huripoki e huri nei
i runga i te taumata o te kaha.[1]

Te Ao Hurihuri
is a world revolving:
a world that moves forward
to the place it came from;
a wheel that turns
on an axle of strength.[1]

✳

This book is concerned with the interrelationship between indigenous peoples and the development of global order. It is written as both a history of the present and a signifier for the future. The book tells two stories. The first story recounts the history of indigenous peoples' relationships with the world order of nation states and the impact of the twin capitalist logics of accumulation and expansion on indigenous peoples. Its starting point is the early recognition of the indigenous peoples of the Americas as sovereign nations and the changes in international law that brought about the dispossession of indigenous peoples' sovereignty and their exclusion from political status in the world of nations. It also speaks of indigenous peoples' active interventions in these processes and the resultant changes and advances in international law. This story is thus one of resistance and transformation and, at the same time, of cooptation and hegemonies. But most importantly, it is a story of the possible.

The other story is concerned with the development of the world order of nation states and its transformation into a global order. This story traces the contested ideologies that have been the driving forces in the development of global order from the sixteenth century until the present. It interrogates particular aspects of these transformations, such as the contested sets of ideologies that operated at the conjunction of particular formations of power and knowledge, the development of government and the construction of peoples as populations

1

to be governed. In particular, this story is one of the vigorous promulgation of particular ideologies through transatlantic networks of elites and of the construction of the global politico/economic architecture. The tale ends with the emergence of American unilateralism as the predominant characteristic of the contemporary global order, a unilateralism that is now openly referred to as empire, yet neither of these stories has reached its ending.

Throughout the book, these two stories are interleaved, as neither can be told without the other. This is the nature of the dialectic relationship between indigenous peoples and the political world order. In the final analysis, my intention is to raise questions about the shape and form of the emerging global order and the nature of our response. Among the responses to the multiple and increasing crises of globalization in the twenty-first century are calls for a new political ontology of global order. This book is one response to those calls.

A World in Crisis

'Crisis awareness', Edward Tiryakian points out, has been part of sociological consciousness from the beginning of sociology as a discipline.[2] In its earliest days, he recounts, Claude Henri de Saint-Simon's call for the development of a 'science of social physiology' was in response to the global crisis of the period. Saint-Simon envisaged a new social order that would be 'more inclusive and universalistic in nature'.[3] The role of this new science was to deal with social phenomena that would facilitate the transition from one social order to another. Immanuel Kant's treatise on perpetual peace in which he foresaw a world polity as a means of solving forever the problem of 'violence among nations', was written in the aftermath of the political crisis that saw the 1795 signing of the Treaty of Basel between France and Prussia. Kant's ideal was a peaceful federation of nations operating under a new form of cosmopolitan law by which means war would be forever extinguished. Based on humankind's natural propensity for greed, 'the power of money' would ultimately guarantee a striving for peace between nations, thus serving 'reason as the means of procuring ... to the state the establishment and sure maintenance of an external and even internal peace'.[4] Karl Polanyi's seminal work *The Great Transformation,*[5] first published in 1944, was a response to the global economic crisis of the 1930s. His work explored the socially disruptive tendencies in the world economy driven by the self-regulating market. Polanyi's analysis of the 'double movement' of unprecedented market expansion and the political responses of societies, which demanded that states counteract the dislocating and polarizing tendencies generated by this expansionism, has gained increased relevance in a world dominated by ever-expanding global markets and the multiple crises of global capitalism.

One of the most potent aspects of the global crises is 'the crisis of multilateralism'. In the lead up to the 9/11 attack on the World Trade Centre, the world witnessed America's rebuttal of new treaties which aimed to make the world a safer place, and withdrawal from established treaties. These two groups of international treaties included a treaty to control the world's traffic in small arms, a treaty to eliminate land mines, the Kyoto Accord, the Biological and Toxins Weapons Convention, and many other international agreements. Following the attack of 9/11, America terminated the Anti-Ballistic Missile Agreement with Russia, actively opposed the establishment of the International Criminal Court and blatantly opposed the UN Security Council in declaring war on Iraq.[6]

By the end of the twentieth century, the view most frequently articulated in the literature was that the bi-polar nature of the post-war world order had given way to something quite different that, as David Held suggests, was variously described as tri-polar, multipolar, multicentric and post-hegemonic.[7] Four years into the twenty-first century and in the wake of two wars in the Middle East, a great deal has changed. The possibility for multipolarism has given way to an aggressive unipolarity signified by the prevailing discourse of empire. The inescapable conclusion is that, depending on one's vantage point, we are witnessing either the revival, or the overt emergence of American empire.

For critical theorists, scholars and activists, the challenge is to identify strategies that go beyond resisting empire. It is my contention that the most urgent task facing us today is to effect transformation of the ontological underpinnings of the terms in which world order is conceived and the meaning of existence is articulated. It is from that viewpoint that I present the central task of this book, to argue the salience of traditional indigenous ontologies as key principles for a transformed global order.

Empire Reborn?

As we have seen, prior to 2002, the age of empire was widely regarded as over. Thus, despite its centrality to indigenous theories of world order, the concept of imperialism rarely entered into mainstream analyses of the current world situation.[8] This is not to say, Foster notes, that critiques of twentieth-century US imperialism have been completely absent from the literature of the Left. Foster draws attention to Magdoff's *Age of Imperialism* (1969) which provided a strong critique of the received view of US relations to the rest of the world, and his later work in which he argued that narrow, economic explanations of imperialism fell far short of a true account. In Magdoff's account, the ultimate source of imperialism was the historical development of capitalism since the sixteenth century.[9] Nonetheless, prior to the publication of Hardt and Negri's seminal work, *Empire*[10] in 2000, political theorists largely ignored imperialism as an explanation for contemporary policies and strategies. In their analysis of contemporary globalization, Held, McGrew, Goldplatt and Perraton contend that the end of the Cold War and the break-up of the Soviet Union represented the giving way of 'one of the world's last imperial structures'.[11] In their account, the US had 'abandoned any pretensions to global empire or overt hegemony since its enormous structural power has remained deeply inscribed into the nature and functioning of the present world order'.[12] Seen thus, the historical uniqueness of this contemporary phase of globalization derives from its lack of association with 'the expansionary logic or coercive institutions of empire'.[13]

In contrast, Hardt and Negri's thesis, written between the end of the Persian Gulf War and the beginning of the war on Kosovo, is that the new formation of empire represents a new global paradigm in which empire is the political subject that effectively regulates global exchanges of markets and production. This new empire, they declare, is not locatable within the US or any other state.[14] Andrew Bacevich (*American Empire. The Realities and Consequences of US Diplomacy,* 2002) notes that this analysis is in marked contrast to the view that was openly promulgated by former US President Clinton and his advisers. In the words of former security adviser Samuel Berger, the drive for openness that was the central imperative of the Clinton administration, was 'the President's strategy for harnessing the forces of globalization for the benefit of the United States and the world'.[15] In fact, Bacevich notes, the concept of American empire had been openly promulgated in the reports and writings of senior US officials and strategists since at least the mid-1990s. One such work is that by former US policy adviser Zbigniew Brzezinski who declared

America as 'not only the first, as well as the only truly global superpower but ... also likely to be the very last'.[16] Brzezinski considered as the three critical imperatives of American geopolitical strategy, 'to prevent collusion and maintain security dependence among the vassals, to keep tributaries pliant, and to keep the barbarians from coming together'.[17] In this account, control of the world's energy and resources are critical to the maintenance of global order and US domination. Thus Brzezinski's geostrategy centres on control over the Caspian/Central Asian region viewed as 'America's chief political prize', upon which America's global primacy is utterly dependent. The imperative, therefore, is to prevent the possibility of any other power emerging in the region.

In a similar vein, the Wolfowitz doctrine of military intervention and pre-emptive behaviour – first articulated in the US Defence Planning Document for 1994–9 and again in the 2000 *Report of the Project for American Century, Rebuilding America's Defences* – called for increased militarism as a proactive measure for the deterrence of contenders. This view was given official sanction in the global policy document, the 2002 National Security Strategy of the United States of America. In the aftermath of the US pre-emptive strike against Iraq in March 2003, launched despite failure to win support from the UN Security Council and in the face of opposition from fifteen European Union heads of state, the terms 'empire' and 'imperialism' now appear regularly in print, both in political analyses and in mainstream print media such as *Time* magazine. Today the most commonly held view is that we are not only witnessing the re-emergence or rebirth of empire, but also one that is unequivocally American. Others see the current form of American empire as the fulfilment of a historical vision that has always seen US accumulation and expansion in global terms. From being denied, the concept of American empire is now taken for granted. What is in question is whether this 'informal' empire should become formalized, as conservatives would have it, with America becoming the world's benevolent imperial power.[18]

In the burgeoning body of literature concerning contemporary American imperialism, there are two readily identifiable and related debates. One concerns its historical origins and extent. While much of the literature identifies the Spanish–American War of 1898 as the formative moment of American imperialism, there is rather less consensus regarding its historical trajectory. The second is the question of whether or not US foreign policy has been taken over by a cabal of

hawkish neoconservatives, or whether the neoconservatives themselves are part of a broad consensus around the concept of America as
the moulder and shaper of the globalized world. That there is some
consensus around this seems evident, although Wallerstein argues
that, rather than a consensus, a cabal of hawks has tired of the 'velvet
glove' approach and aggressively intervened.[19] This perspective also
finds favour with Bacevich, who sees critical key principles as
common to the administrations of US presidents George Bush Snr,
Bill Clinton, and George W. Bush. Comments such as that by US
Secretary of Defence Rumsfield, who stated that another Pearl
Harbour would open the way for America to reshape the world as it
had in 1945, support this view. A third related debate centres on the
possibilities for transformation through the emergence of a challenger
hegemon in the form of either a state such as China, or a regionalized
structure such as the European Union.

Both John Foster[20] and Leo Panitch argue for a much deeper
analysis of the historical underpinnings of US imperialism, including
its causes and the actors involved. Foster, for example, cites Magdoff's
contention that rather than stemming from a liberal desire to contain
communism, US interventionism in the Third World was based on
capital's need for accumulation and expansion, twin processes which
have since been subsumed under the constructs of globalization.[21]
Immanuel Wallerstein and David Harvey present similar arguments,
as does Bacevich. Bacevich cites Ronald Steel's argument that
'incessant warnings about the omni-present danger of Communist
aggression', combined with the imperative for defending America's
freedom, concealed from view the 'twin anchors' of containment and
expansion that formed US policy during the Cold War.[22] In those
years, Bacevich states, globalization became the vehicle and the
rationale for open US expansionism. Its 'ultimate promise', he writes,
was 'peace, prosperity, and democracy, all reinforcing one another in
a self-perpetuating cycle'.[23]

Globalization – Its Promise …

At the end of the 1980s, the collapse of Communism was widely seen
as denoting the triumph of Enlightenment and of the modernity
project, and the beginning of a new global era that embodied the
West's ideals of freedom, justice and democracy. This was represented in declarations of a New World Order whose key signifiers
were economic globalization through structural adjustment, trade

liberalization and the free market. Through these measures, wealth would eventually accrue to the poor as structural imbalances were ironed out and the principles of the free market were embedded across the globe.

New international treaties and regimes promised the protection of human rights, of the oceans, the environment, the commons, democracy and free speech. They promised non-intervention in state sovereignty, and the right of states to have control over their own natural resources. In the prevailing view, globalization would ensure access to the basic necessities of life for all and a free and democratic world in which trade was the guarantor of peace and multilateral regimes the guarantors for fair and equal distribution of wealth and protection of the global environment.

... And Failure

In the 1990s, globalization was still a contested notion, with much debate as to whether it was a meaningful concept at all. Some, for instance, asserted that the world economy continued much as always and that the world had not radically changed.[24] Since then the focus of the debate has shifted from whether or not it exists, to its actual consequences. In the last 20 years, as John Ralston Saul pointed out in the *Financial Review*,[25] we have witnessed the abject failure of globalization and the free market to meet its promises – of an international balance of trade, of peace through prosperity, of justice through internationally agreed human rights principles, and of the equal distribution of wealth. Some of the markers of globalization's failure include extreme disparities of wealth and poverty, the resounding failure of many Asian economies in the late 1990s due to the exigencies of footloose capital, the gross exploitation of Third World countries and minority populations, the continuing dispossession of indigenous peoples, and finally, the return of pre-emptive strikes and the notion of the 'just war'.

It has become all too obvious that profound crises in the world system are increasing rather than decreasing. These crises are multilevel and multicausal. What they have in common is their impact in shaping a world system, a new global order that is struggling to be born. The new global order is a site of huge contestation and enormous polarities, of competing visions and discourses. The rise of anti-systemic movements seeking the overthrow of current paradigms of power and global capitalism is one form of response to these crises. These movements are manifest in the groundswell of protest that began with the 1999 meeting of the World Trade Organization (WTO) in Seattle, and have been witnessed thereafter at every major global economic forum.

'Humanity is divided into two parts,' Lyotard writes:

> One faces the challenge of complexity, the other that ancient and terrible challenge of its own survival. This is perhaps the most important aspect of the failure of the modern project.[26]

Cox points out that theory is 'never autonomous but is always for someone and for some purpose'.[27] Gill and Law similarly argue that in political economy theorizing is not something that occurs only within some isolated academic space; it also enters into and becomes part of the global economy.[28] On both accounts, for political transformation to occur, critical examination of the premises which underlie current conceptualizations of world order within contemporary political theory is urgently required.

Conceptualizing Globalization

Hardt and Negri comment on two common and competing conceptions of the global order; first, the notion that the present order 'somehow rises up spontaneously out of the interactions of radically heterogeneous global forces, as if this order were a harmonious concert orchestrated by the natural and neutral hand of the market', and second, that it is dictated by 'a single power and a single centre of rationality transcendent to global forces' which guides the historical development of order 'according to its conscious and all-seeing plan'.[29]

Jan Scholte sees a major site of struggle between three broad and competing discourses – conservative, liberal and critical views of globalization.[30] Conservative views include those that reject the notion of a globalized and borderless society in favour of territorial units such as regionalized formations. Liberalist discourses encompass those that generally promote ideologies of benign economic expansion and shared wealth, and see internationalisation and globalization as interchangeable concepts.[31] Two important liberal variations are neoliberalist views which take for granted the 'end of history' thesis, namely, that the ending of the Cold War signalled the end of the dialectic of history and the triumph of capitalism,[32] and a reformist liberalism which holds that any imperfections that might accrue from the expansion of global capital and the market can be addressed by minor adjustments to global system.[33] Held categorizes the three major approaches to globalization as hyperglobalists, sceptics, and transformationalists.[34] Hyperglobalists include neoconservatives such as Kenichi Ohmae, for whom the notion of 'a borderless economy, a single global market and global competition as the harbingers of human progress' mark the beginning of a new epoch of a borderless world. In this view, the imposition of a neoliberal economic discipline on all governments means that 'politics is no longer the "art of the possible" but rather the practice of sound economic management'[35] – hardly a new vocation for the state, according to Foucault.

The sceptic view, on the other hand, conceives of current levels of economic integration as merely representing heightened levels of interaction between national economies, rather than a new phenomenon. Here the increasing regionalization of the world economy, which is seen as contradicting globalization, evidences a significant lessening of the integration of the world economy.[36] For some in this camp, national governments are deeply implicated in the intensification of world trade and foreign investment through their function as agents of monopoly capital. The transformationalist view is one in which contemporary processes of globalization are seen as unprecedented. Thus while the processes of globalization are transforming the global landscape, the direction of the future trajectory is yet unknown.[37]

Conservative views such as are expounded by Konichi Ohmae[38] and Martin Albrow[39] see globalization teleologically, as the inevitable outcome of an evolutionary movement. Historical materialist analyses such as those by Immanuel Wallerstein[40] and Robert Cox,[41] on the other hand, conceive globalization as the convergence of multiple politico-economic processes that have brought humankind to the brink of disaster. In this perspective, by the close of one of the most conflictual centuries in Western history, humankind had reached the edge of the precipice and, in 2004, gazed into the abyss of our own destruction.

Political Economy of World Order

The first task of a contemporary political theory', Cox insists, 'is to declare its ontology.'[42] Cox compares two quite different theoretical approaches that he sees as linked to different modes of knowledge: positivism and historicism. These two approaches correspond to two broad purposes – a problem-solving purpose which 'tacitly accepts the permanence of existing structures, served by the positivist approach', and 'a critical purpose, envisaging the possibilities of structural transformation, which is served by the historicist approach'.[43] Both approaches can be found in the political ontologies and theoretical explanations that shaped the political world order in the aftermath of the First and Second world wars, as well as in contemporary theoretical explanations.

Vasquez's classic study of power politics[44] provides a useful entry point to understanding the competing political ontologies that dominated the theorizing of international relations after the Second World War and still, to a large extent, inform political conceptions of the current world order. Two competing conceptual paradigms were embedded in the international institutions of the new political order, realism and idealism, the latter being exemplified in liberal internationalism. Realists saw relations of power, the interests of states, and rationality as the key components of any adequate analysis of world politics. Liberal internationalists, on the other hand, saw the political world eventually becoming one unified body and thus sought to study and improve the processes by which the nation state would eventually be replaced by international institutions as the organizing principle of world order. The idealist vision saw individuals as the most important actors, the real world as inherently peaceful and the establishment and maintenance of peace as the primary goal of international relations. In this account, the realist assumption that international politics was inherently about a struggle for power and peace contradicted the real world in which global order could be achieved by the use of reason.[45] These principles, at least in part, guided the negotiations regarding the Treaty of Versailles and the first international institutions of world order. The failure of the League of Nations to fulfil the expectation of international peace and the subsequent outbreak of another world war even more horrific than the first gave strength to a conflictual paradigm of international relations that sees states as driven by self-interest and a global hegemon as the only way to ensure stability.

Morgenthau's *Politics Among Nations*, published in 1948, provided a strong critique of liberal internationalist idealism. Strengthened by liberal internationalism's failure to prevent a second world war, Morgenthau's development of the realist paradigm both shaped and explained post-war politics.[46] He delineated particular patterns of behaviour by states as a set of general laws about international relations; that all politics are a struggle for power, that nations strive to protect their national interests, and that the power of a nation could be most effectively limited by another nation.[47] In this view, the logical outcome of nations acting to protect their own interests and security was the consolidation of power with an attendant arms build-up. The concept of a Leviathan or global state was therefore the rational method for the maintenance of international order. In the absence of a global state, a global empire or hegemony on the part of an overwhelmingly powerful nation that would discipline other states and maintain order was seen as the preferred alternative. An intermediate step towards that was the carefully constructed and rationally maintained balance of power to maintain the *status quo*. During the Cold War period, the dominance of classic realism gave way to new formulations of realism theory that nonetheless maintained the notion of the balance of power as the primary determinant of order and stability in a state–centric world order.

Hegemony and World Order

Debates about the nature and decline of US hegemony were central to political theories regarding the future shape of world order in the aftermath of the economic crisis of the 1970s and the collapse of the Eastern Bloc at the end of the 1980s. Hegemony, Harvey states, is understood in a variety of ways. One of the most influential theories during the late 1980s and 1990s was Keohane's 'hegemonic stability' thesis and his exposition of regime theory.

The emergence of a transnational form of society based upon linkages between interested parties is a central concept in regime theory. Linkages are seen as playing an important role in the development of multilateral regimes across disciplines. States in particular are seen as caught in a 'complex system of linkages' in which regimes are constituted under the protection of dominant powers.[48] Hegemonic stability is critical to the success of these arrangements. 'Hegemonic structures of power, dominated by a single country,' Keohane states, 'are most conducive to the development of strong international regimes, whose rules are relatively precise and well-obeyed.'[49]

The incorporation of the hegemonic stability thesis in post-Cold War international political economy perspectives reflected particular assumptions about the nature of hegemony. Orthodox international political economy theory came to be seen as a discourse constructed around a particular view of the hegemonic state. While these analyses successfully maintained the *status quo*, the limited notion of hegemony that they embraced failed to provide a satisfactory explanation for the emergent historic bloc of transnational forces and their role in the reconfiguring of a post-Westphalian world order.[50]

The strongest challenge to assumptions regarding the hegemonic state came from historical materialist analyses, of which the most notable was Cox's 'new realism' theory, defined by the author as a framework for action embedded in historical materialism.[51] His analysis of hegemony is particularly pertinent as a critique of the hegemonic stability model and for interrogating the discourses of globalization and empire that hold the high ground in contemporary debates.[52]

Cox critiques the reduction of hegemony to 'the single dimension of dominance, i.e. a physical-capabilities relationship among states'[53] and redefines hegemony as 'a fit between power, ideas and institutions' through which the hegemonic frameworks of coercion and cooptation operate.[54] Elaborating this, he explains world hegemony as 'an outward expansion of the internal hegemony established by a dominant social class'.[55] Cox writes,

> Hegemony at the international level is thus not merely an order among states. It is an order within a world economy with a dominant mode of production that penetrates into all the countries and links into other subordinate modes of production. It is also a complex of international social relationships that connect the social classes of the different countries. [56]

Despite critiques such as these, the widespread and largely uncritical adoption of the hegemonic stability thesis, coupled with the fostering of a problem-solving approach, significantly limited the possibilities for a wider more inclusive framework for transformation. By assuming the decline of US hegemony as a given, the notion of a post-hegemonic or non-hegemonic world order was taken for granted. Thus in the early 1990s debates about the possible shape of a new non-hegemonic and multipolar world order proliferated. These assumptions were given added strength by the rise of new regionalized formations.

The Regionalization Debate

Like globalization, definitions of regionalism are heavily value-laden. 'Against the background of US hegemony,' Mittleman writes, 'regionalism in its various formats is an important feature of hegemonic geopolitics.'[57] Regional arrangements between geographically aligned countries or areas are a familiar phenomenon within the capitalist world system. As Mittleman elucidates, formations of regionalism that emerged during the 1930s were strongly protectionist in nature. During the post-Second World War period, the geopolitical model that developed in the Asia-Pacific region centred on a view of the world divided into military power blocs that were 'sometimes competing, sometimes aligned'. In the 1970s, Third World formations of regionalism were again grounded in the goal of 'collective self-reliance'. In Europe during the 1950s and 1960s, the revival of regionalism both as concept and practice was fuelled by increasing regional integration between both nation states, as in the case of the European Community, and federal states, as in the US. These new regional formations have become increasingly significant within the global context.

Bjorn Hettne provides a useful perspective of the contradictions and tensions inherent in current formations and theoretical analyses.[58] He sees three broad and sometimes competing theoretical perspectives of regionalism. From a liberal internationalist perspective, new regionalism is seen as part of a new geopolitics in which growth is occurring equally across all three levels of regions, nations and transnationalism, allowing for more participative forms of international politics and holding the possibility for a new multipolar, non-hegemonic world order. Here the three capitalist world centres are seen as taking a cooperative, shared hegemonic role in what is essentially an international world order. The benign open-economy liberalist model includes the notion of diminishing state sovereignty in favour of regions, such as Ohmae's 'borderless world' in which the increasing permeability of nation state borders sees the sovereignty of nation states give way to new political regional formations or 'region states'.[59] Neorealist perspectives view regionalism as one level of the complex web of linkages that define the international or global order and are part of the growing transnationalism that is matched by a 'revived nationalism'.[60]

Elsewhere regionalism is viewed as a conduit for the development of the global economy as well as an arena for the struggle over economic and political power, as in the trading bloc or 'megamarket' model. The latter version of trilateral regionalism gives rise to the notion of fortress trading blocs or 'megamarkets' based on competitive, trilateral capitalist centres within a more closed and regionalized world economy. A third model is concerned with transnational formations described as 'extended nationalism'. In the European Union paradigm, an important characteristic of the new regionalism is the adoption of a regional identity.[61]

As the increasing economic integration of the European Community in the 1990s gave rise to fears of 'fortress trading bloc' models, these competing perspectives became the subject of increasing debate. Paradoxically, as these views demonstrate, regionalism is conceived on one hand as potentially the most viable framework for a cooperative, multilateral, non-hegemonic world order and, on the other, as the redefining of the struggle for global supremacy in terms of economic power. One of the important issues in these competing views is the relative sovereignty of the nation state.

Globalization and the State

Competing views about the nature and impact of regionalism are reflected in competing theoretical perspectives of the impact of globalization on the state. Political theorists generally agree that under the aegis of globalization the role of the state has undergone a significant restructuring. It is the nature and impact of this restructuring that is contested. One of the recast roles of the state is that of mediator between local policy and capital and the global economy. Some analysts see changes in the relationship between states and markets as a reformulation of political authority.[62] Neoliberalists such as Ohmae argue that globalization signals the end of the nation state and a shift to a borderless world. Others such as Cox, Dale and Jessop argue that while globalization has seen changes in the role of the state, the state has always acted as an agent of capital and this role is far from diminished. Cox argues that debates about diminishing state sovereignty invisibilize the reality of the state's role as what he terms a 'transmission belt from the global to the national economy'[63] and of the doctrine of state sovereignty as 'a historical instrument for the advancement and protection of capital and the ownership of property'.[64]

Jessop provides a useful insight into this situation by drawing on Poulantzas's explanation of the relationship between states and capital. Poulantzas focused on the means whereby states, in this case European states, 'take responsibility for the interests of the dominant capital'.[65] In his view, arguments that state powers had been diminished in the face of the 'international giants' of production and capital demonstrate a lack of understanding of the state's role in the international reproduction of the dominant capital. Despite major changes in the form and functions of the national state brought about by the internationalization of capital, national states will not disappear. Rather, in addition to continuing to serve their own nationally based economic capitals, they will function in ways that serve the interests of other economic capitals with which they are affiliated.[66] 'Rather than surpassing or bypassing nation states', Poulantzas wrote, the internationalization of capital included them in 'a system of interconnections that is in no way confined to the play of external and mutual pressures between juxtaposed states and capitals'.[67]

Jessop argues that, far from unravelling, many states are actively involved in constructing the conditions for globalization. Following Poulantzas's line of argument, he asserts that while there has been some erosion in the ability of Keynesian welfare national states (KWNS) to secure state functions linked to specific state projects, this erosion does not apply to all forms of the national state. Importantly, as the boundaries of the KWNS are being rolled back, other boundaries are being rolled forward and/or other forms of politics are becoming more significant. This explanation is particularly relevant to the changes that have taken place in what is now termed the neoliberal state. It also provides an excellent insight into the conditions that occurred in New Zealand, a particular focus of Chapter 6 of thus book, during what Jane Kelsey termed 'the New Zealand experiment' of the mid-1990s.

Changes to the role and function of the state, the central unit in the international world order, impact strongly in all arenas of civil society. Of these, the arena with which this book is primarily concerned is the relationship between the state and indigenous peoples. Changes in the function and role of the nation state impact on indigenous peoples in complex and contradictory ways. In the post-Second World War international order, state sovereignty and the principle of non-intervention were key determinants for the ordering of interstate relationships and provided the terrain across which indigenous rights and other human rights have been contested.

Indigenous Peoples and World Order

Western accounts of the formation of world order generally adopt approaches which, broadly speaking, either trace the evolution of modernity from its beginnings in Western philosophical political thought or, conversely, adopt an international relations approach.

Recent accounts include the proliferation of non-state actors such as non-governmental organizations (NGOs) and other sectors of civil society. Some of these include strong Third World and feminist critiques as well as postmodern analyses of imperialism and more recently, neo-imperialism and the homogenizing of difference. Indigenous peoples are sometimes referred to in these accounts in terms of their marginalization and oppression by the imperializing missions of the West, and as part of the increasingly global movement of social forces that seek to bring about transformation of the world system. More often, however, indigenous peoples are invisible in these analyses.

Indigenous theorists present markedly different accounts of the development of world order and of indigenous peoples' engagement. Their accounts provide detailed analyses of the impact of imperialism and colonialism, of genocide and dispossession, of violence and loss. Some recount treaties between equal nations broken and relationships based on equal partnership and the sharing of knowledge betrayed during what is often described as the first wave of colonization.[68] Others highlight the appropriation of such indigenous knowledge as was deemed useful[69] and the relegation to the realms of 'myth and magic' of indigenous cosmology. Indigenous educational historiographies provide readings of the sustained and deliberate attack on the collective nature of indigenous social and political structures in an attempt to absorb indigenous 'remnants' into the relations of production that sustain Western capitalism, thus facilitating European access to the lands and resources needed for the expansion of capital. These historiographies tell also of the ongoing resistance of indigenous peoples to the dismantling of their social structures and their ontological and epistemological foundations. Despite the amply documented outcomes of colonization – social and familial dysfunction, unemployment, imprisonment, ill-health and what Tewa Pueblo Indian educator Gregory Cajete describes as 'cultural schizophrenia',[70] these ontologies and epistemologies still survive, albeit submerged within traditional stories, chants and other practices.

Indigenous analyses demonstrate the sustained attempts by indigenous peoples to seek justice at the international level and the incremental transformation of international norms that have accrued as a result. These efforts have been predicated on a belief that justice would ultimately prevail and that the light of Western liberal doctrines of freedom, truth and justice, once firmly directed on the factual accounts of legal treaties and relationships between indigenous peoples and the Europeans who 'came to visit', would bring about the fulfilment of the promises and treaties made. To date those hopes remain largely unfulfilled. Indigenous interventions and increased attention by the UN Commission on Human Rights to the plight of indigenous peoples have resulted in UN reports that detail the status of indigenous peoples, their relationship to the natural environment and their spiritual and cultural values of biodiversity.[71] These reports articulate fundamental elements of indigenous ontologies and philosophies of being that provide much of the impetus for indigenous peoples' activism and intervention across multiple arenas.

A considerable body of literature has emerged that details the shifts in international human rights law in recent decades and the impact on domestic law as it pertains to indigenous peoples. Indigenous political theorists and scholars such as S. James Anaya, Glen Morris, Rudolph Ryser, Sharon Venne and Moana Jackson have been major contributors to this body of literature and provide an invaluable resource for understanding the impact of international norms on indigenous peoples.

Recently, non-indigenous political theorists have also turned their attention to the complexities of the position of indigenous peoples within national and international legal frameworks. Theorists such as Stephen May, Joseph Carens and James Tully direct attention to issues of indigenous rights to self-determination and the possibilities for accommodating these rights within liberal democratic theory. Other analyses chronicle the jurisprudential debates of the fifteenth and sixteenth centuries concerning the status of indigenous peoples in the era of Spanish and Portuguese imperialism as well as under later imperializing missions of the Dutch, French and English.

Just as indigenous peoples themselves are not a homogeneous group, so also their experiences of imperialism and colonization are widely varied. Political theorists identify two kinds of colonizing techniques that prevailed during the earliest periods of imperialism and colonization; internal and external colonization. Elaborating the differing treatment of these two forms within international law, Tully defines internal colonization as involving 'the coexistence of colonies and the imperial society on different territories, allowing for the possibility of the colonies becoming free and independent with exclusive control over their own territories, as in the case of Canada, Australia and New Zealand in relation to Britain'.[72] Defined as 'internal' because it is built on the territories of formerly 'free' people, the form of colonization is one in which 'the dominant society coexists and exercises total domination over the territories and jurisdictions which the indigenous peoples refuse to surrender'.[73] Its outcome, Tully writes, is 'continuous unresolved contradictions and ongoing provocation'.[74]

Contradictions predominate also at the international level. After years of endeavour, indigenous peoples have finally been granted a Permanent Forum in the United Nations (UN) system under the aegis of the Economic and Social Council of the Human Rights Commission (ECOSOC). Within this forum for indigenous peoples, states have equal voice and the ability to veto. Most importantly, the UN Permanent Forum on Indigenous Issues has no juridical power. Indigenous peoples are, to all intents and purposes, still in a position of 'wardship'. At the 2004 Second Session of the Permanent Forum, the speech of UN Secretary-General Kofi Annan drew attention to the fact that indigenous peoples continue to be 'subjected to systematic discrimination and exclusion from economic and political power'. As he stated, 'They are denied their cultural identity and displaced from their traditional lands.'[75] From the Pacific to Columbia, from Botswana to Asia and the Middle East, the traditional lands of indigenous peoples are rich in mineral resources. The dispossession of indigenous peoples and the overtly militaristic interventions in these territories by industrialized nations are directly locatable within the logic and processes of globalization.

In the face of increasing globalization, indigenous cultures and identities are being increasingly threatened by the commodification of indigenous culture that is occurring at multiple levels. Beyond the homogenizing influence on material forms of culture is a more funda-mental and profoundly significant issue, that of the homogenization of world views and constructions of reality and the loss and commodification of indigenous knowledge. In his exposition of 'two modernities', Charles Taylor refers to acultural theories that conceive modernity as typified by the growth of reason and as a particular set of transformations through which all cultures must inevitably develop.[76] These include sets of supposedly 'neutral' and 'value-free' facts about the individual as a 'completely self-referential identity' with a maximally instrumental, rationalist approach to life for our own self-benefit, which exhorts us to extract as much as possible from existing resources.

While indigenous peoples are far from being a homogeneous group, they hold in common broad sets of ontologies that define their relationships to all other life forms and to the cosmos. Frequently marginalized or 'occulted',[77] indigenous cosmological and ontological understandings of reality nevertheless present a significant challenge to the orthodoxy of dominant world views. These ontologies challenge dominant rationalist explanations of the purpose of life and the nature of human society and are increasingly being articulated through global networks of indigenous peoples and within international forums. In arguing that indigenous ontologies have an important place in theories of social transformation, it is the ethnocentrism of conservative and liberalist approaches to globalization that I wish to challenge.

Crisis and Transformation

Cox argues that understanding our historical choices in order to seek to effect change requires not just an understanding of current ontologies and their historical condition but also investigation of new, more inclusive ontologies for the reconstitution of society 'from the bottom up'. In order to promote change, he says, critical theorists need to understand the specific historical circumstances in which structures emerged and 'to find the connections between the mental schema through which people conceive action and the material world which constrains both what people can do and how they think about what they can do'.[78] Structures, for Cox, are 'formed by collective human activity over time'. It is a 'picture of reality' and as such 'constitutes the world in which we live'.[79] These intersubjectively constituted realities are developed out of particular ontologies. On this account, historicism is critical to any examination of the ontologies and epistemologies that support current structures of world order.

Wallerstein sees the crisis of the global world system in terms of major shifts taking place across the three interrelated geocultural, political and economic spheres. These major shifts and the accompanying destabilization of the world system, which Wallerstein predicts will increase enormously over the next fifty years, signal that we are in a period of huge change, a transition from one world system to the next. He refers to these moments of 'historical transition', of 'systemic bifurcation' as 'transformational timespace', the opportunity to determine for ourselves the kind of world system that we want and the means by which we may be most likely to get there.

Engagement in this moment of transformation involves the exercise of 'utopistics', defined by Wallerstein as 'the serious assessment of historical alternatives, the exercise of our judgment as to the substantive rationality of alternative possible historical systems.... Not the face of the future, but the face of a historically possible future.'[80] The moral and political obligation to engage in this transitional timespace moment requires us, in Wallerstein's view, firstly to recognize the moment for what it is and of what it consists. To do this, he maintains, requires 'reconstructing the structures of knowledge so that we can understand the nature of our structural crisis and therefore our historical choices for the twenty-first century'.[81]

Increasing calls for a new ontology of world order articulate the imperative that we are not passive but develop considered and proactive ways of transforming this process. In asking critical questions about appropriate ontologies for a new and more equitable world order, Cox, Wallerstein and others point to the urgent need of this time – to understand the historical circumstances that have brought us to this moment and to think critically about the form and shape of future order and our own implication in that shaping. Cox contends that as a terrain of struggle for an alternative world order framework, social movements and forces are the most vital elements in the shaping of the emergent world order. To be effective, he argues, social movements must be capable of penetrating and challenging the multilevel structures that constitute current forms of world order.

This raises questions concerning indigenous peoples' responses and resistance and it is these concerns that I have sought to address. It is to this end that advocating the retrieval and repositioning of traditional indigenous forms of knowledge and understandings of the nature of being and existence became a critical goal of this project.

Issues of Research and Methodology

Particular theoretical perspectives shaped the manner in which I approached this research. My research methodology has been underpinned by what Gadamer calls an 'historically effective consciousness',[82] a consciousness of the way that my own historical understandings and traditions, combined with particular sets of belief systems and values, shape both my interactions with the world and with others, and my interpretations. As is always the case with research regarding human interactions and social issues, my perceptions and interpretation of the issues at hand are, without any doubt, historically conditioned. As Gadamer states, we each stand within particular 'streams of tradition'.[83] These 'lifestreams' determine our consciousness and shape our values and beliefs. My research methodology has involved participation and praxis that are fundamental to a *kaupapa* Maori methodology. This functioned at multiple levels and was driven by multiple factors, the most important being my commitment to social transformation.

Gadamer's theory was profoundly important in my conceptualization of the hermeneutic spiral. Critical international political economy theories offered a framework in which to examine the hegemonies that are decisive in the successful adaptation of nation states to the exigencies of the global economic order. Cox's historical materialist approach to critical international political economy and Wallerstein's 'world systems' approach to the transformation of global order honed the focus of my research. Foucault's nuanced account of power and governmentality during the sixteenth and seventeenth centuries provided the conceptual tools with which to engage the development of governmentality and the role of elite networks. Here Peters's Foucauldian analysis of neoliberalism and its relationship to governance gave important insights in understanding the intersection of governance, the economy and neoliberalism. Having concluded in 2002 that we were witnessing the emergence of a new formation of empire, I was grateful to be directed by Michael Peters to Hardt and Negri's seminal *Empire* and British diplomat Robert Cooper's recent writings on the postmodern state. In the Celtic and Scottish Studies Department at Edinburgh University, a chance discussion with Wilson McLeod regarding David Harvey's work on empire added a vital perspective to my final analysis.

Indigenous critical theoretical analyses were invoked to engage with current discourses and conceptualizations of globalization and models of world order. The development of indigenous critical theories has been a response by indigenous scholars to the ongoing objectification of indigenous peoples by non-indigenous researchers who historically have regarded indigenous peoples as interesting, if inferior, objects of study and whose research has been applied to the benefit of all but those whom they researched. One such critical indigenous theoretical approach is *kaupapa* Maori theory, which has been strongly embedded in my analysis. As a leading indigenous critical response, *kaupapa* Maori theory, originally developed by Maori academic Graham Smith, locates the emancipatory goal of critical theory within a specific context that is at once historical, political and social.[84] As such it articulates a strong challenge to positivist models of research and methodology.

The notion of an unbiased, objective qualitative research methodology is in itself problematic. Debates about positivism and objectivity in research are driven by a notion that objective, quantitative methodologies are somehow more factual, accurate and inherently more valuable than qualitative methodologies. Gadamer offers a two-fold explanation for this debate. In the first place, he identifies a fundamental misunderstanding of the differences in function of natural sciences and human sciences and in the second place, a misunderstanding or misinterpretation of the meaning of the term 'method'.[85] As Gadamer points out, the function of the natural sciences is to apply a methodological approach that objectifies by systematically eliminating every subjective point of view. This concept of an objective, universal methodology was established by Descartes and has come to dominate modern epistemology, whereas 'the term "*Methodos*", in the ancient sense, always means the whole business of working with a certain domain of questions and problems … a "taking part" in something, a participation that more closely resembles what takes place'.[86]

In her ground-breaking work, *Decolonizing Methodologies*, Linda Tuhiwai Smith emphasizes a central characteristic of *kaupapa* Maori research, articulated by a number of Maori academics: that it is premised on the centrality of being and identifying as Maori and as a Maori researcher.[87] One of the issues that arises in qualitative research is the issue of doing research as an 'outside insider', in other words from the position of being a member of the community, but not a member of the inside group.[88] Griffiths sees this in terms of a kind of deception carried out on the part of the researcher, who draws on the rules of social interaction pertaining to reciprocity and trust for research purposes, thus running the risk of exploitation and betrayal. For Maori researchers operating within a *kaupapa* Maori framework, the rules of interaction and reciprocity operate within a particularly complex set of interrelationships and rules. The fine line between revealing too much and stating what is necessary in order to 'give voice' to those who have been generous of their time and trust, to support the goal of transformation and empowerment, and to validate the research, requires a delicate balancing act. As Graham Smith points out, there is a tension between meeting the requirements of the academic community who will provide the 'credentialling' and the needs of the Maori community who, in the end, have – and exercise – the power of excommunication.[89] Negotiating this tension is one of the challenges that are specific to the context of *kaupapa* Maori research methodologies and requires particular sorts of responses that involve maintaining the primacy of Maori world views and objectives.

The reclaiming of invisibilized indigenous histories and the insurrection of subjugated indigenous cosmologies and ontologies are critical aspects of indigenous peoples' resistance to the homogenizing impulse of modernity and its manifestation in current forms of globalization. At the same time, these are complex and contested concepts. In her deconstruction of history as 'a process of epistemic violence' within the imperialist project, Spivak concludes that the notion of 'subaltern history as a project for the retrieval of the subaltern's consciousness and will can be no more than a theoretical fiction to entitle the project of reading'.[90] Furthermore, Spivak argues, it is the 'revisionary impulse' of reverse ethnocentrism, and the nativist project for the recovery of 'lost origins' or 'repressed culture' as a critique of imperialism, that allows for the emergence of the Third World as a convenient signifier.[91] Similar arguments may be constructed about the use of 'indigenous' as an essentializing signifier of indigenous people as 'Other'. On one hand, from an indigenous perspective that sees the past, present and future as operating within one multilevel and continuous paradigm, the re-claiming, retelling and rewriting of our histories is critical to re-affirmation of identities and to healing the deeply embedded scars of the past. On the other hand, indigenous peoples' histories have frequently been so mythologized and reinvented by non-indigenous writers and scholars, as well as by indigenous writers whose main source of self-knowledge is the word of the colonizer, that, as Linda Smith points out, the notion of 'authentic, essentialist' indigenous history is highly problematic.[92]

There is also a tension between oral traditions and the desire of contemporary indigenous academics to ensure the retention of important indigenous knowledge and world views. Marlene Castellano identifies the recording of traditions by sympathetic non-indigenous authors, and even by indigenous scholars who have been trained in non-oral traditions, as one of the problems posed by written indi-genous historical accounts.[93] Although 'what is written down is not necessarily true',[94] as Gadamer states, nevertheless, '[t]he written word has the tangible quality of something that can be demonstrated and is like a proof'.[95] This tension between oral and written accounts of indigenous histories is one manifestation of the ways in which historically indigenous histories have been invisibilized, marginalized and appropriated, and is particularly relevant to the oral histories and traditions drawn on in Chapter 1.

Spiral as Metaphor

The research questions that shaped this work were framed around certain thematic issues I saw as critical to indigenous peoples' experiences of globalization and to which I needed to respond. One is the marginalization of indigenous sovereignty and self-determination within the structural framework of world order. Another is the ongoing subjugation of indigenous ontologies. These themes provide some of the central threads from which this book is woven.

The themes are contextualized within a hermeneutic framework that locates indigenous cosmologies and ways of being at the centre of an expanding spiral of being. I have taken the notion of a hermeneutic 'circle of understanding' and reformulated it as a 'spiral of understanding'. Here the metaphor of the spiral signifies the turning back 'on a wheel of strength', to 'the place it came from': in other words, to the sacred teachings of the ancestors, to the source of 'the primal energy of potential being',[96] and the returning of these to the forefront in a dynamic process of re-creation and transformation.

In the first chapter, I attempt to draw out some of the ontological and cosmological principles shared by many indigenous peoples as key signifiers for a revived, more inclusive indigenous theory of being as an alternative framework for socio/politico/economic order. In my concluding comments, after reviewing the current crisis of globalization and some of the alternatives that have been posited as models for world order, I restate the essence of these central principles and relate them to the crisis of the present. Here my central thesis is fully restated: that, far from being irrelevant in the modern world, traditional indigenous social, political and cosmological ontologies are profoundly important to the development of transformative alternative frameworks for global order.

The book comprises six chapters, a conclusion and a brief epilogue. Chapter 1 provides an exploration of key concepts that broadly may be seen as common to many indigenous peoples' ontological and cosmological principles and as underlying indigenous conceptions of the purpose and nature of socio-political order. The placement of this chapter signals its central role in my argument. It also reaffirms that my research, theoretical paradigm and practice have been informed by a Maori perspective of being and knowing, mediated by the particularities of my ancestral indigenous Waitaha cosmologies and ontologies. Thus, while I propose a broadly unified indigenous ontology of global order, the ontological elements of world order which I postulate are rooted in traditional Waitaha philosophical understandings and cosmologies. Nevertheless they represent a preliminary exploration of the elements of an ecophilosophical indigenous world view as a contribution toward a new ontology for world order.

Chapters 2 and 3 map the historical trajectory of the development of world order. Here I have interwoven the theme of the struggles of indigenous peoples and the development of new frameworks of world order. Chapter 2 traces the emergence of international law as a body of law concerned primarily with the rights of states: I consider its basis in medieval political thought and the concept of natural law, and its development through Enlightenment rationalism and empiricism. The reconstruction of Nature from the holistic ecocentric orientation of the pre-Socratics and indigenous peoples to the mechanistic conceptions of Francis Bacon and Newton occurred simultaneously with the discursive reconstruction of indigenous sovereign nations into dependent populations. The role of education in these processes, particularly in regard to indigenous peoples and their reconstruction as dependent populations of colonizing states, is signalled in the conclusion of this chapter. Chapter 3 historicizes the construction of the multilateral economic order and tracks the transformations in the role and function of international institutions such as the United Nations (UN), World Bank and the International Monetary Fund (IMF). The influence of liberal international networks in the development of the institutions of world order is a focal point in this chapter. The construction of international order has not been an uncontested process, however. In this chapter, I attempt to draw out some of the competing agendas involved in the process and the impact of these in the reshaping of world order.

The central theme in Chapter 4 is the development and articulation of indigenous resistance strategies within the international political arena and their impact within international law. Included in these 'arts of resistance' is the articulation and affirmation of indigenous cosmologies and ontologies. Held suggests that, having developed alongside the international world order of sovereign states, international law – originally viewed as 'law between states only and exclusively'[97] – has come to encompass groups as well as individuals.[98] This chapter maps the evolution of indigenous rights within international law in the latter part of this century, against a backdrop of the contested concepts of state sovereignty and indigenous self-determination.

Chapter 5 spans the last fifty years of twentieth century inter-nationalism and tracks the shift from post-Second World War trans-atlantic post-Fordism to a regime of global interdependence. Important features of this process were the emergence of the Third World as a significant power bloc within the UN and the monetarist response from the industrialized world. In the aftermath of the social and economic crises of this period, the re-emergence during the 1970s of new forms of classic liberalism in a context of shifting power relations, ideological struggles and the restructuring of economic and political systems of governance contributed to the legitimating of new forms of militarist interventions, the recolonizing of wealth and resources and the recapture and integration of 'rogue' states within contemporary capitalist frameworks. During this process, notions of democracy and freedom were transformed and the groundwork for global imperialism was laid. Occurring alongside these interventions was a critical shift in the locus of hegemony.[99] The discussion concludes with the increase in militarist interventionism and the insertion of the interests of capital within the structures of the UN as key strategies in the hegemonic transformation of international order.

The final two chapters are concerned with identifying some of the specific geopolitical transformations that characterize the transition to global order and new formations of empire. As noted earlier, one of the theoretical debates taking place within globalization discourses concerns the transformation of the state. Chapter 6 explores the redrawing of politico-economic boundaries and the shifting role of the state in the development of new regional formations. These formations are a critical site within which the contested power relations underpinning the emerging global economic order are played out and they also have significance in terms of the incorpora-tion of indigenous peoples within these frameworks. Here I draw together debates around the changing role of the state, the role of new regional formations and attempts by the state to mediate between the local and the global. Debates about the changing function of the state within industrialized countries in relation to the globalizing of capital and new regional formations form a backdrop against which to examine the tensions and contradictions involved in two specific cases of state engagement with indigenous peoples over their aspirations to self-determination and development in the final decade of the twentieth century.

The final chapter attempts to conceptualize the hegemonies and ideologies that comprise empire in the twenty-first century within the context of the constitutive framework of global economic order. Important signifiers of the problematics of globalization identified in this chapter include the privatization of goods and services and the interface of property rights and indigenous knowledge within the context of the WTO as the constitution for global economic order. Of enormous significance in the current context, the connecting roles of militarism and the economy and the increase in technologies of surveillance and control have become key elements of a new form of biopower and the exercise of global domination. In this regard, the re-emergence of the 'just war' doctrine and the racialized rhetoric of global terrorism have become dominating metaphors for a post-modern imperialism. Two views of new empire are compared in my conclusion. Both support the argument that what we are facing in this current phase of globalization is far from a multipolar order; instead, it is a new and dangerous form of imperialism. Drawing on Hardt and Negri's analysis of empire and the response of the multitude, increasing calls for a new ontology of world order provide the impetus for advocating one informed by indigenous world views and understandings of Being.

NOTES

1 Cited King, Michael (ed.) (1992) *Te Ao Hurihuri: Aspects of Maoritanga*. Auckland: Reed Books, p. 191.

2 Tiryakian, Edward A. (1984) 'The global crisis as an interregnum of modernity', *International Journal of Comparative Sociology*, 25 (1–2), pp. 123–30.

3 *Ibid.*, p. 4.

4 Kant, Immanuel (1939) *Perpetual Peace*. New York: Columbia University Press, pp. 34–5.

5 Polanyi, Karl (1957) [1944] *The Great Transformation. The Political and Economic Origins of Our Time*. Boston: Beacon Press.

6 Presotwitz, Clyde (2003) *Rogue Nation. American Unilateralism and the Failure of Good Intentions*. New York: Basic Books.

7 Held, David, McGrew, Anthony, Goldplatt, David and Jonathan Perraton (1999) *Global Transformations: Politics, Economics and Culture*. Stanford, CA: Stanford University Press.

8 Cf. Foster, John Bellamy (2001) 'Imperialism and "Empire"', *Monthly Review*, online at http://www.monthlyreview.org/1201.jbf.htm, accessed 13 May 2004; Panitch, Leo (2004). '2004: The New Imperial Challenge', *Socialist Register*, online at

http://www.york.u.ca/spcreg/, accessed 12 May 2004.

9 Foster, John Bellamy (2002) 'The Rediscovery of Imperialism', *Monthly Review*, November 2002, online at http://www.monthlyreview.org/1102jbf.htm, accessed 18 May 2004; Magdoff, Harry (1969) *The Age of Iimperialism: the Economics of US Foreign Policy*. New York: Monthly Review Press.

10 Hardt, Michael and Antonio Negri (2000) *Empire*. Cambridge, MA: Harvard University Press.

11 Held *et al.* (1999), p. 425.

12 *Ibid.*

13 This view may very well have changed in the light of the second war on Iraq.

14 Hardt and Negri (2000), p. xi.

15 Bacevich, Andrew J. (2002) *American Empire. The Realities and Consequences of US Diplomacy*. Cambridge, MA and London: Harvard University Press, p. 102.

16 Brzezinski, Zbigniew (1997) *The Grand Chessboard. American Primacy and Its Geostrategic Imperatives*. New York: Basic Books, p. xiii.

17 *Ibid.*, p. 40.

18 Ferguson, Neill (2004) *Colossus: The Rise and Fall of the American Empire*. London: Allen Lane, Penguin.

19 Wallerstein, Immanuel (2003) 'US weakness and the struggle for hegemony', *Monthly Review*, July–August 2003, online at http://www.monthlyreview.org/0703wallerstein.htm#Volume, accessed 10 May 2004.

20 Foster, John Bellamy (2004) 'The New Age of Imperialism', *Monthly Review*, July–August 2004, online at http://www.monthlyreview.org/0703jbf.htm, accessed 10 May 2004.

21 *Ibid.*

22 Bacevich (2002), p. 87.

23 *Ibid.*, p. 42.

24 For example, see Hirst, Paul and Grahame Thompson (1996) *Globalization in Question: the International Economy and the Possibilities of Governance*. Cambridge: Polity Press; Cambridge, MA: Blackwell.

25 Saul, John Ralston (2004) 'The end of globalism', *Financial Review*, 26 February 2004, online at http://www.financialreview.com.au/articles/2004/02/19/1077072774981.html.

26 Lyotard, Jean Francois (1984) *The Postmodern Condition: a Report on Knowledge* (translated by Geoff Bennington and Brian Massumi, foreword by Fredric Jameson). Manchester: Manchester University Press, p. 79.

27 Cox, Robert W. (1996) [1981] 'Social forces, states ands world orders: beyond international relations theory', in Robert W. Cox (with Timothy Sinclair), *Approaches to World Order*. Cambridge: Cambridge University Press, p. 128.

28 Gill, Stephen and David Law (1984) *The Global Political Economy: Perspectives, Problems and Policies*. Baltimore: Johns Hopkins University Press.

29 Hardt and Negri (2000), p. 3.

30 Scholte, Jan (1996) 'Beyond the buzzword: towards a critical theory of globalization', in Eleanore Kofman and Gillian Young (eds.), *Globalization: Theory and Practice*. New York: Pinter, pp. 43–57.

31 Cf. Waltz, K. N. (1993) 'The new world order', *Millennium*, 22 (2), pp. 187–95; Krasner, S. D. (1994) 'International political economy: abiding discord', *Review of International Political Economy*, 1(1), pp. 13–19.

32 Cf. Camelleri, J. and R. Falk (1992) *The End of Sovereignty? The Politics of a Shrinking and Fragmented World*. Aldershot: Elgar.

33 Scholte (1996), p. 51.

34 Held *et al.* (1999), pp. 3–7.

35 *Ibid.*, p. 4.

36 E.g., Hirst and Thompson (1996).

37 The most comprehensive representation of this perspective can be found in the work of Manuel Castells, particularly (1996) *The Rise of the Network Society*. Oxford: Blackwell; (1997) *The Power of Identity*. Oxford: Blackwell; (1998) *End of Millennium*. Oxford: Blackwell.

38 Ohmae, Kenichi. (1996) *The End of the Nation State. The Rise of Regional Economies*. London: Harper Collins.

39 Albrow, Martin (1996) *The Global Age*. Cambridge: Polity Press.

40 E.g., Wallerstein, Immanuel (1999) *The End of the World as We Know It. Social Science for the Twenty-First Century*. Minneapolis and London: University of Minnesota Press.

41 E.g., Cox, Robert W. (with Timothy J. Sinclair) (1996) *Approaches to World Order*. Cambridge: Cambridge University Press.

42 Cox, Robert W. (1995) 'Critical political economy', in Bjorn Hettne (ed.), *International Political Economy. Understanding Global Disorder*. Halifax, Nova Scotia: Fernwood Publishing, p. 36.

43 *Ibid.*

44 Vasquez, John A. *The Power of Power Politics. From Classical Realism to Neotraditionalism*. Cambridge: Cambridge University Press.

45 *Ibid.*, p. 38.

46 *Ibid.*, pp. 36–7.

47 *Ibid.*

48 The concept of international regimes was developed in 1975 by John Ruggie, who defined it as 'a set of mutual expectations, rules and regulations, plans, organizational energies and financial commitments, which have been accepted by states'. See Ruggie, John G. (1975) 'International responses to technology: concepts and trends', *International Organization*, 29 (3) (Summer), p. 570.

49 Keohane, Robert O. (1989) 'The theory of hegemonic stability and changes in international regimes, 1966–77', in Robert O. Keohane (ed.), *International Institutions and State Power. Essays in International Relations Theory*. Boulder, San Francisco and London: Westview Press, p. 75.

50 *Ibid.*, pp. 92–3. For the peace treaties of Westphalia, see Chapter 2 below, pp. 71–2.

51 Cox (1996) [1981], pp. 85–123.

52 An important essay in which Cox sets out his interpretation of Gramsci's concept of hegemony is Cox, R. (1996) [1983] 'Gramsci, hegemony and international relations: an essay in method', pp. 124–43.

53 Cox (1996) [1985], 'Realism, positivism and historicism', p. 55.

54 Cox (1996) [1981], p. 104.

55 Cox (1996) [1983], p. 137.

56 *Ibid.*

57 Mittleman, James H. (2000) *The Globalization Syndrome. Transformation and Resistance*. Princeton, NJ: Princeton University Press, p. 132.

58 Hettne, Bjorn (1997) 'The double movement: global market versus regionalism', in Robert W. Cox (ed.), *The New Realism. Perspectives on Multilateralism and World Order*. Tokyo: United Nations University Press; Basingstoke: Macmillan Press; New York: St Martin's Press, pp. 223–42.

59 Ohmae, Kenichi (1990) *The Borderless World. Power and Strategy in the Interlinked Economy. Management Lessons in the New Logic of the Global Marketplace*. New York: Harper Collins; see also Ohmae (1996).

60 Cf. Palmer, Norman D. (1996) *The New Regionalism in Asia and the Pacific*. Toronto: Lexington Books; Mack, Andrew and John Ravenhill (1994) *Pacific Cooperation: Building Economic and Security Regimes in the Asia-Pacific Region*. Australia: Allen and Unwin.

61 Mittleman (2000), p. 115.
62 See, for instance, Held *et al.* (1999).
63 Cox, Robert W. (1994) 'Global restructuring: making sense of the changing international political economy', in Richard Stubbs and Geoffrey R. D. Underhill (eds.), *Political Economy and the Changing Global Order*. Basingstoke: Macmillan, p. 49.
64 *Ibid.*
65 Poulantzas, Nicos (1975) *Classes in Contemporary Capitalism*. London, New Left Books, cited by Jessop, Bob (2003) 'Globalization and the national state', published by the Department of Sociology, University of Lancaster online at http://www.lancs.ac.uk/fss/sociology/papers/jessop-globalization-and-the-national-state.pdf, p. 3, accessed 14 March 2005, previously published at http://www.comp.lancaster.ac.uk/sociology/soc012rj.html in 2000. As outlined by Jessop, Poulantzas identified three overlapping stages of capitalist development on a world scale – 'a transitional phase, competitive capitalism, and monopoly capitalism or imperialism'. These stages were in turn divided into phases. Jessop explains that 'different phases of imperialism correspond to specific forms of capital accumulation and to specific forms of the global relations of production and the international division of labour' (*ibid.*, p. 5).
66 Cited *ibid.*, p. 11.
67 Poulantzas (1975), cited ibid., p. 8.
68 Cf. Jenkins, Kuni E. H. (2000) 'Haere Tahi Tauua. An Account of Aitanga in Maori Struggle for Schooling'. Unpublished PhD thesis, University of Auckland.
69 Cf. Smith, Linda T. (1999) *Decolonizing Methodologies. Research and Indigenous Peoples.* London and New York: Zed Books; Dunedin: Otago University Press.
70 Cajete, Gregory (1997) *Look to the Mountain. An Ecology of Indigenous Education.* Skyland, NC: Kivaki Press.
71 Key points highlighted in these reports are also outlined in the following chapter.
72 Tully, James (2000) 'The struggles of indigenous peoples for and of freedom', in Duncan Ivison, Paul Patton and Will Sanders (eds.), *Political Theory and the Rights of Indigenous Peoples.* Cambridge: Cambridge University Press, p. 40. Prior to the 1776 Declaration of Independence, this also included the United States of America.
73 *Ibid.*
74 Tully delineates four dimensions of internal colonization historically: (1) the reduction of the population; (2) the usurping of existing forms of government; (3) the displacement of the decreasing native population to reserves, etc.; and (4) treaty making, which often preceded usurpation and appropriation. The long-term effects of these four dimensions have been thoroughly documented.
75 Secretary-General Kofi Annan's message to the Second Session of the UN Permanent Forum on Indigenous Issues.
76 Charles Taylor (1995) 'Two theories of modernity', *Hastings Centre Report,* 25 (2), p. 32.
77 Mushakoji, Kinhide (1997) 'Multilateralism in a multicultural world: notes for a theory of occultation', in Robert. W. Cox (ed.), *The New Realism. Perspectives on Multilateralism and World Order.* Tokyo: United Nations University Press; Basingstoke: Macmillan Press; New York: St Martin's Press.
78 *Ibid.*, p. 52.
79 Cox (1995), p. 33.
80 Wallerstein, Immanuel (1998) *Utopistics, or Historical Choices of the Twenty-first Century.* New York: The New Press, p. 65.
81 *Ibid.*, p. 88.
82 Gadamer, Hans-Georg (1998) *The Beginning of Philosophy* (translated by Rod Coltman). New York: Continuum, p. 28.
83 *Ibid.*

84 Smith, Graham Hingangaroa (1997) 'The Development of Kaupapa Maori: Theory and Praxis'. IRI PhD Thesis Series No. 3. Te Whare Wananga o Tamaki Makaurau: International Research Institute for Maori and Indigenous Education, University of Auckland.

85 Gadamer (1998), pp. 30–1.

86 *Ibid.*

87 Smith, L. T. (1999).

88 Griffiths, Morwenna (1998) *Educational Research for Social Justice. Getting off the Fence.* Buckingham and Philadelphia: Open University Press.

89 Smith, G. H. (1997), p. 62.

90 Spivak, Gayatri Chakravorty (1987) 'French feminism in an international frame', in *Other Worlds: Essays in Cultural Politics.* New York: Methuen, pp. 134–53, cited by Young, Robert J. C. (1990) *White Mythologies: Writing History and the West.* London: Routledge, p. 160.

91 *Ibid.*

92 Smith, L. T. (1999), p. 72.

93 Castellano, Marlene Brandt (2000) 'Updating Aboriginal traditions of knowledge', in George J. Sefa Del, Budd L. Hall and Dorothy Goldin Rosenberg (eds.), *Indigenous Knowledges in Global Contexts. Multiple Readings of Our World.* Toronto, Buffalo and London: University of Toronto Press, p. 31.

94 Gadamer, Hans-Georg (1989) *Truth and Method.* [*Wahrheit und Methode*] (translation revised by Joel Weinsheimer and Donald G. Marshall), second revised edition. New York: Crossroad, p. 272.

95 *Ibid.*

96 Marsden, M. [1975] 'God, man and the universe', in King, M. (1992), p. 135.

97 Oppenheim, L. (1985) *International Law*, Vol. 1. London: Longman, cited by Held *et al.* (1999), p. 62.

98 Held *et al.* (1999).

99 Cox (1996) [1992] 'Multilateralism and world order', p. 494.

CHAPTER 1

※

Of Order and Being

Towards an Indigenous Global Ontology

This chapter presents the central theme of this book. It provides the foundation for my claim that despite having been devalued, marginalized, disenfranchised and frequently submerged throughout the history of Western imperialism, traditional indigenous knowledge forms have a profound contribution to make towards an alternative ontology for a just global order.

The search for meaning, for the essence of 'man' and 'being', has occupied humankind possibly since the beginning of thought itself. In the disorder and uncertainty of the contemporary moment, the need for meaning is more potent than ever as identities, structures and subjectivities get reordered in the flux of rapid integration, disintegration and reintegration. As Touraine eloquently depicts this condition in his *Critique of Modernity*,[1] modernity's separation of Reason and Spirit has in large measure given birth to 'the crisis of the new millennium'.

Responses to this crisis include the reconfiguration of civil society–state relationships. Another significant response has been the enormous rise of anti-systemic movements seeking the overthrow of current paradigms of power and global capitalism; Stavenhagen asserts that this development 'signifies another level, another reality, that of "ontological becoming", in the problematic of multilateralism and world order'.[2] We are indeed in a moment of 'transformational timespace'. In Wallerstein's terms, we are required to engage in an exercise of 'utopistics', of deciding on the basis of 'substantive rationality' our overall goals for the future and the best means of getting there.[3]

Ontology and Being

Robert Cox's response to the crisis of this time has been to call for what he terms 'a new ontology of social and political existence'.[4] 'Ontology', Cox states, 'lies at the beginning of any enquiry.'[5] The ontology Cox refers to here consists of the presuppositions that people make in thinking about, for instance, the entities and inter-relationships that make up the system broadly referred to as world order. According to Cox, 'the ontologies people work with derive from their historical experience and in turn become embedded in the world they construct'.[6] Historical experiences, however, are under-stood subjectively. Their interpretation is contingent upon the world view, the values (moral, spiritual and otherwise), the sets of ideas and notions of being and existence held by the subject, and it is in this philosophical sense that the notion of ontology is most contested.

In poststructuralist discourses in particular, 'ontology' is often seen to imply the notion of a 'fixed essence', a concept most notably disputed in contemporary philosophy by thinkers such as Sartre, who argues that the only reality by which man can be conceived as existing lies in 'how he acts and what he does',[7] and Foucault, whose suspicion of ontologies as representing essentialist notions of universal truths lead him to declare that, rather than looking for universal truths, we should be looking instead at the functioning of power within Western society.[8] In contrast, Heidegger argues that questions of being have ontological priority, yet these questions, he points out, have today been rendered empty and meaningless.[9] Here Heidegger refers to his argument that the Western philosophical tradition has forgotten to interrogate adequately its own taken-for-granted *meaning* of being.[10] Similarly, I suggest that in bringing us to acknowledge-ment of the plurality of histories and of the self, contemporary post-structuralist and deconstructivist discourses – in successfully disman-tling modernism's 'grand theories' and the divide between 'self' and 'other' – have deconstructed notions of truth and the meaning of existence to the degree that there has ceased to be any fundamental notion of the meaning of being.

Recent years have seen an increasing acknowledgement of the potential contributions to new ways of coexistence inherent in other civilizational modes. Similarly, the search for new ontologies may be seen as the motivation behind the revived interest in ancient Greek thought and in the hermeneutic interrogation of ancient meanings and world views as a response to the multilevel crisis of the contemporary world society. To date, however, outside of indigenous scholarship itself, within academic circles little serious attention has been paid to examining the possibilities inherent in indigenous ontologies.[11] It is precisely this possibility that I hope to demonstrate. Thus in this chapter I seek to identify certain fundamental principles of the nature of being that are common to most indigenous ontologies and cosmologies, and to postulate these as a response to calls for a new ontology of social and political existence.

Here the ancient symbol of the double spiral provides the central metaphor or motif for my thesis and, indeed, for the nature of being. Within some Maori tribal traditions, the double spiral is known as *takarangi*, literally meaning chaos, and represents the concepts of pre-existence and potentiality, concepts that are central to Maori cosmological understandings. In this sense, then, the symbol of the double spiral points to an ontological form and structure for world order that indicates solutions, I suggest, to the current disorder: a new/old way of thought and action embedded in the participatory forms of creation and existence of indigenous ecological humanisms. The symbolism inherent in the various representations of the spiral sits at the centre of Maori epistemologies and ontologies. The interrelationships of past, present and future, of time and space, of spirit and matter that are integral to Maori cosmologies and ontologies are profoundly represented within the symbol of the double spiral form. In Maori art forms such as carving, the placement of the double spiral pattern within meeting houses or on canoes signifies specific meanings all of which speak in various ways to the principle of being and existence within the different domains of being. In some forms, the spiral symbol represents the energy of pre-creation, of *Te Kore*, the potential of being. In other forms the spiral symbolizes coming into beingness, a progression from potential being, *Te Po*, towards actual existence, *Te Ao Marama*. In its representation as the seed-stuff of the universe from which existence comes into being, the three-dimensional double spiral also represents the relationships between the world of pre-creation, the world of pre-existence, and the world of existence. It is in its encapsulation of these meanings that the double spiral form provides a framework as well as a metaphor for this book.

In the necessarily brief discussion of indigenous, Maori and Waitaha ontologies that follows I have adopted the concept of ontology described by James Marshall as 'a branch of metaphysics which is concerned with a theory of what exists, or as a structure of reality, or as a categorical schema'.[12] Pointing to Quine's argument that there is no such thing as non-relative fact concerning the ontology of a theory but that all ontology of any theory or theorists is relative, Marshall argues that 'different systems of ontology then propose different systems of being, or a range of objects which must exist if a theory is true'.[13] There are certain broadly shared and funda-mental beliefs about the meaning of meaning and the nature of inter-relationships that are central to notions of indigeneity. While I acknowledge the essentialist nature of this endeavour, it can nonethe-less be argued that these broad groupings of beliefs and values comprise what might be called an indigenous ontology of being. In privileging Waitaha cosmologies and ontologies, I acknowledge two points of critical importance. The first is that in universalizing certain aspects of indigenous belief systems, I recognize that ontologies are relative and that the particularities and historicality of indigenous peoples and nations, as with those of individual Maori sub-tribes, give rise to unique characteristics and differences, some of which are identi-fiable within variations in stories of origin, in interpretation, and in *kawa* or protocols. The second point connects to the fact that, with respect to indigenous cosmologies, the bulk of my personal learning and experience has occurred within the extended family structure of Waitaha and that the knowledge systems thus acquired have made an inestimable contribution in shaping my conceptualizations of the crisis of globalization.

The Nature of Knowledge

'Traditional knowledge', Dearborn River Metis scholar Carl Urion writes, 'is living knowledge.'[14] By this he means that rather than being limited to a 'codified canon', traditional or indigenous knowledge is an expression of life itself, of how to live, and of the connection between all living things. Knowledge is regarded as having come from the Creator; hence knowledge is also understood as sacred. Urion describes indigenous knowledge as having four components: physical, mental, emotional and spiritual.[15] For many indigenous authors, one of the signifiers that differentiate indigenous and Western forms of knowledge is the holistic nature of indigenous knowledge. Cree educationalist Franke Wilmer comments on the profoundly different understandings of the nature and uses of knowledge in West-ern and indigenous world views. In indigenous ontologies, knowledge is both accumulated and applied in ways that involve the 'inner tech-nologies' of heightened consciousness as well as technologies of biodiversity and ecosystem management.[16] Seen as the highest attainment of human beings,[17] the acquisition of these 'inner technologies' involving consciousness of both the inner and outer realities of existence has been intrinsic to indigenous peoples' existence and to their storehouse of knowledge. Cree scholar Willie Ermine refers to traditional Aboriginal peoples' insight into the presence of an immanence 'that gives meaning to existence and forms the starting point for Aboriginal epistemology', an insight derived from their exploration of the 'universe of being within each person'.[20]

A number of authors critique the conceptualization of indigenous knowledge and Western forms of knowledge as being diametrically opposed to one another.[18] Thierry Verhelst refers to indigenous cultures as containing the seeds for the birthing of potential alternative societies to 'the standardized and devitalized model that has spread over the world'.[19] He cites the terms used by Indian philosopher Pannikar in his distinction between non-Western peoples and the 'European spirit' as 'anthropocentric' and 'cosmocentric'. For Verhelst, the appropriateness of these terms stems from the linear nature of post-Enlightenment Western conceptualizations of the universe as opposed to cyclic conceptions, the perception of humanity in a position of dominance, and 'the priority accorded to doing and having as opposed to a sense of being'.

Lakota scholar Vine Deloria Jnr provides a useful and important commentary on indigenous scientific knowledge and methodologies. Deloria identifies indigenous conceptions of knowledge as intrinsically connected to the lives and experiences of human beings, individuals and communities. He points out that whereas Western scientific knowledge draws conclusions by excluding some forms of data and including others, within traditional and indigenous systems of knowledge, all data and all experience are relevant to all things. In the Sioux traditions, for instance, the universe was a moral universe in which all knowledge and experience was drawn together in order to establish the 'proper moral and ethical road' or direction for human beings. Knowledge did not just exist in abstract form but was drawn from every gamut of individual and collective human experience. No experience, no piece of data was excluded or seen as invalid. All human experiences and all forms of knowledge contributed to the overall understandings and interpretations. The important task was to find the proper pattern of interpretation.[21] Similarly, Maori knowledge is temporally and spatially located within a particular cosmological paradigm of existence and pre-existence through which the social fabric of Maori societies was continuously remade and regulated. Integral to this concept is the emanation of an accumulated body of knowledge that incorporates the historical experiences of Maori people and their interactions with each other and the world.[22]

Western perceptions frequently interpret indigenous peoples' lack of mechanical methods for controlling nature as well as their information-gathering methodologies as evidence of the 'prescientific', precausal nature of indigenous knowledge systems, and an inability to conceptualize in an objective symbolic manner.[23] Yet, as Deloria points out, traditional indigenous knowledge systems involve both highly abstract symbolic thought and measurable and observable data collecting. Indigenous scientific knowledge includes minutely detailed knowledge of the natural world and a comprehensive understanding of the smallest phases of change that occur in the natural world, as demonstrated in the extremely specific inscription of names by characteristics or phases of growth. Arihia Smith's work in exploring the diverse inscriptive traditional Maori names for insects and spiders, their place in Maori mythology and use in classroom texts is one of many examples.[24] In her work, *He Ingoa Ngarara*, Smith identifies the way in which names are inscribed according to the activities or the characteristics of the creatures. For example, the caterpillar that merely eats its way around the edges of a leaf is known as *awhato kai paenga*, in contrast to the all-devouring caterpillar, which is known as *awhato ngongenga roa*. Similar examples abound in all indigenous vocabularies. This view of knowledge can be compared with Western scientific paradigms of knowledge that include and validate certain kinds of data and experiences and exclude others.

The Nature of Existence

A central principle of indigenous peoples' relational ontologies and cosmologies is the inseparable nature of the relationship between the world of matter and the world of spirit. In this view, the laws that govern the universe and determine and maintain the constitutive elements of material existence are fundamentally spiritual in nature. In Maori traditions, these worlds are woven together by *Te Aho Tapu*, 'the sacred thread', a concept that expresses the sacredness of all existence. Where the meaning of existence and the relationship between being and action are contested within existentialist and postmodern philosophical frameworks, Maori understandings recognize creation as a process of continuous action or coming into being, the impetus for which emanates from *Kore*, or *Te Korekore*, the world of potential being. In this process of coming into being, particular forms of sound and thought play an essential role. For Maori, as well as being a vehicle for the expression of human thought and language, sound has deep metaphysical and creative connotations that go beyond its use as the practical instrument of ordinary communication. The cadences of ancient songs, of ritual calls, of sacred chants, through which the world is sung into existence, the flesh is sung onto the bones, and the relationships are sung which bind all together within the cosmos, express what Knudtson and Suzuki refer to as bringing 'a measure of harmony to the Cosmos' and breathing 'life into the network of subtle interconnections between human beings and the entire natural world'.[25]

The interactive nature of the relationship between the spiritual and physical worlds is articulated through indigenous narratives that are frequently interpreted by the Western world as myth. Discussing the medicine stories of tribal people in North America, Native American author Paula Gunn Allen refers to interchanges with supernaturals as 'the bedrock of native spirituality',[26] affirming that while frequently called myths and conceived of as 'primitive spiritual stories that articulate psychological realities',[27] these accounts detail actual exchanges and interchanges between humans and the supernaturals that occupy the same environment. Allen argues that while these accounts do 'inform consciousness' and 'connect with deep levels of being',[28] their significance and their ability to inform and connect in these ways stems from the fact that they are real accounts rather than explanations of psychological states. As such, these oral narratives – like the rituals through which these relationships between the corporeal and spiritual are expressed, and which play a critical role in meditating the multiple states of existence – form part of what Allen refers to as a 'great body of articulated experiential knowledge' that underpins indigenous cosmological and ontological knowledge.[29]

This principle of the spiritual nature of existence has been the lynchpin of many traditional indigenous social and political structures and frequently remains so today. Chief Oren Lyons of the Iroquois Nation states: 'The primary law of Indian government is the spiritual law. Spirituality is the highest form of politics, and our spirituality is directly involved in government.'[30] For Lyons, the Iroquois see spirituality and politics as two powerful forces, two fires, which work together in coalition with the spiritual fire at the centre. Similarly, in the African view of reality elaborated by Senghor, the various kingdoms and different forms of existence represent different aspects of a single reality. Senghor describes it thus:

> this reality is being in the ontological sense of the word, and it is life force. For the African, matter, in the sense the Europeans understand it, is only a system of signs which translates the single reality of the universe: being, which is spirit, which is life force.[31]

The implications of these practices and the application of the principles expressed therein demonstrate something of the nature of indigenous peoples' understanding of the physical and metaphysical worlds. As Wilmer suggests, whereas Western peoples' explorations of technology took an outward direction, indigenous peoples' prioritizing of 'inner technologies'[32] enabled the advancement of particular ways of knowing centred around the interconnections between the molecules of existence and the nature of the energy that binds them.

This esoteric and scientific, highly specialized knowledge, which forms the highest level of Maori cosmological wisdom[33] and the ridgepole of Waitaha ontologies and epistemologies, reflects particular understandings of the nature of existence, understandings that some contemporary physicists have recently begun to conceptualize in similar ways. One expression of this understanding reflects the essential energy or *hihiri* that is the primal force of pre-existence, the binding energy or *mauri* that knits together the elements, the life force or *mauri-ora* inherent in all existence, and the spiritual force or *hau-ora* by which life itself is animated. This concept of *mauri* as the unique living force that is present in all the kingdoms of existence extends to inanimate as well as animate objects and, indeed, to concepts and forms of knowledge.[34] Within the natural world, each individual rock and stone, each individual animal and plant, as well as every body of land and of water, is recognized as having its own unique life force.

There are many implications, interpretations and meanings that connect to the concept of *mauri*. One such is the concept of each living thing being guarded by its own supernatural being, explained by leading Maori scholar Mason Durie as an expression of the need to acknowledge and protect the life force present in all aspects of the natural world. Understood thus, *mauri* is an essential element of wellness. As an expression of interrelationships, Durie states, *mauri* or life force 'spirals outwards seeking to establish communication with higher levels of organization and to find meaning by sharing a sense of common origin'.[35] At the level of metaphysics, protection of *mauri* is essential for spiritual wellbeing. The ability to manipulate *mauri* encapsulates the concept of *mauri* as the powerful force or energy of 'bringing into being'. In Indian cosmology, the primordial energy of pre-existence in its manifested form is conceptualized as *Prakti*.[36] As such, Indian academic and author Vandana Shiva suggests, it is both 'a highly evolved philosophical category' and 'one through which ordinary women in rural India relate to Nature'.[37] In the Cree language, this ability to tap into the energy of the life force is known as *mamatowisowin*, and is applied to the ability to co-create by accessing the life force of existence. Ermine explains this as an expression of 'being in connection with happenings'.[38]

The Nature of Relationships

As articulated and given expression in many ways, some of which have been briefly touched on here, the interrelationship between all forms of existence is fundamental to Maori cosmology and ontology. It is inscribed within Maori stories of origin and genealogies. It is this notion of interconnectedness that governs Maori understandings of and relationships to the physical world and to the world of metaphysics. It is the principle that governs reciprocity, the principle of life itself. Coupled with the notion of interconnectedness of all existence and pre-existence is the notion of balance. Inherent in Maori epistemologies and ontologies, the requirement of balance is reflected in Maori notions of the reciprocity of all things, a principle that permeates every aspect of Maori social and political life, and is expressed in the relationship between the dimensions and layers of existence comprising being and non-being.

Within Waitaha ontology, the binding together of all the elements of existence occurs in a particular order within which human beings coexist in direct genealogical relationship to all the other elements of existence. As with other indigenous perceptions, this relationship extends beyond this universe to the entire cosmos. It extends also to the world of spirit and the inhabitants of that realm, to those supernatural beings whose existence in the world of pre-creation performs a vital function in the ordering of existence, and to the cosmos itself.

The concept of interrelatedness is emphasized by indigenous authors and scholars as being integral to indigenous understandings of knowledge and being. Compared to Western knowledge systems, which are largely seen as linear and concerned primarily with empirical data and materiality, indigenous knowledge systems are often defined as circular or spiral in nature and inclusive of both experiential and intuitive data. Founded on notions of separation and opposition, the traditional field of European knowledge and philosophy is for Leopold Senghor, as for many other indigenous writers, characterized by its separation of matter and spirit and its distinction between body and soul. Senghor sees African ontology as diametrically opposed to the traditional philosophy of Europe which he describes as 'essentially static, objective, dichotomic … dualistic'.[39] Like other indigenous authors, including most notably Oren Lyons, Willie Ermine, Vine Deloria Jnr and Gregory Cajete, Senghor expresses the principle of the interrelated nature of all existence as underpinning African ontologies.[40] Exploring indigenous notions of power and justice, Alfred refers to the indigenous belief in a universal relationship expressed as a circle of interdependency involving all the elements of existence.[41]

In Maori orderings of time and space, *whakapapa* or genealogy is both the differentiator and the regulator of time/space. Discussing the importance of the particular as well as the universal, in his submission to the New Zealand Royal Commission on Genetic Engineering, Peter Wills notes that, within Maori tradition, knowledge of anything is concerned with the 'proper perception of its location in time and space'.[42] As Wills argues, the particularities of *whakapapa* are crucial to understanding knowledge of things and events, for the location of their origin within time and space provides the map for understanding the true nature of anything that is. In this sense, the physical and temporal origins of all things define the nature of their relationships to one another and to the land. This relationship to the land is seen as the *pito*[43] by which the connectivity of Maori identity is bound and held. It is also explanatory of the encoding of philosophical and metaphysical knowledge that, along with *whakapapa* and the ancient rituals of sacred encounter, is embedded within the geographical landscape. Like those of other indigenous peoples, Maori understandings of temporality are conceived of in a way that is fundamentally at variance with contemporary Western empirical scientific thought. Like *whakapapa*, time has many layers of meaning, some of which exist at the metaphysical level and others at the level of physical temporality. Shirres tells us that, at the deepest level of Maori understandings of being and time, located at the core of the cosmos, there is a 'singularity', where there is neither space nor time. The whole universe comes from that point, *'i te kore ki te po, ki te ao marama*, from the nothingness, to the night, to the full day'.[44]

Thus time and space exist only at the level of the material world, where they are firmly intertwined. In the world of pre-existence and the world of spirit, time and space do not exist. These worlds are beyond time and beyond space. Within the world of corporeality, however, as Nepe suggests, time is of great significance and highly valuable.

Te Maire Tau provides an example of this in his critique of Peter Munz's view of genealogy as the basis for indigenous peoples' measure of time.[45] In Te Maire Tau's explanation, Maori and non-Maori views of time are differentiated by their understandings of what constitutes both time and history. As Tau points out, Maori perceptions of the past are not the same as those held by *Pakeha* (the British). For Maori, the past is continuously in front of us, one manifestation being the acknowledgment of the presence of the ancestors on ceremonial occasions, another being the fundamental concept that as we proceed forward, we also hold the past constantly in front of us. Beyond being a historical record of the past, time provides circuitous continuity in which the ancient past, the present and the future are indissolubly connected. Through genealogical recitals and the rituals of encounter, the past is linked directly back to *Papa-tua-nuku* and *Rangi-nui-i-tu-nei*, the original parents.

Within Maori ontological and cosmological paradigms it is impossible to conceive of the present and the future as separate and distinct from the past, for the past is constitutive of the present and, as such, is inherently reconstituted within the future. Here the symbolism of the spiral speaks to Maori understandings of time and space. Each circumambulation of the spiral incorporates the past into both the present and the future and, in so doing, reconstitutes both. In the same manner, both the present and future are constitutively incorporated into the past, thus changing the nature or understanding of the past.

At the same time that the spiral is going forward, it is returning, *'Te torino whakahaere, whakamuri'*.[46] 'This', Ihimaera tells us in his novel set in the time of the prophet Rua at the turn of the twentieth century, 'is the esoteric nature of the spiral. It is the first law of the universe.'

Modernity and the Attack on Nature and Holism

Conflicting views regarding the nature of being and the relationship between spirit and reason have dominated the thinking of philosophers and scientists since at least the fifth century BC. Arnold Davidson, in his introductory words to Pierre Hadot's inaugural lecture to the Chair of the History of Hellenistic and Roman Thought at the College de France, 'Forms of Life and Forms of Discourse in Ancient Philosophy',[47] points to Hadot's insights into the ancient physics of the Stoics and Epicureans as a 'spiritual exercise that allowed one to see the human world "from above"',[48] and the work of the ancient philosophers as a 'spiritual exercise in the degree to which, elevating thought to the perspective of the Whole, it liberates it from the illusions of individuality'.[49] In the metaphysical philosophy of Pythagoras there was no opposition between religion and science. Number was not only a universal but also a sacred principle, 'the principle, the source and the root of all things';[50] it was a living reality to be approached experientially. One, the monad, or unity, was the principle underlying number, and numbers themselves were 'manifestations of diversity in a unified continuum'.

In the early centuries of Christianity, some of the holistic ideals of ancient Greek philosophy survived by becoming submerged within the doctrines of the early church. Ancient belief systems and religions that celebrated the Mother Goddess and the fecundity of the Earth Mother became incorporated into the Marian doctrines of the Catholic Church. The Celtic Church also became known for its celebration of Nature and for the ecclesiastical leadership of women. The writings of Pelagius in the fifth century demonstrate the influence of Celtic spirituality in the early British Church, an influence that ultimately led to his expulsion and excommunication.[51] However despite the Church's attempts to discredit doctrines such as the St John tradition of the love of creation and the essential goodness of humanity, the influence of Celtic spirituality and of great mystics like Dionysius in the sixth century continued, at least in pockets, well into the eighth and ninth centuries. Ultimately, the dominance of power-driven patriarchal ideologies within the Church led to the marginalization of both women and Nature.[52] Contemporary feminist philosophers point to the influence of patriarchal ideologies of dominance and power, these being notably demonstrated in the assassination by a sect of fanatical monks of the outstanding neo-Platonist astronomer, mathematician and philosopher Hypatia of Alexandria in approximately 415 CE.[53]

In his work *The Gendered Atom* (1999),[54] Theodore Roszak focuses attention on the impact of the patriarchal austerity of the Calvinist Reformation, which by the mid-sixteenth century had not only driven the Mother of God out of European religious and spiritual practice, but had also attempted to destroy every vestige of the ancient traditions of holism, of community, and of earth as primal mother. As Roszak contends, the Puritanism of Calvin prepared the way for the emergence of modern science and the positivist emphasis on mathematics and empirical knowledge heralded by Galileo in the late sixteenth and early seventeenth centuries.[55] In the Aristotelian anthropocentric tradition, Judeo-Christian ideologies, in which humankind was located at the top of the Chain of Being, conceived of land and its creatures as existing for man's benefit. The confining of worship to a distant, lawgiving Father God occurred concurrently with the birth of new forms of science that eschewed holism and imagination in favour of cold logic and an atomized reality.

The development of Western philosophical thought did not rest on a universalist teleology, and Roszak notes that reductionism has an ancient lineage traceable to the Athenians of the fourth century BC.[56] Arguing against the popular view that Greek atomism was overthrown by the 'dark ages' of religion and superstition, Roszak points out that, unlike the atomism of the Enlightenment philosophers, the atomism of the ancient Greeks was located within a tradition of humanism that sought peace of mind and tranquillity through 'the evidence of things unseen'.[57] Henryk Skolimowski, in his discussion of changes in historical differences in basic positions regarding the relation of values to knowledge, points to the contrasting ideologies of the twelfth century, most notably represented in the ecocentric philosophy of Francis of Assisi and that of Thomas Aquinas, whose hierarchical view of creation located all creatures, by virtue of their lack of intellect, as subject to human beings.[58] The integration of Aristotelian logic into Christian theology had a profound impact on Western thought, giving rise later to the 'doctrine of discovery' discussed in Chapter 2.

The spread of hermeticism in the fifteenth and sixteenth centuries, helped by the development of the printing press and the translation of the Hermetica[59] by the Italian mathematician Ficino, was a strong influence on the nature-centred, holist strand in Renaissance humanism. Frances Yates traces the expansion of hermeticism from Italy and Venice into England and its adoption by leading intellectual figures such as William Grocyn, John Dee, Francis Bacon[60] and, later, Isaac Newton.[61] In Europe, where it was largely driven underground, hermeticism was embraced by scholars such as the German alchemist and philosopher, Michael Maier and the charismatic Italian Giordano Bruno, in whose magical variant of neoplatonist hermeticism, Yates states, the unity of the All in the One was a constant theme.[62]

The sixteenth and seventeenth centuries saw a radical transformation in the conceptualization of nature and existence. The development of scientific academies such as the British Royal Society and French Académie des Sciences, both established in 1660, created meeting places for like-minded souls whose study and application of both hermetics and science, it has been argued, reflected the emergence of 'an historically unprecedented will to power'.[63] René Descartes based his view of Nature on a fundamental division into two separate and independent realms, that of mind (res cogitas) and matter (res extensa). For Descartes, the search for a true method, the aim of which was 'arriving at knowledge of everything my mind was capable of grasping', had as its goal 'a practical philosophy' that would make humankind the 'masters and possessors of nature' through 'the invention of an infinity of devices through which we might enjoy, without any effort, the fruits of the earth and all its commodities as well as the preservation of health, which is undoubtedly the first good'.[64]

While men were seen as both physical and mental beings, the rationality of the human mind and the ability of men to develop 'various automata which move without thought' provided proof that animals were merely 'natural automata'.[65] Influenced by Cartesian mechanism and the impact of the attack on 'heresies', this period marked the turning away from hermetic principles of interconnectedness, reverence for existence, and the symbiotic reciprocity between male and female. While, on one hand, leading thinkers such as Pascal, Leibniz and Spinoza in the seventeenth century, and Rousseau and Kant in the eighteenth century, challenged the empiricism that became dominant in Western thought, on the other hand, the Cartesian division of matter and mind described by Heidegger as 'the implantation of a baleful prejudice' in a 'seemingly new beginning proposed for philosophizing'[66] provided the rationale for scientific hypotheses that atomized matter into isolated fragments and saw scientific knowledge as distinct from, and superior to, intrinsic values.

The Hermeneutic Mode

Robert Cox suggests that inquiry into complex and comprehensive change requires a 'historically oriented, interpretive and hermeneutic epistemological approach' that 'sees subject and object in the historical world as an interrelated whole'.[67] As I seek to demonstrate in this section, the hermeneutic epistemological model most recently developed within Western philosophical thought is an articulation, albeit in a reduced form, of concepts and understandings that have always existed in indigenous epistemological and ontological thought. My intention in tracking very briefly the historical development of critical forms of hermeneutics is to demonstrate one of the spaces within which, anticipating Western philosophical thought, indigenous epistemologies and ontologies provide pathways towards a more meaningful and inclusive form of global society. I maintain that the continuity of pathways they provide has profound relevance for the future.

As a methodology for the uncovering of meaning within the human sciences, the origins of hermeneutics are locatable within the Reformation controversies concerning the proper interpretation of the Bible.[68] As Connolly and Keutner show, the two contradictory approaches that formed the basis of these disputes centred around whether the proper method for illuminating the meaning of the text was to discern the author's intention, in what became the author-intentionalist position,[69] or – the Lutheran view – to stress an interpretation of meaning in the context of the whole, a precursor to the hermeneutic rule that any part of a text must be understood in the context of the whole, while the whole must likewise be understood in terms of its constituent parts.[70] This rule, Gadamer explains, 'stems from ancient rhetoric and was carried over by modern hermeneutics from the art of speaking to the art of understanding'.[71] This more or less circular process of understanding, which, as Hogan suggests, involves an evolving interplay between the reader and the text, has been the basis of the central debate involving what is referred to as 'the hermeneutic task'.[72]

The sacking of Constantinople by the Christian Crusaders, through which the philosophical thought of the ancient Greeks was brought to the Western world, saw the development of a new form of textual hermeneutics initially centred on the interpretation of the complete works of Plato.[73] In the late eighteenth and early nineteenth centuries, led by the work of the German philosophers Friedrich

Schleiermacher and, following him, Wilhelm Dilthey, textual hermeneutics emerged as a practical working methodology for the social sciences. Following Schleiermacher's emphasis on the rational character of hermeneutics, Dilthey argued that the hermeneutic circle provided the foundation for a rational reconstructivist methodology that marked off the hermeneutic sciences from the natural sciences. However, where Schleiermacher, in the Romantic tradition, emphasized the creative talent of the individual and, according to Connolly and Keutner,[74] believed that the text was the 'product of the author's personal idiosyncrasy' and that therefore interpretation required intimate harmony with the author, for Dilthey it is the connectedness of 'everything pertaining to mind [or spirit, *Geist*]'[75] that provides the framework for understanding the meaning of the parts which thus determine, and are determined by, the meaning of the whole. According to Dilthey, the intersubjective framework developed by each individual on the basis of his or her own private experience becomes the basis on which 'the transition from private to subjective is accomplished through inferences of analogy and induction'.[76] The probabilistic basis of the functions of inference and deduction thus leads Dilthey to conclude that 'the process of understanding is itself to be conceived as induction'.[77] For the nineteenth century hermeneutic philosophers, then, although different in kind from the natural sciences, hermeneutic disciplines were nevertheless 'scientific'. Interpretation was regarded as both finite and objective, aiming at one objective truth – the true sense or unique meaning of the text, one that is therefore decidable.

It was in the work of Heidegger that the concept of the hermeneutical circle took on new meaning. Developed in *Being and Time*,[78] Heidegger's critique of the notion of a changeless essence of the human focused attention on the hermeneutic circle as operating in all modes of human understanding, rather than as operating only in the interpretation and understanding of texts. Whereas, prior to this point, the circular movement of understanding was confined to going backwards and forwards in the text until it was completely understood, it was in Heidegger, Gadamer states, that historical consciousness in the form of recognizing one's own prejudices and preconceptions became concretized.[79] Heidegger critiqued the separation of interpretation and understanding, arguing that the possibility of 'the most primordial kind of knowing' lies within the hermeneutic circle. For Heidegger, accessing this 'primordial knowing' requires the interpreter to recognize his/her own preconceptions and fancies and the historicality within which they exist. Heidegger contended that all the experiences, networks of institutions and other constituent aspects forming the framework of our perceptions are what shape our projections of the world and our understanding and interpretations of 'the Other', and thus provoke an awareness of our own 'fore-having'. Nonetheless, according to Gadamer's reading of Heidegger, while within the circular structure of meaning 'lies hidden the positive potentiality of the most original knowledge', the task of interpretation is to 'secure the topic under study' by working any pretence of its 'own fore-having, fore-sight, and fore-conception' out of the subject matter.[80] Thus for Heidegger, while it is the historical prejudices of the interpreter that disclose and constitute 'being' and consequently the text – thus making understanding possible – hermeneutic reflection remains concerned with the development of ontologically positive meaning.[81]

The transformation of hermeneutics to the level of a philosophy occurred for the first time in the work of Hans-Georg Gadamer.[82] Deriving his critique of objectivist hermeneutics from Heidegger, Gadamer expanded the notion that all understanding proceeds from the 'positive prejudices' or prejudgements of the reader to encompass what he called 'the anticipation of perfection', the presupposition that 'one can only understand that which presents a unity of meaning'. This anticipation of perfection, or in other words the expectation that what we are about to read is true, which guides our understanding, is in each case dependent on content.[83] According to Gadamer, 'the first of all hermeneutical conditions … remains understanding of the subject matter, i.e., having to do with the same object'.[84] Nevertheless, there is a dichotomy between familiarity with the subject and strangeness that is integral to Gadamer's concept of hermeneutical consciousness. While on the one hand, Gadamer argues, hermeneutic consciousness proceeds from the assumption that for those who seek understanding a necessary connection exists between them and the subject matter, on the other hand, hermeneutical consciousness knows that this connection cannot exist in the notion of 'unquestioned implicit accord' as, for instance, in an 'unbroken continuity of tradition' but exists in the place of Between, described as 'between historically meant, distanced objectivism and belonging to a tradition'.[85]

In a discussion of the implications of Gadamer's work for the philosophy of education Padraig Hogan points to Gadamer's emphasis on the uncovering of preconceptions and prejudices as the constituents of being that most profoundly shape who we are.[86] Hogan identifies six interrelated themes in Gadamer's work which have significance for educational concerns. He cites these as 'the primacy of play in the experience of understanding' (*Spiel*); the principle of 'effective history' (*Wirkungsgeschite*); the predisposing of thought by language; the plurality of tradition; the 'fusion of horizons' (*Horizontverschmelzung*); and the 'dialogue that we are'.[87] As the most important of the six, the principle of effective history identifies Gadamer's hermeneutics as a critical methodology for uncovering submerged meanings and interpretations of events and discourses. Effective history involves the consciousness of the effects of human historicality on our own understandings. This has relevance in terms of the critical awareness of my own biases, which continue to shape my understandings of indigenous knowledge and which I have sought to declare. It has relevance also for the development of critical understandings of the disenfranchisement of indigenous knowledge forms, the events and discourses that have shaped our perceptions and the structures of world order, and the interrelationships between those processes. It is in this ability to bring together all aspects of experience and understanding and to interpret them within a comprehension of the whole and the placement of the self within rather than without, that the transformative potential of critical hermeneutics is most potent.

Critical Hermeneutics and the Transformative Spiral

David Geoffrey Smith points out that, rather than seeking 'some pure ground, some place of objectivity from which to view and analyse people or situations ... the hermeneutic voice attempts to always speak from the centre of action'.[88] He argues that although they have originated within the constraints and limits of European culture and Enlightenment rationality, the insights developed within critical hermeneutics in the sense of the interdependence of human understanding and the acknowledgment of oneself within the larger picture rather than standing objectively without, while not unique, have the potential to achieve the reintegration of that which was 'rent by the objectivist proclivities of science'.[89]

The inherent problematic in the notion of circular understandings originally articulated by Schleiermacher and developed by Gadamer and others as the 'circle of understanding', is that a circle invariably returns to the point of origin. In contrast, the spiral never returns exactly to the point of origin but moves progressively forward in a

process of constant motion and expansion. As a motif for transformation, the double spiral represents all phases of coming into being,
movement, growth, and transformation. One interpretation of the
double spiral within Maori cosmologies, presented by Catholic theo-
logian Michael Shirres in his study of *karakia* (1997), is that of the
unfolding of the entire creation, including the millions of galaxies that
constitute the cosmos as we know it. In a metaphysical sense the
whole of Maori cosmology is represented within the spiral, symbol-
izing the intertwining of the world of spirit with the worlds of potentiality and creation. The spiral thus represents both the potentiality of
being and the actualizing of potential into beingness. As noted in
Shirres's study, for Maori the centre of the spiral represents that place
beyond time and space from which everything, including all knowledge and sound, and all life-giving energy, emanates. Containing
certain similarities to the holistic ontologies and cosmologies of the
ancient pre-Socratic philosophers, these understandings of causality
and existence have been inherent within indigenous ontologies and
cosmologies since time immemorial.

Within the material world, the spiral is found in all the domains of
existence and represents a progression upwards or forwards. In the
complexity of the scheme of evolution, the path of evolution is a
spiral. Each loop of the cycle is a spiral. Inspired by his introduction to
the Indian nine symbols,[90] the number system developed by the
twelfth-century Pisan mathematician Leonardo Fibonacci enabled
new mathematical ways of understanding the composition and
evolution of life, as represented in the alternating spirals in plants, sea
shells and galaxies, a design principle now known as the Fibonacci
spiral. The ground-breaking and sadly neglected work of Austrian
Viktor Schauberger (1885–1958) on energy, motion and the processes of nature identified a form of motion that he referred to as
'cycloid-spiral-space-curve motion' as 'original' motion or a 'form-
creating' dynamic.[91] The discovery of the double-helix spiral structure of DNA by Nobel Prize laureates James Watson and Francis
Crick in 1953 radically changed biology and enabled, in their own
words, 'a possible copying mechanism for the genetic material'.[92]
Gazale contends that spiral galaxies 'constitute the most gigantic
orderly pattern observable by man'.[93] Thus, throughout the natural
world, representations of the spiral signify movement forward,
evolution – in fact, the essence of life and growth.

In the words of Nabokov, 'The spiral is a spiritualized circle. In a
spiral form, the circle, uncoiled, unwound, has ceased to be vicious, it

has been set free.'[94] I contend that a similar argument applies to critical hermeneutics. When the metaphor of the expanding circle and debates about the influence of the self and prejudices in understanding and constituting the past are reframed in terms of a 'spiral of understanding', the transformative potential of critical hermeneutics becomes manifest.

For Smith, 'hermeneutics is about articulating the integrity of the world lying beyond the violence inflicted upon it by ideology, politics and war'.[95] In this sense, Heidegger's claim that interpretation is the 'primordial' work of human experience[96] links to the notion that, as the most profound work of thinking, interpretation is ultimately about showing 'the possibilities for life's continuance'.[97] It is at precisely this moment of possibility, I maintain, that indigenous ontologies and cosmologies have a profoundly important contribution to make.

NOTES

1 Touraine, Alaine (1995) *Critique of Modernity* (translated by David Macey). Cambridge, MA: Blackwell.
2 Stavenhagen, Rudolfo (1997) 'People's movements: the antisystemic challenge', in Robert W. Cox (ed.), *The New Realism. Perspectives on Multilateralism and World Order*. Tokyo: United Nations University Press; Basingstoke: Macmillan Press; New York: St Martin's Press, p. 20.
3 Wallerstein, Immanuel (1998) *Utopistics, or, Historical Choices of the Twenty-First Century*. New York: New Press.
4 Cox, Robert W. (1996) [1992] 'Towards a posthegemonic conceptualization of world order: reflections on the relevancy of Ibn Khaldun' in Robert W. Cox (with Timothy J. Sinclair) (1996), *Approaches to World Order*. Cambridge: Cambridge University Press, p. 144.
5 *Ibid.*
6 *Ibid.*, p. 145
7 Heidegger, Martin (1996) *Basic Writings: from* Being and Time *(1927) to* The Task of Thinking *(1964)* (edited by David Krell, with general introduction and introductions to each selection). London: Routledge, p. 214.
8 Foucault, Michel (1980) 'Two lectures', in C. Gordon (ed.), *Power/Knowledge. Selected Interviews and Other Writings 1972–1977*. New York and London: Harvester Wheatsheaf, pp. 78–108.
9 Heidegger, Martin (1999) [1926]. *Being and Time* (translated by John Macquarrie and Edward Robinson). Oxford: Blackwell.
10 Mulhall, Stephen (1997) *Heidegger and Being and Time*, London and New York: Routledge.
11 A notable exception is *Educational Philosophy and Theory*, 32, 1 (Special Edition), 2000.
12 Marshall, James (2000) 'The boundaries of belief: territories of encounter between indigenous peoples and Western philosophies', *Educational Philosophy and Theory*, 32, 1 (April), p. 15.
13 *Ibid.*
14 Urion, Carl (1999) 'Recording first nations traditional knowledge'. Unpublished

paper, U'mista Cultural Society, p. 11.

15 *Ibid.*, p. 8.

16 Wilmer, Franke (1993) *The Indigenous Voice in World Politics. Since Time Immemorial.* Newbury Park, London and New Delhi: Sage, pp. 205–8.

17 Cajete, Gregory (2000) *Native Science. Natural Laws of Interdependence.* Santa Fe: Starlight Publishers, p. 67.

18 For example, Agrawai, Arun (1995) 'Dismantling the divide between indigenous and scientific knowledge', in *Development and Change*, 26. pp. 413–39. Agrawai problematizes this divide, favouring instead an approach that recognizes 'multiple domains and types of knowledges, with differing logics and epistemologies', arguing for a recognition of the 'multiplicity of logics and practices that underlie the creation and maintenance of different knowledges' as the basis for the preservation and control of indigenous knowledge forms by indigenous peoples (pp. 432–3). The point of my discussion in stressing particular shared conceptualizations of knowledge and existence amongst many indigenous peoples is to highlight the multifaceted principle of interdependence across multiple realms that distinguishes them. This is not to say that these conceptualizations are completely outside what is loosely referred to in the above discussion as 'Western science' or 'scientific knowledge'. The 'discovery' within certain branches of science such as quantum physics of similar principles of existence has done much to transform the thought of particular branches of science. Other areas, however, are much more reluctant to engage with conceptualizations that run counter to the received wisdom of more techno-rationalist views.

19 Verhelst, Thierry G. (1990) *No Life Without Roots. Culture and Development.* London: Zed Books.

20 Ermine, Willie (1995) 'Aboriginal epistemology', in Marie Battiste and Jean Barman (eds.), *First Nations Education in Canada: the Circle Unfolds.* Vancouver: UBC Press, p. 103.

21 Deloria, Vine Jnr (1999) 'If you think about it, you will see that it is true', in Vine Deloria, Jnr, *Spirit and Reason. The Vine Deloria Reader.* Colorado: Fulcrum Publishing, pp. 40–60.

22 Nepe, Tuakana M. (1991) 'Te Toi Huarewa Tipuna Kaupapa Maori. An educational intervention system.' Unpublished MA thesis, School of Education, University of Auckland.

23 *Ibid.*

24 Smith, Arihia (1997). *He Ingoa Ngarara: Insects and Spiders.* Canterbury: Lincoln University Press.

25 Knudtson, Peter and Suzuki, David (1997) *Wisdom of the Elders.* St Leonards, New South Wales, Australia: Allen and Unwin, p. 120.

26 Allen, Paula Gunn (1991) *Grandmothers of the Light. A Medicine Women's Source Book.* Beacon: Boston Press, p. 6.

27 *Ibid.*

28 *Ibid.*, p.7.

29 *Ibid.*, p. 8.

30 Lyons, Oren (1984) 'Spirituality, equality and natural law', in Leroy Little Bear, Menno Boldt and J. Anthony Long (eds.), *Pathways to Self-Determination. Canadian Indians and the Canadian State.* Toronto: University of Toronto Press.

31 Senghor, Leopold Sedar (1993) 'Negritude: a humanism of the twentieth century', *The Africa Reader: Independent Africa.* London, 1970: Vintage, Random Century, reprinted in Laura Chrisman and Patrick Williams (eds.), *Colonial Discourse and Post-Colonial Theory.* London and New York: Harvester Wheatsheaf, p. 30.

32 Wilmer (1993).

33 This form of knowledge was regarded as esoteric knowledge.

34 Here John Rangihau's explanation is instructive in that he explains this as the reason

for the reluctance on the part of elders to divulge certain kinds of knowledge too readily. See Rangihau, J. (1992) 'Foreword: Learning and Tapu', in Michael King (ed.), *Te Ao Hurihuri. Aspects of Maoritanga*. Auckland: Reed.

35 Durie, Mason (2001) *Mauri Ora. The Dynamics of Maori Health*. Auckland: Oxford University Press, p. 88.

36 Shiva, Vandana (1989) *Staying Alive. Women, Ecology and Development*. London: Zed Books, p. 38.

37 *Ibid.*

38 Ermine (1995), p. 104.

39 Senghor (1993), p. 30.

40 See Lyons (1984); Ermine (1984); Deloria (1999).

41 Alfred, Taiaiake (1999) *Peace, Power, Righteousness. An Indigenous Manifesto*. Ontario: Oxford University Press, pp. 43–4.

42 Wills, Peter R. (2001) Testimony to the Royal Commission on Genetic Modification, 8 November 2000, p. 21, online at http://www.gmcommission.govt.nz/publications/PDF_submission.html, also published in an abbreviated and edited form in *Pacific World*, 61 (September), pp. 28–39.

43 Umbilical cord.

44 Shirres, Michael P. (1997) *Te Tangata. The Human Person*. Auckland: Accent Publishers, p. 119.

45 Tau, Te Maire (1998) 'Matauranga Maori as an epistemology', in *Te Pouhere Korero: Maori History, Maori People*, 1, 1 (March), pp. 10–23.

46 Maori proverb cited by Ihimaera, Witi (1997) *The Dream Swimmer*. Auckland: Penguin, p. 90.

47 Hadot, Pierre (1997) 'Forms of life and forms of discourse in ancient philosophy'. Inaugural lecture to the Chair of the History of Hellenistic and Roman Thought at the College de France, in Arnold I. Davidson (ed.), *Foucault and His Interlocutors*. Chicago and London: City of Chicago Press.

48 Hadot, *ibid.*, p. 195.

49 *Ibid.*, p. 198 .

50 Fideler, David (ed.) (1988) *The Pythagorean Sourcebook and Library* (compiled and translated by Kenneth Sylvan Guthrie). Michigan: Thanes Press, p. 21.

51 For a full discussion of this, see Newell, J. Philip (1997) *Listening for the Heartbeat of God. A Celtic Spirituality*. New York: Paulist Press.

52 Ecofeminist authors, in particular, have highlighted the oppression and exploitation of nature and women simultaneously as a result of dominant patriarchal ideologies. See for instance Griffin, Susan (1978) *Woman and Nature: The Roaring Inside Her*. New York: Harper and Row; Merchant, Carolyn (1980) *The Death of Nature*. New York: Harper and Row.

53 Dzielska, Maria (1995) *Hypatia of Alexandria* (translated by F. Lyra). Cambridge, MA: Harvard University Press.

54 Roszak, Theodore (1999) *The Gendered Atom. Reflections on the Sexual Psychology of Science*. Berkeley: Conari Press.

55 *Ibid.*, pp. 139–49.

56 *Ibid.*, p. 35–6.

57 *Ibid.*, p. 36.

58 Skolimowski, Henryk (1981) *Eco-Philosophy. Designing New Tactics for Living*. New York and London: Marion Boyars.

59 The Corpus Hermeticum, a large body of literature in Greek of contested origin, developed under the name of Hermes Trismegistus and which has come down through the Latin translation once attributed to Aupelius of Madaura. Originally viewed as being of profound Egyptian antiquity and now, according to Yates, generally thought to be dated between CE 100 and CE 300, the treatises contained in

the Corpus Hermeticum as well as those of the Asclepius are largely philosophical and provide accounts of the creation of the world, the ascent of the soul and the interrelationships of existence. Other treatises are more strongly focused on the themes of astrology, alchemy and magic.

60 Yates, Frances A. (1972) *The Rosicrucian Enlightenment*. London: Routledge, Kegan and Paul.

61 See Manuel, Frank E. (1979) *A Portrait of Isaac Newton* [1968, Belknap Press], Washington, DC: Harvard University Press, cited in Rich, Bruce (1994) *Mortgaging the Earth, The World Bank, Environmental Impoverishment and the Crisis of Development*. London: Earthscan. According to Manuel, Keynes concluded this from his study of recently discovered manuscripts of Sir Isaac Newton purchased by him from Sotheby's in 1936. Keynes maintained that rather than the first modern scientist, Newton saw himself as 'heir to an esoteric brotherhood' through which he was connected to the 'papers and traditions handed down by the brethren in an unbroken chain back to the original cryptic revelation in Babylonia'. See also Rich, *ibid.*, pp. 211–14 and Yates, Frances A. (1979) *The Occult Philosophy and the Elizabethan Age*. London: Routledge.

62 Yates, Frances A. (1964) *Giordano Bruno and the Hermetic Tradition*. London: Routledge and Kegan Paul, p. 248.

63 Cf. C. S. Lewis (1962) *The Abolition of Man*. New York: Collier Books, cited by Rich (1994), p. 213.

64 Descartes, René (1967) 'Discourse on the Method', in *Philosophical Works of Descartes* (translated by Elizabeth Haldane and G. R. T. Ross). London: Cambridge University Press, p. 78.

65 *Ibid.*, cited by DesJardins, Joseph (1999) *Environmental Ethics, Concepts, Policy, Theory*. Mountain View, CA: Mayfield, p. 38.

66 Heidegger, Martin (1999) [1926] *Being and Time* (translated by John Macquarrie and Edward Robinson). Oxford: Blackwell, p. 46.

67 Cox (1996) [1992], p. 147.

68 Connolly, John M. and Thomas Keutner (editors and translators) (1988) *Hermeneutics vs Science? Three German Views. Essays by H.-G. Gadamer, E. K.Specht, W. Stegmuller*. Notre Dame, IN: University of Notre Dame Press.

69 The divinatory act, Gadamer explains, consists of assuming the author's perspective in order to remove all alien or unusual aspects, in order for understanding to be complete. The Catholic position included reliance on divine interpretation to illuminate the true meaning of scriptural intention.

70 Hogan, Padraig (nd) 'Hermeneutics and educational experience'. National University of Ireland, Maynooth. Previously online at http://www.educacao.pro.br/entries.htm

71 Connolly and Keutner (1998), p. 68.

72 Hogan, Padraig (nd) 'Gadamer and the philosophy of education'. National University of Ireland, Maynooth. Previously online at http://www.educacao.pro.br/entries.htm

73 Significantly, according to authors such as Martin Bernal (*Black Athena*, London: Free Association Books, 1987), this is the moment at which the 'whitening' of Western philosophy began. See also Bernal's reply to his critics in Chioni, David Moore (ed.) (2001) *Black Athena Writes Back: Martin Bernal Responds to His Critics* (Durham: Duke University Press). Other authors who have developed this theme include James, George M. (1992) [1954] *Stolen Legacy* (Trenton, NJ: Africa World Press). Professor James recounts in detail the philosophical legacy of 'Black Egypt' and its appropriation by the Greeks. See also Samir Amin, who, citing Edward Said's *Orientalism* (London: Routledge and Kegan Paul, 1978), points to the invisibilizing of Islam and the Orient in the work of the Romantics, which enabled Christianity to become 'the

foundation of European identity'. See Amin, Samir (1989) *Eurocentricism*. London: Zed Books, pp. 124–35.

74 See Connolly and Keutner (1998), p. 11.
75 *Ibid.*, p. 12.
76 *Ibid.*, p. 13.
77 *Ibid.* In a footnote to their discussion on Dilthey, the authors contrast Dilthey's concept of meaningfulness as being an essential element of the constituents of one's inner world, with Hume's atomistic perspective of these relationships.
78 Heidegger (1999) [1926].
79 Gadamer, Hans-Georg. 'On the Circle of Understanding', in Connolly and Keutner, (1998), p. 74.
80 *Ibid.*, p. 71.
81 *Ibid.*
82 Peters, Michael. Personal communication.
83 Gadamer, 'On the Circle', p. 74.
84 *Ibid.*, p. 75.
85 *Ibid.*, p.76.
86 Hogan (nd) 'Gadamer and the Philosophy of Education'.
87 *Ibid.*
88 Smith, David Geoffrey (1999) 'Experimental hermeneutics: interpreting educational reality', in David Geoffrey Smith, *Pedagon. Interdisciplinary Essays in the Human Sciences, Pedagogy and Culture*. New York: Peter Lang, p. 45.
89 *Ibid.*, p. 46.
90 Fibonacci, Leonardo (1202) *Liber abbaci*. Online at http://www-history.mcs.st-and.ac.uk/~history/Mathematicians/Fibonacci.html, accessed 11 March 2002.
91 Schauberger, Viktor (1998) *Nature as Teacher* (translated and edited by Callum Coats). Bath: Gateway Books, p. 84.
92 Watson, J. D. and Crick, F. H. C. (1953) 'A structure for Deoxyribose nucleic acid', *Nature*, 171, p. 738, online at http//biocrs.biomed.brown.edu/Books/Chapters/Ch%208/DH-Paper.html, accessed 11 March 2002.
93 Gazale, Midhat J. (1999) *Gnomon. From Pharaohs to Fractals*. Princeton, NJ: Princeton University Press, p. 3.
94 Nabokov, Vladimir (1951) cited Gazale (1999), p. 151.
95 Smith, D. G. (1999).
96 Heidegger (1999) [1926].
97 Smith, D. G. (1999), p. 47.

CHAPTER 2

�֎

Indigenous Peoples and the World Order of Sovereign States

The development of international law has been premised upon Western perspectives of the structure of the world and human society, and on the particular forms of knowledge and understanding that rest upon these ontologies. These views, while complex and contested, have become embedded in the everyday legal and social practices of Western societies.[1] My objective in this chapter is to identify these contested knowledge forms and ideologies and to interrogate their impact on the indigenous nations that, at least until the earliest days of imperialism, made up a large part of the world. Here a historical materialist approach allows me to examine the emergence of the political world order of nation states and the operation of historical and contemporary mechanisms for the exclusion of indigenous peoples. In particular, I seek to interrogate the disjunctures in the ideologies that have underpinned the development of world order. Foremost is the disjuncture between indigenous political theories and conceptualizations and the dominating political discourses that shape the world order of nation states.

The first section examines the function of political discourses and juridical power in the construction of indigenous peoples' subjectivities within international law and the contracting out of indigenous peoples from the emergent world order of nation states. In highlighting changes in the international legal discourses and norms that accommodated colonization, my primary focus is the experiences of indigenous peoples within internally colonized territories. The subjugation of indigenous ontologies of being and the emergence of reductionist taxonomies is contextualized by a brief discussion of the impact of Enlightenment technological thought and the processes of human and ecological colonization. Foucault's work on govern-mentality, on power, and on the genealogy of knowledge provides useful insights into the operation of international law on indigenous peoples, particularly with regard to the reconstruction of indigenous nations from sovereign nations to dependent populations. The emergence of notions of governmentality and the economy and the reterritorialization of geographic and cultural space provides the framework for an examination of the contracting out of indigenous peoples from the evolving world order of nations.

Anaya defines international law as a 'universe of authoritative norms and procedures – today linked to international institutions – that are in some measure controlling across jurisdictional boundaries'.[2] In his important and detailed analysis *Indigenous Peoples in International Law* (1996), Anaya argues that 'although once an instrument of colonialism, international law, however grudgingly or imperfectly, has developed and continues to develop to support indigenous peoples' demands'.[3] One of the objectives of this current work is to interrogate the extent to which such objectives have been purely cosmetic. Here Foucault's work is particularly relevant as he draws attention to the generally negative function of juridical power manifested in law, particularly with regard to regulation, limitation, prohibition and control.[4] By virtue of being subjected to this juridical function of law, the productive function of power at an official and personal (physical) level acts to construct and define subjects in terms of particular identities. Foucault divides theories of governmentality into two types, the social contract model in which individuals agree to give up certain freedoms in order to benefit from banding together, and the notion of 'divine' or 'natural' law that suggests that the law existed prior to the formation of society.[5] This latter notion of juridical sovereignty ignores the fact that law is something that is produced by the processes of history and, in the same way that it is made by people, can be unmade. As such, Foucault argues, rather than being the originator of the rule of justice and reason, the law works to cover up the acts of violence that are so often part of the establishment of communities and which involve the contracting in of certain groups and the contracting out of others.[6]

In the second half of the chapter, a discussion of the concept of state sovereignty and its application within the 'family of nations' is followed by a consideration of the notions of trusteeship within which sovereign indigenous peoples were redefined as populations and wards of nation states. Education has been a key tool in the development of biotechnologies for the construction and subjugation of populations. My concluding comments therefore draw attention to the function of education in the construction of indigenous peoples as populations to be governed and the attempted subjugation of their minds and souls.

International Law, Indigenous Nations and Imperialism

International law has been described as having its roots in the jurisprudential treatises that originated in classical Western thought, the legacy of medieval humanism.[7] Authority was rooted in the concept of natural law, conceived of by the Spanish school of thought (and in particular the theorist Francisco de Vitoria) as divine law, the law of God, and, a century later, by Grotius (1625) as a 'dictate of high reason'.[8] From the earliest days of Spanish and Portuguese imperialism, however, tension between the high reason of natural law and greed for territorial expansion and for resources saw these principles bitterly contested.[9] Maori lawyer Moana Jackson sees ideologies that ultimately became manifest in the nineteenth century colonization of New Zealand as originating in 'the discourses which accompanied the Catholic Crusades to drive out the Moslem infidels from the Holy Land'.[10] Inherent in these discourses was an assumption of the divine right of Christianity to dispossess all who stood in its way, an assumption that was later to be evident in the peremptory running up of flags and proclamations of discovery or annexation.[11]

Columbus's 'discovery' of the Americas in 1492 precipitated a period of rigorous European expansion. Ironically, it also saw early European acknowledgement of the sovereign nation status of the indigenous peoples of the Americas. The papal bull 'Inter Cetera Divini' of 4 May 1493, which contained references to the 'certain remote islands and also mainlands' discovered by Columbus, included the crucial acknowledgement that 'these nations living in the said islands and lands believe that there is one God and one Creator in the heavens',[12] an imperative condition for sovereign nationhood. In the context of the imperialist missions, however, the sovereignty of indigenous nations represented a moral barrier to the acquisition of lands and resources 'discovered' through exploration. Columbus's journey to indigenous America was undertaken on the basis of an agreement that he would retain one-tenth of the 'pearls, precious stones, gold, silver, spices, and other things and other merchandise whatsoever, of whatsoever sort,' to be found in the lands that 'should be discovered and gained'.[13] Venne notes that within 50 years of Columbus's visit to the Americas, the right of conquest over indigenous nations by Christian nations became the subject of widespread and intense secular and religious debates intensified by the horror of Spanish colonization in America.[14]

At issue was the humanity of indigenous or aboriginal peoples and accompanying rights. Central to these debates were concerns for the acquisition of lands and resources and a territorial struggle between Portugal and Spain over the right to claim ownership. Throughout this early period of imperialism, dominant notions of European intellectual and moral superiority saw these norms hotly debated.[15] Morris's study of fifteenth-century international law and its application to indigenous peoples details the theological debates initiated by the papal bulls of 1493 legitimating Spanish territorial claims. These debates over the right to possess gave rise to the concept of the doctrine of discovery. This was definitively outlined in the Inter Cetera Divini, which declared that

> The Pope could place non-Christian peoples under the tutelage and guardianship of the first Christian nation discovering their lands as long as those peoples were reported by the discovering nation to be 'well disposed to embracing the Christian faith'.[16]

Glen Morris makes the important point that the ongoing genocide and dispossession of indigenous peoples of the Americas by Spain was in defiance of papal bulls that declared such acts illegal. Throughout these debates, both Aristotelian notions of slavery as the natural state of the American Indians and the notion of the just war as applied to the indigenous peoples of the Americas were strongly refuted by Bartolomé de Las Casas, who later estimated that by the middle of the sixteenth century conquistadors had killed 15 million natives in South and Central America.[17] In his work *Concerning the Rule of the Kings of Spain over the Indians*, De Paz argued that indigenous nations had the right to self-defence, thus affirming the sovereignty of indigenous peoples and the illegality of Spanish dispossession of indigenous nations of their lands and their 'inherent sovereign right to govern themselves'.[18] In 1532, on the basis of natural law, Vitoria advocated the creation of a wardship for indigenous peoples by the 'more civilized' European states whereby 'in their own interest the sovereign of Spain might undertake the administration of their own country ... so long as this was clearly for their benefit'.[19]

[T]he indigenous nations of the Americas exercised true dominion over their property in both public and private matters, just like Christians … and neither their princes nor their private persons could be despoiled of their property on the ground of not being true owners.[20]

Widely regarded as the founding fathers of international law, both Vitoria and Grotius drew on the dictates of natural law, according to which legal sovereignty was ascribed to indigenous nations on the basis of their humanity and modes of social organization. Alexander Murphy states that, in using 'high reason' as the basis for his view of natural law, Grotius drew on concepts of property rights with roots in ancient Greece and Rome and also on the theory of sovereignty articulated in the same period by his French contemporary Jean Bodin.[21]

From the perspective of the prevailing legal norms of the period, like other civilizations with which the Western world had been in contact for much longer, indigenous peoples in newly discovered lands had equal sovereign status in the Law of Nations. Accordingly, the initiating of trading arrangements by imperializing powers with the inhabitants of other lands required the formulation of treaties and other similar arrangements.[22] Tully nonetheless contends that, in the early stages of imperialism, treaty making was a means of modifying the open usurpation and appropriation of indigenous territories where effective resistance by indigenous peoples was encountered.[23]

Following a lengthy period of acrimonious debates, the Council of the Indies was established in Spain in 1550 for the purpose of finally determining the moral and legal rights of discovery. Representations were heard by Juan Gines de Sepulveda, who based his argument for the subjugation of indigenous peoples upon the Bible, and Las Casas, who, horrified by the enslavement and genocide of the indigenous peoples of the Americas by the conquistadors and colonists, argued for the human rights of indigenous peoples.[24]

The findings of the Council foreshadowed the conviction of Christian/European superiority that underpinned the establishment of world order and international law. The right to win souls became the justification for the seizure of indigenous lands and the waging of war on indigenous peoples. By the end of the sixteenth century, Spanish, Portuguese, French, Dutch and English imperialist policies of expansion and resource extraction for export to core countries saw the invasion of many indigenous peoples' territories throughout the 'known' world, accompanied by genocide of unimaginable magnitude.

In England, the doctrine of a just war was extended on the basis of an Elizabethan Protestant doctrine that declared the English to be in covenant with God to bring 'true' Christianity to 'heathen natives'. Morris contends that English legal doctrines regarding colonization were heavily influenced by the English jurist George Peckham's adaptation of Vitoria's writing to support his own justification of English colonization.[25] According to Peckham, English Christians had an inalienable right to trade with indigenous peoples throughout the world and by association, the right to wage war and dispossess them of their lands, should they refuse to trade or to accept missionaries. In Morris's account, the Barkham case (1622) – which, in contradiction to the writings of legal theorist Vattel and others, held that 'the legal and political authority of 'heathen infidels' was necessarily abrogated when it came into contact with Christian sovereignty'[26] – demonstrates the manner in which English 'self-serving justifications' became legitimated in legal precedent. These beliefs were grounded in rationalist ideologies about the nature of being which linked modernity and Enlightenment to notions of the expansion of 'civilization' across the face of the earth. Repeated throughout the 'discovered' world, including the Pacific, the translation of these ideologies into the doctrine of *terra nullius*[27] saw the indigenous populations decimated. In Australia, in the province of Queensland alone, Martin Taylor reports, by 1920 the indigenous population was reduced from at least 120,000 to 20,000.[28]

Territorialization, Ecological Imperialism and the Taxonomizing of the World

In the empiricist tradition, the influence of Hobbes and Locke saw the natural law function of protecting the common ownership of land and its produce transformed to protection of 'the freedom to act, trade and to own property'.[29] The Enlightenment and the rise of its corollary, capitalism, established the acquisition of territory and resources as the rationale for capitalist expansion. Lockean ideologies that linked Christianity with trade and were underpinned by notions of an overriding right to profit, continued as a dominant motif throughout the era of modernity. In Locke's canon, individual ownership was defined thus:

whatsoever then, he [man] removes out of the state that nature hath provided and left it in, he hath mixed his labour with and joined to something that is his own, and thereby makes it his property. It being by him removed from the common state nature placed it in, hath by this labour something annexed to it that excludes the common right of other men. For this labour being the unquestionable property of the labourer, no man but he can have the right to what that is joined to, at least where there is enough and as good left in common for others.[30]

In his *Critique of Modernity*, Alain Touraine identifies Locke's rationalism as supplying 'new foundations for the divorce between individual and society'.[31] According to Touraine, Locke establishes a total discontinuity between the state of nature and social organization by giving the state of nature 'political expression' in which '[t]he analysis of a community and the needs of its members is replaced by an analysis of labour and property which must be protected by laws'.[32] The creation of a private sphere that was separate from but exercised a constraining influence over the public sphere was central to Locke's theory of civil government. Predicated upon principles that equated civil rights with property ownership, the separation of the public and private spheres was held to be critical for political order and stability as well as for personal liberty.

Ultimately, the growing opposition between the empiricism that leads to positivism and the idea of natural law that 'inspires all the social movements that resist the established order' culminated in the separation between traditional holism and modern individualism that, for Touraine, represents the divorce or separation between the two faces of modernity.[33] These disjunctures are reflected in the transition from indigenous peoples being perceived as international citizens with natural law rights and their discursive reconstruction as uncivilized savages incapable of self-governance, whose dispossession of their traditional lands could be legitimated on the basis of positivist ideologies driven by racialist rationalizations. The transition from traditional holism to the rationalist empiricism and Cartesian dualisms of modernity also legitimated the negation of indigenous epistemologies and cosmologies. In this regard, Robert Young's discussion of the role of the Hegelian dialectic within political oppression and eurocentric historicism[34] highlights the manner in which declarations such as Hegel's 'Africa has no history' saw the historical realities of civilizations thousands of years old invisibilized within universalized world histories, and their resources absorbed by the universalizing mission of liberal modernity.

Rationalist empiricism, atomistic scientific theories and the invention of new technologies had a profound effect on geographical space and indigenous environments across the globe. Contemporary environmental historians who locate ecological issues in cultural, economic, political and anthropological contexts[35] have brought attention to bear on the impact of European technologies of domination on indigenous environments, cultural practices and locations from the fifteenth century onwards. Most notably and controversially, Alfred Crosby, in *The Columbian Exchange*,[36] argued that the complex of diseases, plants and animals that accompanied European colonization had a far more devastating impact on indigenous cultures and ecosystems than European weaponry, a theme that he elaborated fourteen years later in his work *Ecological Imperialism*.[37] Critiqued by some historians for its biological determinism and by others for arguing that European colonialism had less ecological impact in the Old World than in the New World, Crosby's work is nonetheless valuable for its detailing of the impact of European preoccupation with reconstructing the landscapes of Europe or new 'Utopias' wherever they went, an activity which reached its zenith in the late seventeenth century.[38] Richard Grove and John MacKenzie describe how the scientific fervour of the late eighteenth and nineteenth centuries, combined with technological and scientific change, stimulated European convictions of their innate superiority and their moral and scientific duty to tabulate everything that they saw.[39] The appropriation of indigenous flora and fauna for the great botanical collections of Europe and England was accompanied by the colonization of indigenous terrains by foreign weeds and animals.

Having remained in relative isolation until the eighteenth century, the uniqueness of the landscape of New Zealand, despite the similarity of its climate to that of England, was a source of fascination for colonial naturalists whose role, Grove notes, had long been one of curators of collections belonging to the wealthy.[40] Crosby details the transformation of the unique biological and 'profoundly un-European'[41] landscape of New Zealand – a transformation, Crosby points out, that owed as much to colonization by weeds and animals as it did to the land wars that sought the dislocation and enclosure of Maori on behalf of European expansionism. In his sensitive examination of the impact of imperialism on New Zealand's ancient landscapes, ecologist Geoff Parks points to the fact that, by the end of the nineteenth century, some of the world's oldest and strangest plants and animals, the result of seventy million years of isolation from other land masses and the support system for the physical and spiritual life of the indigenous inhabitants of New Zealand, were brought to extinction.[42] Enlightenment rationalism and the new technologies of science and warfare, combined in scientific expeditions which sought to codify and tabulate the flora and fauna of the globe, also codified and tabulated any indigenous knowledge of the environment that would contribute to the scientific coffers of European biologists and taxonomers.

In his work documenting the origins and early history of environmentalism and the influence of Utopian, physiocratic ideals and medical thinking, Grove notes that the empirical expeditions that brought eminent naturalists such as Joseph Banks in 1768 and, later, Charles Darwin to the South Pacific provided the setting for 'a new kind of scientific critique extending beyond the discovery of the empirical to embrace a detached kind of social empiricism' – including a fascination with the impact of climate upon human society.[43] Grove discusses how the impact of Baconian science and the establishment of the Royal Society and the Académie des Sciences provided the intellectual infrastructure for the development of new desiccation and climatic as well as wider environmental and agricultural theories. Newtonian physics provided the impetus for studies on air quality and vegetation. Many of these studies contributed to concerns for the impact of environmental degradation. For millennia, indigenous peoples' practices had enabled the successful coexistence of humans with nature, yet now these practices were blamed for the degradation of the environment, thus affording a rationale for the enclosure of the indigenous inhabitants into reservations and the preserving and/or the introduction of game for colonial sport.[44] At the same time, as Linda Tuhiwai Smith points out, indigenous knowledge identified as relevant to European ecological interests was appropriated by naturalists and botanists for their own scientific purposes.[45] The reinscription of political space by the establishment of the colonial state occurred through a territorialization of flora and fauna as well as of indigenous peoples' lands and knowledge.

Governmentality, the State and the Political Economy of Exclusion

Foucault's work on governmentality demonstrates a relationship between the emergence of the problematic of government in the period between the sixteenth and eighteenth centuries and the exercising of new technologies of power that developed in conjunction with the scientific and technological inventions of the seventeenth and eighteenth centuries.[46] Foucault's focus on the importance of this technology of power as its ability to incorporate itself in the bodies of individuals through their behaviour and attitudes – an incorporation that was an essential prerequisite to obtaining 'productive service' from them[47] – informs our understanding of the disciplinary procedures that were applied to indigenous peoples during this period. These techniques of power relied for their effectiveness on discursive and disciplinary strategies and were indispensable in the controlling of 'populations', a category that emerged between the sixteenth and eighteenth centuries as part of the 'problematic' of governance.

The theoretical conceptualizations that underpinned the emergent body of international law assumed the state as the paragon of human aspiration and association, a Hegelian concept that became embodied in the world order of Westphalian nation states.[48] Inherent in this body of international law were ideologies based on racist notions of culture and civilization that determined who and what counted as 'nations'. Written in 1758 by the Swedish diplomat Vattel, the legal treatise *The Family of Nations* became the defining work that established international law as a body of law concerned exclusively with states. Although Vattel's definition of states included 'all political bodies, societies of men who have united together and combined their forces, in order to procure their mutual welfare and security', Vattel himself distinguished between what he termed the 'civilized Empires of Peru and Mexico' and the peoples of North America who 'rather roamed over them than inhabited them'.[49] According to Locke's articulation of property rights, rights to land ownership were ascribed only to those of fixed abode. While hunter-gatherers were endowed with the right to own what they killed, the right to own land was denied them – 'the deer is the Indian's that hath killed it – but not the land over which they have travelled in its pursuit'. Lockean distinctions between different types of indigenous societies, ultimately based on a duty in natural law to till the soil, in time became the basis for denying indigenous peoples land rights and status as either nations or states subject to international law. The eventual outcome was a redefining of international norms within a positivist legal theoretical framework legitimated by racist notions of culture and civilization.

Locke's *Second Treatise* defined the principle of individual ownership based on labour and thus legitimated the dispossession of indigenous peoples from their own territories by those who saw land as a resource for the extraction of wealth and the allocation of citizenship rights on the basis of land ownership. During the seventeenth and eighteenth centuries, dissimilarity between indigenous and non-indigenous peoples became the dominant ideology by which moral exclusion from the family of nations was operationalized. As the polygeneticist ideologies of Voltaire and others gave way to doctrines of social evolutionism, the division between sedentary and hunter-gatherer peoples as the criteria for distinguishing civilized from non-civilized or savage societies became the justifying principle for imperialism and for the exclusion of particular groups from the world of nations. It also enabled the enactment of genocidal practices upon indigenous peoples within colonial nation states to continue without fear of punitive legal measures and became the legitimizing principle for viewpoints such as that of Tom Paine, who in 1776 said that America was 'happy as she pleases she hath a blank sheet to write on'.[51]

Legal norms and discourses that defined relationships between indigenous peoples and states within internally colonized territories concretized the reconstruction of indigenous peoples' status from sovereign nations to dependent populations within international law. During the nineteenth century, the exclusion of indigenous peoples in internally colonized territories from sovereign status and therefore protection within international law was elaborated by doctrines such as US Chief Justice John Marshall's 'dependent nations' in 1823 and Henry Wheaton's treatise on the *Elements of International Law* (1846). Introduced in 1821 in a report from special Indian Commissioner Jediah Morse to US President James Monroe, the exercise of juridical rights over 'the Indian territory' and the exclusive right over its soil was legitimated on the basis of the law of nations by which, 'the whole Indian population is reduced, of necessary consequence, to a dependent situation'.[52] Thus legal decisions of the time that functioned to legitimate Western imperialism and the doctrine of discovery became part of the foundational jurisprudence of the international system of nation states and the means by which indigenous peoples became both dispossessed and disenfranchised within their own territories. These decisions legitimated the Indian Removal Act of 1830 – which saw the forced march of thousands upon thousands of Indian people, many of whom either died or were murdered along the way – and termination policies such as that which abolished the

Choctaw Nation in 1830 and dismantled tribal governments, forcing members of heretofore sovereign nations to seek places within mainstream society.

In the US, the adoption into law of Chief Justice John Marshall's Christian Doctrine of Discovery was predicated on the claim that during the 'Age of Discovery' Christian European nations had assumed 'ultimate dominion' over the lands of America. Further, it was maintained that upon 'discovery', in most cases, the Indian nations had lost their rights to complete sovereignty as independent nations and retained only a right of 'occupancy' in their lands.[53] Based on a Hegelian reinterpretation of international law norms holding that, when it gained its independence in 1776, the US inherited from Britain the right of 'discovery' and with it the power of 'dominion', the Marshall doctrine as expressed in three major decisions was influential in determining the status of indigenous peoples and their relationship to nation states; it continued long after to provide legitimation for the dispossession of indigenous peoples' sovereign rights. In the same era, the work of Marshall's compatriot, Henry Wheaton, concretized the view that while some Indian nations could be included among what was then referred to as the 'family of nations', others were deemed 'an unsettled band of wandering savages not yet formed into civil society'.[54]

In the late nineteenth and early twentieth centuries, the conjuncture of reified constructions of the state as the signifier of modernity arising from nationalism, and positivist interpretations of international laws, culminated in the exclusion of indigenous peoples from the international legal system and the world system of sovereign nation states. Western definitions of civilization that were used to evaluate non-Western polities defined a 'civilized' state according to such practices as 'freedom of traffic, guarantees of the life and liberty of foreign nationals, the egalitarian application of law, acceptance of European international law including the rules of war, and the maintenance of continuous diplomatic relations with other members of the system'.[55] These conditions were decisively stated as not applying to 'organized wandering tribes' who were emphatically excluded from the law of nations. Treatises of the nineteenth and early twentieth century were embedded in revived forms of positivism upon which were constructed notions of race and civilization. These further reinforced doctrines of 'discovery' and of 'dependent nations' in international legal norms. Anaya cites as particularly significant John Westlake's *Chapters on the Principles of International Law* (1894) which distinguished between 'civilized and uncivilized humanity' and deemed international society to be limited to the civilized, and W. E. Hall's *A Treatise on International Law* (1924), which, declaring international law to be a product of the special civilization of modern Europe, took the exclusion of indigenous peoples from international law for granted as 'such states only can be presumed to be subject to it as are inheritors of that civilization'.[56] The principle of recognition – which, David Strang points out, is peculiar to the Westphalian state system of international order[57] – was elaborated in Lassa Openheim's *International Law* (1920 edition). Here it was declared that 'statehood alone does not imply membership of the Family of Nations .... Through recognition only and exclusively a State becomes an International Person and a subject of International Law', and the conditions under which acceptance and recognition might occur were delineated.[58]

The shift from 'divine' or natural law to the Law of Nations legitimated the invalidation of the many treaties that had been made with many indigenous nations, for international law now upheld treaties only among states that were deemed to be sovereign under international law.[59] These principles were demonstrated in the case of the island of Palmas in which Judge Heuber declared that

> contracts between a state and native princes or chiefs of peoples that are not recognized as members of the community of nations, they are not, in the international law sense, treaties or conventions capable of creating rights and obligations such as may, in international law, arise out of treaties ... [because] ... native chiefs and tribes are neither states nor international organizations; and thus possess no 'treaty making capacity'.[60]

In 1877 in *Wi Parata v Bishop of Wellington*, Chief Justice Prendergast similarly denied the validity of the Treaty of Waitangi. Prendergast described the treaty as a 'simple nullity', arguing that indigenous tribes did not have the capacity to cede sovereignty,[61] a position that for a hundred years was the orthodox view in New Zealand law. Thus empiricist legal decisions based on Darwinist constructions of indigenous peoples became embedded in domestic and international law. The fiction that indigenous peoples had *never* been seen as capable of possessing rights within international law and that indigenous peoples had no territorial rights that states or monarchs were bound to respect, prevailed over earlier natural law notions and became embedded in legal norms and discourses.[62] At one level, this reflected the universalizing mission of the project of modernity, within which indigenous peoples were expected to vanish either by extinction or by assimilation into the nation states that had imposed juridical rights over them. At another level, the denial of treaties entered into on the basis of equal sovereign nations was about the appropriation of land and the redrawing of landscapes within a framework of the colonial home country.

Cultural Space, Populations and the Economy

Stephen Rosow writes that the global economy of the eighteenth century was constructed around Enlightenment notions of luxury, consumption and commercial society.[63] According to the ontology advanced by the Scottish Enlightenment philosopher David Hume, the need for consumption and the social benefits that it endowed were the driving force behind the development of the rational self. As a powerful means of transforming the self from being passion-driven to needs-driven, luxury was considered as 'a spur to accumulation and a moral discourse that civilizes men'.[64] In this sense therefore, luxury and consumption provided a civil means for comparison and competing with others and a framework within which human needs could be met without recourse to war. For Hume, the expansion of international trade for the purpose of satisfying the need for consumption was integral to the creation of civil order. Rosow points out that by linking his theory of luxury consumption to the division of labour within a universalist framework of a single, global economy based on the commercial practices of European capitalism, Hume endowed political economy with its own moral sanction within a global trading system that made civil society possible.

Robert Young's articulation of Deleuze and Guattari's dynamic of 'deterritorialization' and 'reterritorialization' in *Anti-Oedipus*[65] attributes the deterritorialization of indigenous peoples' territories and the dismantling of their social and political structures to capitalism's need for territorial expansion. As Young contends, 'Colonialism is not simply a discursive operation but a seizure of cultural (in all senses of the word) space'.[66] 'Above all', he argues, 'colonialism involves the physical appropriation of the land, its capture for the cultivation of another culture'.[67] The violation of treaties signed between colonizing powers and indigenous nations was critical to the formalized process of dismantling of indigenous peoples' institutions and social structures, to the reinscribing of absolutist forms of power, and to the subjugation of their minds and bodies, a process which Young describes as the physical and ideological procedures of colonization, deculturation and acculturation, by which the territory and cultural space of an indigenous society must be disrupted, dissolved and then reinscribed according to the needs of the occupying power.[68]

The rewriting of geographical space is an essential aspect of the process of expansion and the reduction of everything to the abstract value of money.[69] In his discussion of eighteenth-century processes of demographic and capital expansion, Foucault points to the emergence of the notion of population in a way that 'interconnected the science of government, the recentring of the theme of the economy ... and the problem of population'.[70] The introduction of the economy into political practice was seen as the essential aspect of good government. Citing Quesnay's eighteenth-century definition of good government as 'economic government', and Guillaume de La Pierre's statement that 'government is the right disposition of things, arranged so as to lead to a convenient end', Foucault identifies as the juridical principle which defined sovereignty in public law, that 'sovereignty is not exercised on things, but above all on a territory and consequently on the subjects who inhabit it'.[71] Government, on the other hand, is not to do with territory so much as with a 'sort of complex composed of men and things', of which 'property and territory are merely one of its variables'.[72] As with the governance of a family, on which the art of government is modelled, all of these 'things' are ultimately issues of economy and management and it is towards this end that questions of government and policing are directed. Thus, Foucault states, 'the very essence of government – that is, the exercising of power in the form of economy – is to have as its main objective what we are today accustomed to call "the economy"'.[73]

Steve Webster's discussion of the ideologies governing British colonization in the nineteenth century highlights the convergence of government and the economy in the colonization of New Zealand.[74] As Webster points out, those responsible for British settlement of its colonies, such as Edward Gibbon Wakefield, had specific theories about colonial regimes that would support capital accumulation. In Wakefield's view, a ready availability of land in the colonies impeded the accumulation of capital. Because economic independence on the part of the colonists inhibited them from needing either to produce a surplus of commodities or to sell their labour, the price of land was inflated to ensure both a constant supply of labour and the under-writing of the cost of human migration.

State Sovereignty and the Problem of Government

Foucault explains that the theory of government that at the end of the sixteenth century and throughout the seventeenth century was linked to the development of the administrative apparatus of territorial monarchies, and to the emergence of governmental apparatuses, was connected to the development of particular forms of knowledge and sets of analyses. Organized around what Foucault calls the theme of the reason of state,[75] the central principle of state sovereignty as both a theoretical question and a principle of organization was the fundamental impediment to the development of the art of government in a specific and autonomous manner.[76]

The concept of sovereignty that became embodied in Western political thought was heavily influenced by political theorists such as Hobbes, whose absolutist notions of sovereignty were expressed in *Leviathan* (1651), and Locke, for whom natural law placed man in a position of dominance. This pre-eminence was coupled with particular notions of responsibility in relation to the rest of creation, and positivist rationalism which denied the existence of natural law and the notion of moral rights and obligations. As Rosow shows, from the fourteenth century, sovereignty, understood as 'the presence of a supreme ruler and power',[77] was used in at least three ways: for political rulers, for males in the context of family, and for divinity. During the sixteenth century, the new use of sovereignty as a way of differentiating these different spheres led to sovereignty increasingly being restricted to the political realm. Prior to the seventeenth century, the state was mainly seen as a means to an end – the glory of the sovereign, the welfare of the people. Inextricably linked to the emergence of the modern nation state, sovereignty was the basis of the medieval struggle for political power between feudal rulers, the Church and the king or emperor. From this period forwards, the state came to be seen as an end in itself.[78] Whereas notions of 'divine' law saw the prioritizing of both the glory of the state and the welfare of its people, from the eighteenth century onwards the strength and wealth of the state became the driving force. Peoples were no longer conceived of as ends in themselves, but as resources to be used to ensure the development and viability of the state.

The peace treaties of Westphalia, which established the end of thirty years of political and religious wars and the religio-politico reconstruction of medieval Europe from *Respublica Christiana* to an international society of sovereign states, are widely held to be the foundation of secular international law, or what came to be known as the 'public law of Europe'.[79] Hobbes's concept of sovereignty was developed against this background and the struggle between feudalism, the monarchy and the Church. In *Leviathan*, Hobbes conceived of the state as having unlimited sovereignty. Individual sovereignty was to be forfeited voluntarily by man to the state in a contractual arrangement that would ensure social order. Without this mechanism of absolute authority, law and order could not prevail and man would descend into the 'brutishness' and civil war which Hobbes conceived as man's natural state. In this absolutist concept of sovereignty, the state became the sole interpreter of right and wrong and the only mechanism for the determination and exercise of justice. In the climate of the post-Thirty Years War period and the emergence of autonomous European state societies, Vattel's *Law of Nations* was the precursor to the doctrine of state sovereignty as a central precept in international law and the mercantilism that underpinned the formation of the modern state.[80]

The notion of absolute or unlimited sovereignty was further developed by Hegel (1770–1831) and used, as Lapidoth states, 'in support of totalitarianism and expansionism'.[81] While expansion through colonization by countries such as Spain, Portugal and later Britain had begun two centuries earlier, the doctrine of absolute sovereignty became a rationalist justification for further expansionist imperialism. Jean Bodin's theory of unlimited and indivisible sovereignty, propounded in his *Six Books of the Commonweal* – published in France in 1576, during the Thirty Years War – was important for the later development of political theory. Bodin argued that state power had its basis in force and that 'an absolute sovereign is one who, under God, holds by the sword alone'.[82] Jonathan Schell points out that, for Bodin, sovereign power amounted to what is today referred to as coercive power. Although absolute, unlike Hobbes's conceptualization, there were limits on Bodin's view of sovereignty, for the sovereign remained subject to the laws of God and nature.

For Locke and his contemporaries, civil liberty, natural rights and popular sovereignty exercised through a fiduciary government was fundamental to the development of society based upon the principles of liberty and equality and within which laws would derive from natural reason. Writing in 1667, Locke asserted that the authority of magistrates was only to be exercised for 'the good, preservation and peace of men in that society'[83] and that therefore their conduct must be determined solely by this principle. The Glorious Revolution

(1688) in England and the replacement of one royal dynasty by another provided the context in which Locke developed his contention that political sovereignty resided in the nation, which was thus able to transfer it from one sovereign to another.[84] The concepts of liberty and sovereignty expressed by Locke and other English political philosophers found a response in France, where thinkers such as Montesquieu, Voltaire and Rousseau drew on the English model of popular sovereignty. This was subsequently refined in Jean-Jacques Rousseau's *Du Contract Social*, and given its ultimate expression in the French Revolution and the French Declaration of Rights (1789).[85] Notably, some authors have also ascribed influence from the federated democracies of the indigenous nations of the Americas on the political thought of the time, particularly in the case of Voltaire, Rousseau and Montesquieu.[86] While this may be contestable, the important point in this discussion, as Thomas Musgrave also emphasizes,[87] is that the concept of sovereignty that developed in Central and Eastern Europe was significantly different from that which developed in Britain and France. France and Britain had politically unified states and relatively homogeneous cultures, a view which many Irish and Scots might nonetheless contest vigorously. In contrast, there was no correlation between ethnic groups and states in Central and Eastern Europe. Examples include the Austro-Hungarian and Russian empires in which many diverse ethnic groups existed within a single state.[88]

In his analysis of the conjunction of power, knowledge and the production of discourses of truth, Foucault identifies the seventeenth and eighteenth centuries as the point at which a new phenomenon in the exercise of power emerged. In contrast with the mechanisms of power manifested through the theory of sovereignty, and which Foucault describes as being exercised over the earth and its products, this new mechanism of power is concerned with the exercise of power over 'human bodies and their operations',[89] in particular the extraction of time and labour for the production of wealth. What is important here is that, according to Foucault, this form of power, which he labels 'disciplinary power' and which is external to and radically different from the form of sovereignty, has been, in his words, 'a fundamental instrument in the constitution of industrial capitalism and the type of society that is its accompaniment'.[90] At the same time, Foucault explains, the persistence of the theory of sovereignty as the organizing juridical principle enabled the concealment of the procedures by which the mechanisms of disciplinary power and forms of subjection were exercised within and through-out society. The democratization of the constitution of a public right upon collective sovereignty was at the same time fundamentally determined by and grounded in mechanisms of disciplinary power continuously exercised, including through means of surveillance. The conjunction of state sovereignty, on one hand, and the inter-vention of disciplinary power as the means for the ongoing subjugation of populations on the other, saw indigenous peoples reconstituted as subjects under the tutelage of nation states. Accord-ing to the prevailing discourses of truth, this project was driven by the honourable instincts of humanitarianism and moral obligation.

Liberal Internationalism, Self-determination and the Doctrine of Wardship

In the mercantilist societies of Europe from the sixteenth to the eighteenth centuries, the ability to accumulate wealth and power relative to other states was seen as the key factor in protecting the economic and territorial integrity of states.[91] The 'scramble for Africa' was motivated by the Romantic nationalism of dominant European ideologies in which the building of nationalist empires was a precondition of power and prestige. In the late nineteenth century, the re-emergence of powerful positivist legal ideas that rejected natural law as the juridical basis for society and viewed the state as the guarantor of individual rights, coincided with the tide of European nationalism and Darwinian doctrines of evolutionism.[92] During the nineteenth century, the new science of ethnography redefined the darker-skinned races as 'childlike', lacking intelligence, incapable of internal systems of governance.[93] In what McKenzie calls the taxono-mizing of the whole world, the emergence of paleontology saw a renewed preoccupation with codifying and classifying nature, a venture that included the reclassification of mankind.[94] Barry Hindess explains this as the obverse side of 'the familiar liberal claim that government should rule over, and as far as possible through, the activities of free individuals', a claim containing the assumption 'that substantial portions of humanity consist of individuals who are not at present capable of acting in a suitably autonomous fashion'.[95] Kees van der Pijl draws attention to the fact that this period also saw the emergence of a transnational elite network committed to economic liberalist ideals and imperialist aspirations rationalized by Darwinist ideologies.[96] Liberal economic statesmen and financiers – Pijl's list includes Lords Escher, Grey, Milner, Rothschild and Balfour – joined with British South African politician and financier Cecil Rhodes in translating their 'aristocratic, "ethical" racist concept of an Anglo-Saxon civilizing mission into a secret society of concentric circles'[97] dedicated to furthering their ambitions. For Rhodes, this was nothing less than 'The furtherance of the British Empire, the bringing of the whole of the uncivilized world under its rule, the recovery of the United States of America, the making of the Anglo-Saxon race into one Empire'.[98]

Some of these networks were reorganized by Lord Milner at the beginning of the twentieth century into the Round Tables in the British Empire and the United States. In conjunction with the trans-national Rhodes Trust educational network and other networks, these organizations became important vehicles for the ambitions of leading political and economic figures. Thus, during the nineteenth and twentieth centuries, the economic liberalism that was the driving force behind the race for possession of the remaining lands and resources of the world saw the re-emergence of discourses that recast indigenous peoples as naïve and dependent, a legitimating construction for their new role as wards of the imperializing powers. Wilmer argues that the trusteeship principles adopted by Great Britain during the nineteenth century arose less from liberal humanitarian concerns than from the establishment of an international system of colonial administration.[99] The 1885 Treaty of Berlin that portioned out the lands and territories of Africa, the Brussels Treaty of 1890 and the Treaty of Algiers in 1913 formalized within international law the reconstruction of indigenous peoples as trustees of the 'Great Powers' of imperialism.[100] The arguments that legitimated these paternalistic policies linked philanthropy to industrial development and created human commodities as workers in a new division of labour predicated upon ideologies of civilization and Christianity. The same ideologies of trusteeship and the exercise of state sovereignty were applied to the indigenous inhabitants of both internally and externally colonized territories throughout the British Commonwealth. A comparative review of the legal status of indigenous peoples within domestic and international law undertaken in 1919, which used the Morse Report as its benchmark, found that

> the general nature of the jural relationship which a civilized State exercises over all of its colonies and all of its dependent communities … is best described by the word trusteeship, using this word in its literal sense as implying a fiduciary relationship essentially personal, though

extending to property as well as person; the fiduciary power is plenary, in the sense that ... as a power over political personalities it is an incident of sovereignty of each civilized State, and is governed by the law of nations ... and that the closest analogies to this relationship which occur in private law are those of patron and apprentice and guardian and ward.[101]

The construction of the League of Nations as a liberal international institution – the first modern international institution of world order – obfuscated the realities of a political and economic space contested by the major colonizing powers, whose competition for control and exploitation of the world's resources was couched in ideologies of universal progress. The reallocation of what were formerly seen as German-occupied territories, in what was nothing less that a disguised colonization and annexation, re-divided the natural and human resources of indigenous territories throughout Africa, Europe and the Pacific amongst the victors of the First World War – the sharing of the spoils theatrically played out as international benevolence through the League of Nations.[102] In his exploration of the sequence of discourses that led to the 'development era', Gilbert Rist points out that the re-division of the world within an international system of colonial administration was driven by the three principles of expansion, philanthropy and politics.[103] Formalized in June 1919 following the ending of the First World War in November 1918, the Treaty of Versailles comprised a redrawing of the political map of the world by the four victors, Britain, the USA, France and Italy. The result of a compromise between the idealist ideologies of US President Woodrow Wilson, the expansionist position of France and Britain, and the combined power of the Labour Party and the humanitarian movements, the Treaty also formalized the construction of the Covenant of the League of Nations.

The Covenant of the League of Nations confirmed the contracting out of indigenous peoples and nations from the new international order by formalizing the doctrines of wardship and trusteeship over indigenous peoples and their territories. Rist points out that Article 22 of the Treaty of Versailles explicitly linked together two types of evolutionary classification systems: the social evolutionist model underpinned by Darwinist ideologies and an economic and industrial development model underpinned by positivist economism. In both models, the 'developed' industrial nations represented by Britain and the USA were seen as the evolutionary ideal and provided a model for the advancement of civilization. Central to the universalizing project of modernity, the civilizing mission of the trusteeship system was couched in semi-religious terms such as 'sacred trust', thus invoking the highest aspirations of liberal progressivism. The exploitation of indigenous peoples' resources and labour as a means of social and economic development was submerged beneath humanitarian discourses which constructed indigenous peoples as beneficiaries of their own exploitation, while the resources utilized by indigenous peoples for thousands of years were to be held in trust by Western powers who would apply industrial methods of development to their exploitation.[104] Wardship doctrines embedded in liberal racist ideologies premised on notions of indigenous peoples as 'primitive', lacking 'civilization' or 'culture' according to eurocentric criteria for social organization, became the means by which ultimately traditional cultures and indigenous peoples were to become subsumed within a universal family of nations. These doctrines located indigenous peoples on the bottom rung of a hierarchical division of labour within a society predicated upon ideologies of capitalist expansionism.

The mandate of the International Labour Organization (ILO), created under the terms of the Treaty of Versailles, included the protection of indigenous peoples as wards towards whom the imperializing nations had a special responsibility, thus perpetuating the prevailing view of indigenous peoples as backward and destined to disappear once given the opportunity to join modern, civilized structures. Strong recommendations for the 'protection of certain minorities, particularly ethnic, linguistic and religious' which 'assured the rights of internal minorities in countries whose majority populations were understood to be different ethnically, nationally or religiously'[105] were predicated on the assumption that indigenous peoples and minorities would ultimately become assimilated into the states that had been imposed upon them. Hegelian definitions of what could be regarded as states maintained the exclusion of indigenous peoples from participation within the new world order. While the provisions of the League provided for the protection of the 'ethnic, linguistic and religious character' of minorities within defeated states, no such provision was made for minorities within the victor states. The assimilation of indigenous minorities within these states was taken for granted. In the case of internally colonized territories, assimilation efforts by the colonizing states initially took on renewed impetus before becoming discursively reinvented as integration. Education and social policies in internally colonized territories targeted the integration and subsuming of indigenous practices and belief systems within the mainstream world view.

The Subjugation of Indigenous Knowledge and the Construction of Populations

Throughout the expansionist period of imperialism, access to tribally owned land for development by settler colonies and for the establishment of capitalism was uppermost on the agenda of colonizing governments. Strategies for the social control of aboriginal populations and their assimilation into the new colonial societies were essential to the success of these agendas and nothing was discounted as a means of accessing the lands and resources of indigenous peoples. In Australia, as in many indigenous peoples' territories, Darwinist ideologies justified declarations of *terra nullius* and legitimated policies of physical and cultural genocide of aboriginal inhabitants.[106] In countries such as New Zealand, where the processes of colonization began somewhat later, the mediating effect of humanitarian influences frequently saw assimilation rather than extermination become the primary focus of native policy. Nonetheless, the primary goal of native policy in colonized territories and the primary agenda in the provision of colonial education for indigenous peoples was the acquisition of land and labour as resources to be exploited for the expansion of capitalism. The colonization of indigenous minds and the disciplining of populations were integral to the success of this mission.

Foucault's interrogation of the relationship between discourse and power illuminates the historical processes in which education was a primary tool for the perpetuation of hegemony over indigenous peoples. In particular, his historical analysis of the strands of discourse and practice dealing with knowledge and power provides important insights into both the subjectification of indigenous peoples and the subjugation of indigenous forms of knowledge through the medium of colonial education. In engaging the nature and operation of power and the rules of right in the disqualification of certain genealogies of knowledge, he provides a pertinent and insightful examination of the mechanisms through which particular forms of regional genealogies of 'local, discontinuous, disqualified, illegitimate knowledges' become disqualified from regimes of truth,[107] and the production of discourses of truth. Foucault explains his use of the term 'genealogies' as referring to 'the union of erudite knowledge and local memories which allows us to establish a historical knowledge of struggles and to make use of this knowledge tactically today'.

He defines subjugated knowledges in two ways; first, as 'historical contents' which functionalism and/or formal systemization buried or disguised, and second, as whole sets of knowledges that have been disqualified from the hierarchy of knowledge and sciences on the basis of their alleged naïveté or irrelevance. According to Foucault, most analyses of power are conducted within the context either of the power relations embedded in juridical power and questions of sovereignty, or of the economic functionality of power and its role in the maintenance of relations of production. The real focus of concern, he maintains, should be the way in which power surmounts the rules of right and becomes embodied in techniques and interventions that result in subjects being 'gradually, progressively, really and materially constituted through a multiplicity of organisms, forces, energies, materials, desires, thoughts, etc.'[108] Next to genocide and enclosures, the undermining of indigenous ontologies and cosmologies was the most persistent strategy of the first wave of colonization. What First Nations author Willie Ermine describes as 'the relentless subjugation of Aboriginal People' and the discounting of their ways of knowing was accompanied by the 'dissemination of acquired knowledge and information', as if Western voyages and discoveries were 'the only valid sources to knowing'.[109] As a consequence, states Ermine, indigenous peoples' mission of the exploration of inner knowledge and cosmologies 'has come perilously close to being aborted'.[110] While war and conquest waged in the name of religion and imperialism subjugated the physical being of indigenous peoples, Ngugi wa Thiong'o argues, European-style education, which within colonized territories targeted indigenous peoples' modes of organization and aimed to undermine indigenous cosmologies and epistemologies, ultimately brought about the 'subjugation of the soul'.[111]

Education as a Technology of Domination ...

Analyses by indigenous historians and educationalists highlight the marginalization and mythologizing of indigenous cosmologies and ontologies and the undermining of essential qualities and characteristics of indigenous community life such as extended family structures, notions of shared ownership and collective methods of decision making. Critiques by Maori educationalists draw attention to the impact of colonial education on Maori knowledge, on the collectivity of Maori social structures[112] and on gender relationships. Revisionist educational historiographies show the impact of strongly assimilationist policies for 'native education' by missionaries and other emissaries of Christianity in the first instance, and in the second instance, colonial governments. The extinguishing of aboriginal land rights, the denial of the validity of treaties signed between sovereign nations, the discursive construction of sovereign indigenous nations as 'populations' within Western-style states and the disestablishment of indigenous frameworks for the study of specialist and metaphysical knowledge were accompanied by the disciplining of minds and bodies. The recruitment, training, education and employment of indigenous peoples and minorities, viewed as fundamental to achieving the goal of their construction as docile and productive providers of labour, was accompanied by the targeting of the fundamental elements of indigenous cultural values and forms of knowledge as a means for dismantling indigenous political and social structures. In conjunction with legislation outlawing indigenous traditional ceremonies and structures,[113] education was the primary tool for the submerging of indigenous peoples' highly developed 'inner' ways of knowing under a layer of colonizing ideologies.[114]

In New Zealand, Judith Simon's examination of the function of ideologies in missionary and state-provided education for Maori exposes the deliberate and systematic targeting of Maori modes of organization through government policy, the deliberate relegation of Maori to second-class citizenship within what had become *pakeha-*dominated society, and the concerted attack on Maori values of collectivity, deemed a barrier to the acquisition of collectively owned Maori land under British law.[115] Drawing on the theoretical insights of scholars such as Andy Green and Roger Dale, Maxine Stephenson's recent study of the role of schooling in the construction of the state demonstrates the ways in which schooling was not only a site for the exercise of biopower at the level of individuals but also a vehicle for the imposition and assertion of new political structures, in particular those of the colonial state.[116] This was 'inextricably linked with attempts to impose *Pakeha* [British] law in the face of Maori resistance to the alienation of land for settlement'.[117] Church residential schools such as those provided for 'native education' in Canada and the denominational boarding schools for Maori in Aotearoa were sites within which the exercise of 'technologies of power' aimed at transforming autonomous, independent indigenous communities into resources for the production of capital. The enclosing of indigenous children away from the 'beastly influence' of the community[118] sought the production of healthy, docile, and productive populations. Demonstrated in the curricula of denominational boarding schools for Maori, labour combined with moral training and the inculcation of notions of citizenship formed a major part of the daily timetable.

... And a Site of Resistance

Indigenous peoples were not passive victims in this process but had well-developed strategies of resistance. Having made the decision to participate in European-provided education as a means of enhancing their own knowledge base,[119] the subsequent withdrawal of their children from the native school system was a response by Maori to both their lack of access to the kind of knowledge that would enhance their role within colonial society and the harsh regimes meted out to Maori children within the schools.[120] Under the leadership of Thornton, an enlightened and supportive principal, Te Aute College for Maori boys demonstrated the potential of education as a site not only for the subjugation and assimilation of Maori but also for resisting the ideologies and disciplinary techniques that were inherent within colonial education for Maori.[121] Stephenson's historical interrogation of Karakariki Native School, a school attended by several members of one extended family (*whanau*) and taught by a family member, demonstrates the way in which, despite *whanau* structures being targeted for disruption through the native schools system, native schools themselves became, on occasions, significant sites for resistance to European-imposed ideologies of individualism and for the reinforcement of the collective values and pedagogies that the colonial state sought so assiduously to eliminate.[122]

In the latter part of the twentieth century, the counter discourses of indigenous peoples played a strategic role in the affirmation of indigenous rights and in the reclaiming and revalidating of indigenous forms of knowledge and world views. During the reconscientization period of the 1970s, the reassertion of traditional indigenous values and pedagogies became central strategies of resistance and a main plank in the development of education strategies and policies by and for indigenous peoples. Foucault's conceptualization of the insurrection of subordinated knowledge as 'the reactivation of local knowledges ... in opposition to the scientific hierarchization of knowledges',[123] as the problematizing of unitary, scientific discourses and the defining of a terrain of struggle, speaks to the return to and revalidating of traditional knowledge so central to indigenous peoples' reclaiming of political and cultural space. Education strategies became a critical pathway in the revitalization of indigenous languages and cultures. More importantly, they became centres for the reclaiming of indigenous ontologies and epistemologies whose full potential has yet to be recognized. In addition to being the basis of demands for the recognition of indigenous peoples' rights within international law, the insurrection of subjugated indigenous knowledge has become a vehicle for the expression of the spiritual beliefs and rights of indigenous peoples. These discursive strategies, which continue to be integral to the emergence of a politics of indigeneity within the national and international arenas, have contributed in large measure to ideological changes towards indigenous peoples' rights across a range of contexts, and their enumeration and acknowledgement in international legislative documents and instruments.

Faced with highly developed strategies of resistance to assimilation and the imposition of foreign political structures by indigenous peoples, states have demonstrated ongoing and determined efforts to confine indigenous peoples and nations to positions of relative subjugation in the liberal international order. Despite these endeavours, as we shall see in Chapter 4, indigenous strategies of resistance have had a profound impact on the shaping of international law within the political framework of world order.

Notes

1   Cf. Tully, James (2000) 'The struggles of indigenous peoples for and of freedom', in Duncan Ivison, Paul Patton and Will Sanders (eds.), *Political Theory and the Rights of Indigenous Peoples*. Cambridge: Cambridge University Press, p. 36; Kymlicka, W. (2000) 'American multiculturalism and the "nations within"', in Ivison, Patton and Sanders (eds.), *Political Theory*.

2   Anaya, S. James (1996) *Indigenous Peoples in International Law*. New York: Oxford University Press, p. 4.

3   *Ibid.*

4   Dotyl, Roxanne (1996) 'Sovereignty and the nation: constructing the boundaries of national identity', in Thomas J. Biesteker and Cynthia Weber (eds.), *State Sovereignty as a Social Construct*. Cambridge: Cambridge University Press, p. 129.

5   Danaher, Geoff, Schirato, Tony and Jen Webb (2000) *Understanding Foucault*. St Leonards, Australia: Allen and Unwin.

6   *Ibid.*, pp. 84–5.

7   Anaya, S. J. (1996).

8   Grotius, Hugo (1925) [1625] *The Law of War and Peace*. Translated Francis W. Kelsey, Classics of International Law, cited *ibid.*, p. 27.

9   Cf. Anaya (1996), p. 12; Havemann, Paul (ed.) (1999) *Indigenous Peoples' Rights in Australia, Canada and New Zealand*. Auckland: Oxford University Press, p. 14.

10 Jackson, Moana (1995) 'Sovereignty as culture, culture as sovereignty: Maori politics and the Treaty of Waitangi'. Paper presented at the Global Cultural Diversity Conference Proceedings, Sydney, p. 2.

    http://www.immi.gov.au/multicultural/confer/speech56a.htm, accessed June 2001.
11 *Ibid.*, p. 3.
12 Cited in Morris, Glen T. (1992). 'International law and politics. Toward a right to self-determination for indigenous peoples', in M. Annette Jaimes (ed.), *The State of Native America: Genocide, Colonization and Resistance.* Boston: South End Press, reproduced by the Fourth World Documentation project at http://www.halycon.com/pub/ FWDP/International/int.txt, accessed April 1999.
13 Gutierrez, Gustavo (1993) *Las Casas – In Search of the Poor of Jesus Christ.* New York: Orbis Books, cited in Venne, Sharon (1998) *Our Elders Understand Our Rights: Evolving International Law Regarding Indigenous People.* Penticton, BC: Theytus.
14 *Ibid.*, p. 5.
15 In particular, see Havemann (1999); Anaya (1996); Wilmer, Franke (1993) *The Indigenous Voice in World Politics. Since Time Immemorial.* Newbury Park, London and New Delhi: Sage; Morris (1992).
16 Muldoon, James (1979) *Popes, Lawyers and Infidels: The Church and the Non-Christian World, 1250–1550.* Philadelphia: University of Pennsylvania Press, cited in Venne (1998), p. 4.
17 See Gutierrez (1993).
18 Morris (1992).
19 Vitoria, Fransciscus de (1917) *De Indis et De Ivre Belli Relectiones* (ed. E. Nys, translated J. B. Bate) in *The Classics of International Law,* J. B. Scott Reprint, New York: Oceana, 1964, cited in Morris, Glen (1993) 'International structures and indigenous peoples', in Marc A. Sills and Glenn T. Morris (eds.), *Indigenous Peoples' Politics: an Introduction. Vol.1.* Denver: Fourth World Centre for the Study of Indigenous Law and Politics: University of Colorado, p. 23.
20 Cited in Morris (1992).
21 Murphy, Alexander B. (1996) 'The sovereign state as political-territorial ideal: historical and contemporary considerations', in Thomas J. Biersteker and Cynthia Weber (eds.), *State Sovereignty as a Social Construct.* Cambridge: Cambridge University Press, p. 85.
22 Martinez, Miguel Alfonso (1999) *Study on Treaties, Agreements and Other Constructive Arrangements between States and Indigenous Populations,* Final Report, Special Rapporteur, UN Commission on Human Rights Sub-Commission on Prevention of Discrimination and Protection of Minorities, 24 June.
23 Tully (2000), p. 28.
24 Venne (1998). The humanitarian views of Las Casas, a member of the Spanish mission, stemmed from his conviction of the oneness of humankind. However, in Las Casas's view, as Hardt and Negri point out, the oneness of humanity equated to a sameness in which all men were seen as potential Europeans and Christianity was viewed as the highest expression of Europeanism. Hardt, Michael and Antonio Negri (2000) *Empire.* Cambridge, MA: Harvard University Press, p. 116.
25 Morris (1992).
26 *Ibid.*
27 The *terra nullius* doctrine was a fiction created within international law by which indigenous lands prior to any colonial presence were considered unoccupied. As Anaya explains, by this means the doctrine of discovery could be used to uphold colonial claims to indigenous lands, thus bypassing any indigenous claims to possession or ownership.
28 See Pilger, John (2002) *The New Rulers of the World.* London and New York: Verso.
29 Touraine, Alaine (1995) *Critique of Modernity* (translated by David Macey). Cambridge, MA: Blackwell, p. 49.
30 Locke, John (1988) [1690] 'The Second Treatise of Government. An Essay Concerning the True, Original, Extent and End of Civil Government, II', in

Laslett, Peter (ed.), *Two Treatises of Government*. Cambridge: Cambridge University Press pp. 287–8.

31 Touraine (1992), p. 49.

32 *Ibid.*

33 *Ibid.*, pp. 52–4.

34 Young, Robert J. C. (1990) *White Mythologies: Writing History and the West*. London: Routledge.

35 MacKenzie, John M. (1997) *Empires of Nature and the Nature of Empires. Imperialism, Scotland and the Environment*. East Linton: Tuckwell.

36 Crosby, Alfred W. (1972) *The Columbian Exchange: the Biological and Cultural Consequences of 1492*. Westport: Greenwood Press.

37 Crosby, Alfred W. (1986) *Ecological Imperialism. The Biological Expansion of Europe, 900–1900*. Cambridge, New York and Melbourne: Cambridge University Press.

38 Grove, Richard H. (1995) *Green Imperialism. Colonial Expansion, Tropical Island Edens and the Origins of Environmentalism, 1600–1860*. Cambridge: Cambridge University Press, p. 153.

39 *Ibid.*, p. 36.

40 *Ibid.*, p. 312.

41 Crosby (1986), p. 222.

42 Parks, Geoff (1995) *Nga Ururoa. The Groves of Life. Ecology and History in a New Zealand Landscape*. Wellington: Victoria University Press.

43 Crosby (1986), pp. 313–16

44 MacKenzie (1997), pp. 43–8.

45 Smith, Linda Tuhiwai (1999) *Decolonizing Methodologies. Research and Indigenous Peoples*. London and New York: Zed Books; Dunedin: Otago University Press, p. 59.

46 For instance Foucault, Michel (1991) 'Governmentality', in Graham Burchell, Colin Gordon and Peter Miller (eds.), *The Foucault Effect. Studies in Governmentality*. Chicago: University of Chicago Press.

47 Foucault, Michel (1994) 'Truth and power', in James D. Faubion (ed.), *Michel Foucault. The Essential Works, 3: Power*. London: Allen Lane Penguin, p. 125. For the Westphalian peace treaties, see this chapter, pp. 71-2.

48 Anaya (1996), pp. 13–14.

49 Vattel, cited *ibid.*, p. 16.

50 Locke (1988), p. 269.

51 Cited by Chomsky, Noam (1997) *Perspectives on Power. Reflections on Human Nature and the Social Order*. Montreal, New York and London: Black Rose Books, p. 239.

52 Snow, Alpheus Henry (1972) [1919] *The Question of Aborigines in the Law and Practice of Nations*. Reprint. Northbrook, IL: Metro Books, cited in Wilmer (1993), pp. 119–20.

53 Case (*Worcester v. Georgia*) cited in Anaya (1996).

54 Wheaton, Henry (1846) *Elements of International Law*, cited in *ibid.*, pp. 18–19.

55 Gong, Gerrit W. (1998) 'Asian Financial Crisis: Culture and Strategy', ICAS Fall Symposium, 'Asia's Challenges Ahead', University of Pennsylvania and Institute for Corean-American Studies, 29 September, cited in Strang, David (1996) 'Contested sovereignty: the social construction of colonial imperialism', in Biersteker and Weber (1996), p. 32.

56 Cited in Anaya (1996), p. 21.

57 Strang (1996), p. 23.

58 Openheim, cited in Anaya (1996), p. 35, note 108.

59 Magallanés, Catherine J. Iorns (1999) 'International human rights and their impact on domestic law', in Havemann (1999), pp. 235–76.

60 Cited in Anaya(1996), p. 23.

61 Cited in Brookfield, F. M. (1999) *Waitangi and Indigenous Rights. Revolution, Law and Legitimation.* Auckland: Auckland University Press, p. 99.

62 Anaya (1996), p. 21; Havemann (1999), pp. 13–17.

63 Rosow, Stephen J. (1994) 'Nature, need and the human world: "commercial society" and the construction of the world economy', in Stephen J. Rosow, Naeem Inayatullah and Mark Rupert (eds.), *The Global Economy as Political Space.* Boulder, Colorado and London: Lynne Rienner, p. 17.

64 *Ibid.*, p. 31.

65 Deleuze, Gilles and Félix Guattari (1977) *Anti-Oedipus: Capitalism and Schizophrenia* (translated by Robert Hurley, Mark Seem and Helen R. Lane). New York: Viking Press.

66 Young, Robert J. C. (1995) *Colonial Desire. Hybridity in Theory, Culture and Race.* London and New York: Routledge, p. 172.

67 *Ibid.*

68 *Ibid.*, p. 170.

69 *Ibid.*

70 Foucault (1991), pp. 98–9.

71 *Ibid.*, p. 93.

72 *Ibid.*, p. 93–4.

73 *Ibid.*, p. 92.

74 Webster, Steve (1990) 'Maori land, Maori labour. Studies in the history of New Zealand political economy'. Unpublished paper, Department of Anthropology, University of Auckland.

75 The notion that the state was governed according to a rationality that was both inherent in and peculiar to the state.

76 Foucault (1991), p. 97.

77 Rosow (1994), p. 25.

78 Danaher, Schirato and Webb (2000), p. 64.

79 Hinsley, F. H. (1966) *Sovereignty.* New York: Basic Books, cited in Biersteker, Thomas J. and Cynthia Weber (1996) in 'The social construction of state sovereignty', in Biersteker and Weber (1996).

80 Cox, Robert W. (1994) 'Global restructuring: making sense of the changing international political economy', in Stubbs, Richard and Geoffrey R. D. Underhill (eds.), *Political Economy and the Changing Global Order.* Basingstoke: Macmillan, p. 45.

81 Lapidoth, Ruth (1992) 'Sovereignty in transition', in *Journal of International Affairs*, 45 (2) (Winter), p. 326.

82 Bodin, Jean (1967) *Six Books of the Commonwealth.* Translated M. J. Tooly, Oxford: Basil Blackwell, p. 36, cited in Schell, Jonathan (2003) *The Unconquerable World. Power, Nonviolence and the Will of the People.* New York: Metropolitan Books, p. 282.

83 Locke (1988), p. 3.

84 *Ibid.*, p. 367.

85 See Schell (2003).

86 For a comprehensive discussion of this, see Young, Iris Marion (2000) 'Iroquois federalism', in Ivison, Patton and Sanders, (2000).

87 Musgrave, Thomas D. (1997) *Self-Determination and National Minorities.* Oxford and New York: Oxford University Press.

88 See also Hobsbawm, E. J. (1990) *Nations and Nationalism Since 1780.*Cambridge: Cambridge University Press.

89 Foucault, Michel (1980) 'Two lectures', in C. Gordon (ed.), *Power/Knowledge. Selected Interviews and Other Writings 1972–1977.* New York and London: Harvester Wheatsheaf, p. 104.

90 *Ibid.*, p. 105.

91 Gill, Stephen (1994) 'Knowledge, politics and the neo-liberal political economy', in Stubbs and Underhill (1994).
92 Murphy (1996), p. 99.
93 Strang (1996).
94 MacKenzie (1997), p. 36 .
95 Hindess, Barry (2000) 'Not at home in the Empire'. Unpublished paper. Australian National University, p. 4.
96 Pijl, Kees van der (1995) 'The second glorious revolution: globalizing elites and historical change', in Bjorn Hettne (ed.), *International Political Economy: Understanding Global Disorder*. Halifax, Nova Scotia: Zed Books.
97 *Ibid.*, p. 106.
98 Cited in Shoup, Laurence H. and William Minter (1980) 'Shaping a new world order: the Council for Foreign Relations' blueprint for world hegemony, 1939–1945' in Holly Sklar (ed.), *Trilateralism. The Trilateral Commission and Elite Planning for World Management*. Boston: South End Press, pp. 135–56.
 99 Wilmer (1983), p. 173.
100 Daes, Erica-Irene (1996) 'The Draft United Nations Declaration and the definition of the concept of Indigenous Peoples'. Workshop on the United Nations Draft Declaration on Indigenous Peoples, Inaugural Indigenous Peoples of the Pacific Workshop, Suva, 2–6 September 1996; Wilmer (1983), p. 173.
101 Snow (1976) [1919], cited in Wilmer (1983), p. 121.
102 Rist, Gilbert (1999) *The History of Development. From Western Origins to Global Faith.* Cape Town: University of Cape Town Press, p. 52.
103 *Ibid.*
104 Wilmer, F. (1993), p. 188.
105 Weisbrod, Carol (1993) 'Minorities and diversities: the "remarkable experiment" of the League of Nations'. *Connecticut Journal of International Law*, pp. 366–7, cited in Venne (1998), p. 69.
106 For a well-researched, detailed and highly readable account, see Reynolds, Henry (1999) *Why Weren't We Told?: A Personal Search for the Truth about Our History.* Ringwood, Victoria: Viking.
107 Foucault (1980), p. 83.
108 *Ibid.*, p. 97.
109 Ermine (1995), p. 101.
110 *Ibid.*
111 Thiong'o, Ngugi wa (1986) *Decolonizing the Mind: The Politics of Language in African Literature.* London: James Currey; Portsmouth, NH: Heinemann, p. 7.
112 For a detailed account, see Stewart-Harawira, M. (1995) 'Whakatupuranga Ngaro: Kei Te Whai Ao, Kei Te Ao Marama. The impact of colonization on Maori *whanau*', Unpublished MA thesis, School of Education, University of Auckland, pp. 83–105.
113 In New Zealand, the *Tohunga* Suppression Act 1907, ostensibly aimed at preventing 'charlatan' *tohunga* or medicine people, was also aimed at undermining and delegitimating Maori traditional practices. Cf. Simon, Judith and Linda Tuhiwai Smith (eds.) (with Fiona Cram, Margie Hohepa, Stuart McNaughton and Maxine Stephenson) (2001) *A Civilizing Mission? Perceptions and Representations of the New Zealand Native Schools System.* Auckland: Auckland University Press. In North America, the banning and criminalization of the potlatch, seen by some analysts as intended to dismantle the distributive economies of the indigenous peoples as part of the drive to impose capitalism, was also part of the systematic dismantling of indigenous ontological and epistemological structures. Cf. Bracken, Christopher (1997) *The Potlatch Papers: a Colonial Case History.* Chicago: University of Chicago Press.
114 Cf. Wilmer (1983); Ngugi wa Thiong'o (1986).

115 Simon, Judith (1990) *The Place of Schooling in Maori–Pakeha Relations*. IRI PhD Thesis Series, No. 1, Te Whare Wananga o Tamaki Makaurau, International Research Institute for Maori and Indigenous Education.

116 Stephenson, Maxine (2000) 'Creating New Zealanders: education and the formation of the state and the building of the nation'. Unpublished PhD thesis, University of Auckland.

117 *Ibid.*, p. 163.

118 Stewart-Harawira (1995).

119 This was strongly articulated by Maori on many occasions and in particular by chiefs who endowed the mission school run by Bishop Octavius Hadfied at Otaki. See, for instance, Appendices to the House of representatives 1858, E1, pp. 4–5 regarding the 1858 Commission of Inquiry into mission schools held at Otaki, and comments by Tamihana Te Rauparaha, who sought for 'a really good English master to take charge of the schools'.

120 Writing to Bishop Hadfield in 1867, Pora Tuhaere of Oraki complained that Maori children were being 'treated like slaves' and given only two hours of education a day instead of being educated. See New Zealand Government, Appendices to the House of Representatives, 1867, A 31, Wellington, p. 15.

121 Cf. Simon (1990).

122 Stephenson, Maxine (1993) 'Karakariki School: a revisionist history'. Unpublished MA thesis, School of Education, University of Auckland.

123 Foucault (1980), p. 85.

CHAPTER 3

❋

Shaping the
Liberal International Order

The intellectual work of social explanation, Stephen Gill suggests, is frequently linked to political strategies developed from varying viewpoints.[1] The shaping of the multilateral world system of Westphalian nation states reached its culmination in the closing years of the Second World War. From a liberal internationalist perspective, the international institutions established in the wake of that war were widely held to be the framework for a new form of democratic world governance that was embodied in the 1945 Charter of the United Nations. From the viewpoint of indigenous political theorists, the international order of nation states that emerged in the aftermath of the Second World War was a continuation of the marginalization of indigenous peoples that typified the inter-war period. Although many indigenous peoples were co-opted by the imperialist powers into fighting on their behalf, the post-war period saw little or no change in their status and, in some cases, exacerbated their marginalization.[2]

In the previous chapter, the establishment of the world order of nation states provided the context for examining the impact on indigenous peoples of the twin processes of modernity and capitalism, and of the development of international law in ways that specifically sought to extinguish their status as sovereign peoples. This chapter examines the construction of the multilateral world order after the Second World War through the lens of the contested political ideologies that shaped its form and functions. The new UN system and the Bretton Woods and other financial institutions can be conceptualized within the metaphor of two tectonic plates – human rights and the rights of capital. It was a world order embedded in a capitalist world economy, the structural framework of which consisted of nation states with, in principle, equal sovereign rights. It was also a world order within which many groups were unrepresented, and for them fundamental human rights were a site of profound struggle. World order was seen largely in political and economic terms with states, producers and financiers the key actors. Production and multilateral trading were its main economic strategies and territorial integrity and non-intervention its political parameters.

As we saw in the introduction, the realist political paradigm which dominated theorizing after the Second World War conceived the post-war world structure as one in which the balance of power was maintained through a hegemon. In the idealist paradigm of early twentieth-century liberal internationalism, however, the establishment of the United Nations and its institutions was viewed as rectifying the omissions of the League of Nations and formally establishing the ideals of Western democracy as the basis for world order. Liberal internationalism, in that sense, gave birth to the UN Declaration of Human Rights and its twin Covenants (one on Civil and Political Rights, the other on Economic, Social and Cultural Rights), as well as the liberal institutions that comprised the post-Second World War democratic world order of nation states.

An important theme in this chapter is the contribution of the liberal agenda for world governance that was articulated within and through elite networks of think tanks. Cox defines a hegemonic society as one in which 'a dominant class has made its conception of social order acceptable to subordinate classes'.[3] In this, transnational elite networks have played a critical role as a forum for the resolution of different strategies, for working out the 'collective will' of the forces represented, and, most importantly, for their articulation and dissemination. Here a preliminary discussion of such networks and their role in shaping the post-Second World War structures is followed by an analysis of the competing agendas and the struggle for hegemony that girded the international institutions of world order. Although contested, the emergence of American globalism through the expansion of its markets across the globe played a major role in the construction of the liberal international order and in determining the balance of power throughout the twentieth century. While the political institutions of the United Nation were intended to maintain the balance of power in favour of the Big Four nations – the US, Britain, the USSR and China – the economic institutions were to support US global ambition for economic expansionism. As I seek to demonstrate, the ideologies that shaped these ambitions were closely bound up with eighteenth-century liberalism and the political philosophies that saw the expansion of capitalism across the globe. After the Second World War, the rhetoric of development became the legitimating impulse for the co-optation of Third World and indigenous elites.

The section that follows considers two views that provide useful insights into the role of elite networks in the shaping of world order. Van der Pijl's historical materialist analysis compares the 1688 Revolution in England and the transformation of state and society under the aegis of globalization.[4] In his seminal work *American Empire. Roosevelt's Geographer and the Prelude to Globalization*,[5] Neil Smith identifies the Spanish–American War of 1898 as marking the earliest beginnings of American expansionism and the earliest signifier of what Henry Luce, publisher of *Life* magazine and described by Theodore White as 'the most powerful opinion maker in America',[6] later named the 'American Century'.[7] The ending of the Cold War and the collapse of the Berlin Wall marked both the close of that century and the beginning of a new phase of what has been dubbed American imperialism. The role of elite transnational networks of finance and capital has been important at both ends of the cycle.

Transnational Networks and the Expansion of Capitalism

The expansion in overseas settlement was accompanied by the expansion of networks of transnational elites which stemmed from the earliest engagement of the English ruling class in economic activity, frequently through joint directorates.[8] The transnational networks of power and influence that evolved parallel to these joint directorates, van der Pijl insists, 'extended beyond the functional connection created by enterprise' and, as in the case of Freemasonry, were often politically as well as economically motivated. For instance, in Britain, Freemasonry provided a vehicle for drawing together the old aristocracy and bourgeoisie, while the liberal Lockean variant expanded overseas. In the US, the Freemasonry variant of Lockean liberalism became notably predominant within the US government and presidency from the time of James Madison to Ronald Reagan (although the same connections were prominent in the Clinton administration). These motivations were strongly linked to the political economy ideologies of those, such as Hume, who linked consumerism and trade to social and political well-being, and Saint-Simon, who similarly conceived of the end of war through international trade.

In van der Pijl's account, the end of the Cold War in 1989 completed 'a century-long process of transnationalization of capital' based on the Lockean model of international integration that was first crystallized in the 1911 Arbitration Treaty and the establishment of the British Commonwealth of Nations.[9] Van der Pijl's analysis draws on the notion of Hobbesian state–society complexes to examine similarities between the 1688 Glorious Revolution in England, which saw the power of the sovereign replaced with 'the supremacy of Parliament over the king and the law over both'[10] and the creation of a particular state–society complex or 'Lockean heartland' through-out the British Isles and other areas of British settlement under the aegis of globalization. Three determining features in the transform-ation from Cromwell's Hobbesian Roundhead Commonwealth to a Lockean framework of aristocratic bourgeois self-government and a market economy regulated by common law were the expansion of civil society, the formation of transnational elite networks, and the impact on interstate relations.

Predating Locke's *Two Treatises on Civil Government*, the advance-ment in overseas settlement from England was underpinned by a transnational civil society.[11] As emigration from Britain gained in momentum during the eighteenth and nineteenth centuries, so too did the transmission of Lockean ideologies – including, most effectively, the public school system. Historical aspirants to Lockean state–society status include France in the late seventeenth and eighteenth centuries, various state-socialist regimes, and, most recently, the multilateral bloc of socialist and developing countries that, during the 1970s, advocated a New International Economic Order.

Key commonalities shared by Hobbesian state contenders include a directive state apparatus, a state mode of production, a pre-emptive confiscation of the social sphere, and revolutions that occur 'from above'. To date, Hobbesian challengers to the Lockean heartland have in most cases collapsed and been integrated into the heartland, while socialist states committed to political alternatives have been subjected to new modes of accumulation and what van der Pijl terms 'the Second Cold War' of economic assault.[12] Thus another important similarity between the first and second 'Glorious Revolutions' is the role of violence as a coercive measure.

The influence of these trans-Atlantic and transnational networks has developed in increasingly purposeful and sophisticated ways, particularly since the expansion of the Rhodes/Round Table networks at the beginning of the twentieth century. Notably, this influence has been felt at the level of government policy and has been disseminated by ministries, prime ministers and presidents, as well as academics, think tanks, foundations and public pressure groups.[13] Held *et al.* describe the period of expansion in the late nineteenth and early twentieth centuries as marking the beginning of a shift from deeply contested imperial and territorial forms of control to 'new, distinctive, non-territorial forms of power and domination'.[14] In the words of Geyer and Bright, these new formations were 'made possible by the formation of communications-based systems of control ... that began to [enmesh] the world in global circuits of power by the end of the century'.[15]

New transnational forms of organization and activity, marked by more autonomous systems of power managed and controlled by new transnational organizations and multinational corporations, signalled the emergence of a new political order in which the hegemony exercised through networks of powerful economic interests was maintained within the emergent regime of international organizations, banks and companies. In this manner, Held declares, the 'visible presence of rule' was replaced with the 'invisible government' of finance and organization.[16] Emerging into more prominence in the second half of the twentieth century, notably through capital and finance as well as military–industrial complexes, the historical impact of these networks of directorates, consultants and advisers has been a powerful hegemonic influence in the formulation of the international as well as local organizations, policies and practices that comprise the formal structures of world order.

The Paris Peace Conference of 1919 was the impetus for what became the most influential organization in US foreign policy, the Council for Foreign Relations (CFR).[17] Launched in 1921 and born out of frustration with the final peace plan at Paris and the reluctance of the American public to relinquish their 'sovereignty' to an international body such as the League of Nations, the CFR was restricted in membership to a select group of 'men of influence': politicians, capitalists, bankers, lawyers, academics and journalists.[18] Close ties were maintained with its British counterpart, the Royal Institute of International Affairs. Whereas the British organization fostered a conservative liberal ideology, the CFR was seen as the vanguard of enlightened liberal internationalism. These ideologies were promoted through the Council's journal *Foreign Affairs*, launched in 1922 and described by the historian Robert Schulzinger as nothing other than 'a plea for a forward United States foreign policy, interested in exploiting the world's natural resources and putting affairs in Washington in the hands of serene, dispassionate experts who, unlike the public at large, knew what they were doing'.[19] The vision of international order articulated in the Treaty of Versailles was one of peaceful coexistence between nations hierarchically organized on the basis of economic access and the exploitation of 'dependent' nations. In the representations by US President Woodrow Wilson at the Paris Peace Conference, Smith argues, global liberal ideals fused with US economic self-interest were clothed in the expression of 'the desire of the people for a new world order'.[20] The resounding failure to achieve this and the failure of the US to gain domestic support for the League of Nations saw winning domestic support for the US global economic agenda become another of the key goals of the CFR. During this period, according to Smith, the US public at large saw the proposed United Nations organization as representing the ultimate evil of world government and the 'emasculation of the nation'. President Roosevelt and the US State Department, on the other hand, saw the UN as 'a pivotal institution for US post-war globalism'.[21]

In order to found a world order, Cox writes, a dominant society 'must be capable of universalizing its own constitutive principles; it must be supremely self-confident in its own internal strength and expansive potential'.[22] In the US, post-war planning for the institutions that would provide a firm foundation for democratic peace and universal rights as well as supporting US global aspirations and economic interests became a priority. Two of the Council's key goals after the Second World War were the preparation of a War and Peace Plan for the redivision of the world and the strengthening and harmonizing of British–American military, economic and political affairs. Another was the guiding of the American public along the path to enthusiasm for a world organization that would uphold the interests of American global ambition. The 1940 transplanting of the Council for Foreign Relations structure into the US government in the form of the Advisory Committee on Post-war Foreign Policy was an important part of this planning. The core of this project was the redesigning of the political geography in a way that would enhance US economic interests.

Contested States, United Nations

The establishment of the United Nations and its Charter was widely viewed as providing a firm foundation for the establishment of world peace, the upholding of human rights and dignity, and the constitution of an evolving world government based on the promotion of equal universal rights and the self-determination of all peoples.[23] In fact, as Smith eloquently demonstrates, the rhetoric of global peace obscured the aim of 'global political and military stability for the new market-based American Empire'.[24] The power relations of the Second World War predetermined the organization of the United Nations as an arena for the playing out of competing agendas, contested political power and the legitimation of a new global hegemony. Where Roosevelt's original vision of a four-way regional sharing arrangement subordinated to the Big Four became superseded by a more global vision, Churchill advocated regional councils, such as a Council of Europe.[25] While the first official blueprint for the structure of the United Nations organization was prepared between the four powers at the August 1944 Dumbarton Oaks Conference in Washington, the final charter that was formally agreed at the San Francisco Conference on International Organization in April 1945 closely reflected the draft prepared by the US State Department in its post-war planning.

Kingsbury and Robert's critique of the United Nations[26] details the contradictions inherent within the UN system, many of which were embedded in the United Nations Charter, a document widely viewed as securing the sovereign integrity of states against aggression, the fundamental human rights of all individual citizens (although not collective rights), and the rights of all peoples to self-determination. Although the UN Charter defined the world system in terms of the sovereign equality and territorial integrity of member states and of non-intervention in their domestic affairs, the recognition required for membership within the world system of nations was then, as now, highly political. Arguably, within the UN system states were neither absolutely sovereign, nor in practice equal to each other in rights, as the theory of sovereignty asserts. The embedded hierarchical structure of the UN system meant that although nominal sovereign equality exists amongst member states, in practice, voting within the General Assembly and other major UN organs was limited to member states. Likewise, access to the International Court of Justice was limited to states and certain UN agencies. The *status quo* of the post-war balance of power was maintained through the designation of five Second World War superpowers as permanent members of the Security Council with the power of veto (whereas others have rotating membership).[27] Despite the rhetoric of a new international order of equal sovereign states, the primary function of the institution created by the 1945 United Nations Charter was to facilitate the maintenance of the *status quo* within an international organization of nation states, membership of which was carefully proscribed. As Wallerstein points out, although five superpowers comprised the UN Security Council, the world quickly came to a common acceptance of the fact that only two powers really mattered, and they were locked into the zero sum game of the Cold War.[28]

Smith views the disputes between Britain and the US over the form and shape of the new international institutions from the perspective of alternative strategies of global accumulation. Whereas Britain saw US economic expansionism as territorially based, for the US, British defence of colonialism was a major obstacle to post-war US economic expansion. With 40 per cent of the world's land shackled by political dependence, an 'intense colloid of seemingly endless global altruism and extreme self-interest'[29] on the part of the US converged with an aversion to colonialism and a desire to open up dependent territories to economic access. For Britain, the US State Department draft on trusteeship represented a disguised assault on the British Empire. As Churchill famously stated, he had not become His Majesty's Prime Minister 'for the purpose of presiding over the dissolution of the British Empire'.

The replacement of the mandate system established under the League of Nations with an expanded system of trusteeship designed to include non-self-governing and trust territories, designated 'dependent countries', was also contentious. Negotiations over dependent territories were based on the Atlantic Charter signed between Britain and the US in 1941, which stated that all nations should have 'access on equal terms'.[30] While some states sought the application of the trusteeship system to all colonial countries, others strongly supported decolonization. Yet others saw nothing wrong with exploiting the resources of the natives whilst maintaining them in a position of subjugation and dependence. In his comments on the British mining of phosphate in Nauru, exported mainly to New Zealand at the rate of 1.3 tons per year, leading CFR member Isaiah Bowman expressed the prevailing attitude towards a combination of total exploitation and benign neglect. 'The phosphate is of no use to the natives …

What could the natives do with the royalties on that amount of phosphate?' Neither did he advocate rasing the living standards of the natives. 'The United States', he said, 'was not going to revise the living standards and raise the status of all the fuzzy-wuzzies in the world at *its* own expense'.[31] Yet Roosevelt, Smith reports, saw no contradiction between the declaration of sovereignty and self-determination, on one hand, and the paternalism of trusteeship under the supervision of 'adult nations' on the other.

A system of regional and international administration was advocated that would both encourage what was viewed as 'timely development' towards the self-determination of arbitrarily determined dependent territories and, at the same time, allow international access. The compromise position that was adopted in Article 73 of Chapter XI of the Charter obliged member states administering non-self-governing territories to transmit regular reports to the Secretary-General regarding the economic, social and educational conditions in those territories, but failed to empower the UN to supervise the attainment of self-government. In the process, collective rights such as those that applied in European states were extinguished and the concept discredited. Thus in the twentieth century reconstruction of post-war world order, the 'wardship' doctrine enshrined in the Treaty of Versailles continued as one of the foundation cornerstones of the United Nations Organization, albeit in a somewhat modified form. The founding Charter, which Wallerstein argues was 'in many respects a restatement of the political philosophy of the modern world system',[32] delineated 'civilized nations' as those that constitute the international order of nation states, reinforcing the doctrines of wardship and of recognition that excluded indigenous nations from entry into the international order of equal nation states. Collective group rights similarly remained outside the scope of the new international structures.[33]

The exclusion of certain groups of indigenous peoples from citizenship within internally colonized territories enabled acts of physical and cultural genocide to continue without recourse of those groups to justice.[34] In Australia, indigenous peoples continued to be denied citizenship status and to be denied basic human rights; as just one of many examples of exploitation and oppression in the Pacific, Nauru continued to be mined for phosphate for the benefit of the West and, having been stripped of all its resources, was forced by foreign creditors into declaring bankruptcy on 18 April 2004; in Canada, the US and New Zealand, assimilation continued as the dominant state policy towards indigenous peoples. In carrying out the function of facilitating political governance and economic access on behalf of dominant Western interests, the United Nations became a vehicle for the perpetuation of a global hegemony in which declarations of common humanity and democratic freedom obscured the reality of US global dominance and the securing of markets for US expansionism. From the point of view advanced by Smith, this can be identified as the second mark of the US Century. For other commentators, this moment marked the beginnings of American imperialism in the twentieth century.[35]

Bretton Woods and the American Agenda

Cox writes that the period of negotiation between the United States and Britain over the formation of the post-Second World War economic order was the specific context for the emergence of the economic concept of multilateralism.[36] The Charter for the organization of the United Nations was drafted by the US State Department. The economic institutions that came out of the Bretton Woods Conference were the brainchild of the US Treasury. The driving impulse was seen by participants and observers as both a determination to prevent the mistakes of the First World War and the Treaty of Versailles with the resultant post-war Great Depression, and a struggle for economic hegemony over the post-Second World War 'New World Order'. According to CFR member Richard Gardner, the negotiations regarding the structure of the post-war framework were based on the assumption of a single world political system that would be devoid of struggles over power and in which the Bretton Woods institutions were to be the basis for a universal monetary system.[37] The critical issue was whose interests would dominate.

Belgian historian Armand van Dormael identifies two levels at which the struggle for power in the formation of a new single world economic system was played out. The competing players in the contest over the form and nature of a Western-driven multilateral economic order were initially Germany and the Western powers as represented by Britain and United States.[38] Germany's proposal for a new economic order was first promulgated in 1940. In Britain, debates regarding the new world economic system occurred mainly between liberal economists, who strongly advocated the removal of trade barriers,[39] and those who favoured the conservative approach advocated by Keynes and his US counterpart, Harry Dexter White, both of whom had been leading figures in opposing the financial liberalism of the 1930s. On the other side of the Atlantic, however, the final institutions for a post-war world order were foregrounded in a series of studies undertaken between 1939 and 1945 by the CFR.

Planning for the New World Order took the form of a vast undertaking known as the War and Peace Project, which involved five study groups – Economic and Financial, Political, Armaments, Territorial, and Peace Aims.[40] From the beginning, Smith states, there was no consensus among Council members regarding the actual extent of US ambition: whether economic hegemony should involve the whole world, or just a designated part. The study of the Economic and Financial Group, which charted approximately 95 per cent of all world trade in every commodity and product, divided the world into blocs and documented the location, production and trade of all important commodities and manufactured goods for each area. Itemized within internal memorandums, each major region was then measured in terms of self-sufficiency, using net import and export figures.[41] Realizing that self-sufficiency for the US would require enormous alteration in the US economic strategy, the study determined that, to maintain the existing system, the minimum area (in 1941 it came to be called the 'Grand Area') required for 'elbow room' included the Western hemisphere, the United Kingdom, the remainder of the British Commonwealth and Empire, the Dutch East Indies, China and Japan.[42] The desired objective, therefore, was to achieve economic integration as a 'subglobal base for post-war US economic prosperity'.[43] Foreshadowing the struggle for control that was to reach crisis point in 2003, the Middle East, recognized then as crucial for geopolitico-economic and military control of the globe, was a significant issue in these discussions.[44]

Facilitated by Britain's indebtedness due to the war, US economic leverage had two significant results for the new multilateral economic order. Britain abandoned the preferential trading payments system – one of many protectionist strategies that attempted to mediate the effects of the worldwide depression of the 1930s – and United States' interests dominated the final proposals for the new multilateral economic order launched at the Bretton Woods conference in 1944. Together, the UN and the Bretton Woods institutions represented the two axes of global governance – economic governance and the interstate system. While the system was transnational in character, its locus of power was firmly based within the US. Its passing marked by the statement of Roosevelt's ambassador-at-large,

CFR leader Norman H. Davis, that 'The British Empire as it existed in the past will never reappear ... and the United States may have to take its place',[45] the *pax britannica* paradigm, which had dominated world order for more than two centuries, was replaced by the *pax americana*.

In broad terms, the Bretton Woods system was predicated upon a combination of liberal internationalist ideologies and Keynesian macroeconomics. Institutionalized in stable currency arrangements supported by the IMF and World Bank and underwritten by US deficits,[46] the focus of this arrangement was the national development of states, the opening up of territories to economic access and the reconstruction and integration of the international economy under American hegemony. As Arrighi and Silver note, the recognition of the legitimate interests of states in protecting the livelihood of citizens was an important part of this arrangement.[47] Relying on the full utilization of national resources, the national development project of the Keynesian national welfare state assumed the integration of indigenous peoples within the state system and the absorption of indigenous territories. Within internally colonized countries such as New Zealand, Australia, Canada and the US, national development projects provided the legitimation for the ongoing confiscation of indigenous lands. The ideology of development had come into its own. The International Development Bank for Reconstruction and Development (IBRD), one of the twin Bretton Woods institutions, was established to support these processes.

Constructing the Institutions of an International Economic Order

The proposals for an International Bank for Reconstruction and Development and a stabilization fund, both established according to the principles of the 1941 Atlantic Charter between Britain and the US, were drawn up by US Treasury Secretary Henry Morgenthau's adviser on international economics, Harry Dexter White, and presented to Morgenthau in 1942.[48] Described by a Treasury memorandum as 'a New Deal in international economics',[49] a substantially modified version of this proposal provided the negotiating document for the 700 delegates from 43 nations who attended the UN Monetary and Financial Conference that began on 1 July 1944 at the Mount Washington Hotel in Bretton Woods, New Hampshire. Outlined in Article 1 of the Bank's Charter, the main purpose of the

IBRD was to 'assist in the reconstruction and development of territories of members by facilitating the investment of capital for productive purposes ... and to promote the long-range balanced growth of international trade ... by encouraging international investment, thereby assisting in raising productivity, the standard of living and the conditions of labour' through guaranteeing private investment as well as its own lending. Reconstruction and development were to be given equal priority, with 'political' and 'non-economic' considerations in the operations of the Bank prohibited in its Charter.[50] Ideologically, however, its roots can be traced to the Saint-Simonian liberalism of the nineteenth century.

Saint-Simon's development ideals were driven by a passion for the improvement of humankind. Inspired by the works of Bacon, Newton and Descartes,[51] he considered that the will to dominate embedded in human nature was the root of all war, violence and disunity. The solution advocated by Saint-Simon was the rechanelling of human aggression into enormous development projects within a unified, global society. In such a society, technocratic, instrumental reason and the 'science of production'[52] would replace politics, and economic development and production would ensure an endless progression of industrial and economic advancement and the elimination of strife. Hence Saint-Simon promoted the idea of a public international development bank. The first private international investment bank, the Credit Mobilier, was established by Saint-Simonian disciples, the Pereire brothers. According to Hayek, the bank's founders described it as a 'centre for administration and control which was to direct according to a coherent programme the railway systems, the town planning activities and the various public utilities and other industries'.[53]

The Bretton Woods system established in 1944 was similarly predicated on what Henry Morgenthau expressed as an 'elementary economic axiom ... that prosperity has no fixed limits'.[54] Described in his opening address at the Bretton Woods Conference as

> the creation of a dynamic world economy in which the peoples of every nation will be able to realize their potentialities in peace ... and enjoy, increasingly, the fruits of material progress on an earth infinitely blessed with natural riches,[55]

the limitless exploitation of the earth's resources was assumed as a given, providing for the infinite expansion of global economic growth to be presided over by the United States. In this system, international trade, unhindered by what Morgenthau described as 'economic evils – the competitive currency devaluation and destructive impediments to trade – that preceded the present war',[56] was again touted as a most effective deterrent to war. In Heideggerian terms, the earth's resources were viewed as a 'standing reserve' existing solely for the profiting of human endeavours. Within this framework, indigenous nations, traditional communities and their territories were similarly viewed. These peoples, territories and resources were to be subsumed within the world economy, remaining available for exploitation and development by industrialized nation states, and their human capital usefully trained in the service of economic capital.

The year 1947 was an epochal year. The launching of the Marshall Plan for the economic reconstruction of war-torn Western Europe provided both a conduit for the enormous production capacity of the US in its post-war conversion phase[57] and a defence against Communist expansion. Not by pure coincidence, 1947 also saw the establishment of the Central Intelligence Agency (CIA). Also launched in 1947, the General Agreement on Tariffs and Trade (GATT), instigated after the non-ratification of the Havana Charter by the US Congress,[58] cemented in place the fourth pillar of a hegemonic, interstate, ostensibly 'democratic' system of world order and secured the dominance of the US economic and trade policy agenda.

The Havana Charter was envisaged by its proponents as the fourth pillar of these new structural underpinnings and was intended to implement an international trade organization (ITO). Its main purpose was to be the overseeing of the world trading system and the imposition of certain obligations on industrial countries. The defeat of the Havana Charter by the United States enabled GATT, which was considerably weaker than the envisaged ITO, to function essentially as the primary post-war international trade agency. In contrast to the ITO, its main role was the facilitation of a controlled process of multilateral trade liberalization among member countries. Discussing the role of GATT, John Whalley argues that while it was not necessarily liberal in its actual principles, in its policies it took an implicitly pro-liberal stance.[59] GATT provided the framework for seven rounds of global tariff reduction negotiations. Included in the obligations of signatory countries was agreement on broad principles governing the use of trade-restricting measures by other governments and providing the basis for a system of rights and obligations between contracting parties. Key principles in GATT were commitments by contracting countries to grant 'most-favoured nation' (MFN) status at the border, as established in Article 1, and the granting of 'national treatment' (NT) within their territories, set out in Article 111. As well as regulating tariffs, parties to GATT also sought to eliminate quotas (Article XI), though with substantial exceptions such as for agriculture, to maintain the balance of payments, or as safeguards. In addition, the right of states to use trade remedy laws was entrenched within the rules of GATT, thus recognizing the sovereignty of states.[60]

With the exception of GATT, the international institutions that comprised the post-war international order were broadly seen as coming under the umbrella of the US-dominated United Nations system and thus being accountable to the UN agencies. Rich, however, demonstrates that, although differently prescribed, the unequal relations of power inherent in the establishment of the United Nations were also inherent in the establishment of the Bretton Woods institutions. Largely the product of Roosevelt's 'New Deal' politics, the Bank and its sister institution, the IMF, were vested with an unprecedented amount of power without any corresponding accountability to those affected by their decisions.[61] Cemented in 1947, an agreement signed between the IBRD (World Bank) and the newly formed UN, and which included the right of the Bank to withhold from the UN all and any information that it deemed confidential, and, further, any information that would 'otherwise interfere with the orderly conduct of its operations', ensured blanket confidentiality coupled with an astonishing degree of secrecy in the Bank's operating procedures, enabling it to defy the UN as it wished.[62]

These then, were the functionalist politico-economic arrangements that constituted the structural framework of the post-war inter-state system. US dominance was embedded in the economic as well as the political arrangements of the post-war structural framework of world order. US industrialism and productivity provided the modernization model for 'development' policies amongst countries that, in the prevailing Darwinist ideologies of development, were hierarchically organized as 'underdeveloped' and 'developing', for post-war reconstruction work in Europe and the Pacific, and led the development of multilateral regulatory regimes for managing interlocking spheres of national interest.

Academic Networks and Neoliberal Economics

Van der Pijl identifies two policy phases in the current period of neoliberalism that indicate the influence of contemporary transnational elite networks in intentionally shaping the processes of globalization. The first such phase he describes as 'the preparation and promulgation of an economic programme aimed, intentionally or otherwise, at the displacement of Keynesian/Fordist corporate liberalism in the West'.[63] The second was direct engagement with socialist states and movements in the latter period of what he terms 'the neoliberal offensive'.[64] The first phase was most notably marked, again in 1947, by the inauguration of the Mont Pelerin Society, an elite group of neoliberal American and European scholars that formed the basis of a 'kind of dispersed worldwide academy of uncompromising liberal scholars and students'.[65]

The roots of the Mont Pelerin Society lay in the politico-economic philosophy of Austrian economist Ludwig von Mises who, together with his key disciple Friedrich von Hayek, promoted the view that there was no alternative to capitalism and that it required for its operation an 'unlimited commitment to the self-regulating market'.[66] Committed to the construction of a 'purer, more uncompromising theory of liberalism' and the aggressive promotion of the universalization of capitalism, the dissemination of this radically conservative version of economic liberalism was facilitated by the dispersal of the Austrian School and Hayek's appointment in the early 1930s to a chair at the London School of Economics. In the United States, the launch of Walter Lippman's book, *An Inquiry into the Principles of the Good Society* published in 1936 and acknowledging the influence of Mises and Hayek, provided the initial impetus for the establishment of the Mont Pelerin Society. The major target of the Mont Pelerin Society in the immediate post-war years was the collectivism of 1945 Europe. It was conceived, according to John Bellamy Foster, as a vehicle for the reconstruction of 'the framework of a free society, with limited government under the rule of law', guaranteeing private property rights but permitting the 'possibility of establishing minimum standards by means not inimical to initiative and functioning of the market'.[67] The Mont Pelerin Society vigorously opposed state interventionism, promoting in its place 'the notion of a "competitive order" arising spontaneously and taking the form of a boundless market economy'.[68]

From its inception, its members sought to minimize public awareness of the organization, preferring instead to broaden its influence by the insertion of its leading thinkers in key academic and political positions. In the words of member Lord Ralph Harris, intellectuals and academics who, 'because of their expert knowledge of their own subjects are listened to with respect on most others',[69] were specially targeted for co-option by the Society on the basis that '[o]nce the more active part of the intellectuals has been converted to a set of beliefs, the process by which these become generally accepted is almost automatic and irreversible'.[70] Like those of other key neo-conservative organizations and think tanks – the Council for Foreign Relations, established in the US in 1921, the Institute of Economic Affairs, established in Britain in 1957 by Anthony Fisher (an early business member of the Mont Pelerin Society),[71] the International Chamber of Commerce, the Trilateral Commission and the Heritage Foundation[72] – the politico-economic ideologies and policies espoused and promulgated by members of the Mont Pelerin Society have exercised increasing influence in the construction of the transnational economic order and in the promotion of new forms of governance centred on the market and the 'enterprise culture'. Discursively con-structed and widely accepted concepts such as 'governance without government' can be directly attributed to the politico-economic ide-ologies promoted by a convergence of the interests of capital and par-ticular forms of liberalism, both of which have dominated the struct-ural and ideological formation of the global economic order. During the post-war years and under the leadership of Mount Pelerin Society members George J. Stigler and Milton Friedman, neoclassical eco-nomics and monetarist policies were widely promoted through the Chicago School of Economics, which, from its earliest phase in the period 1920–45, has been closely associated with neoclassical theories of economics[73] and was influential in the infiltration of neoliberal economics into US foreign and domestic policy. Also influential was Theodore W. Schultz's alignment of development and human capital theories in a manner that saw a renewed emphasis on the role of education in economic growth.

Decolonization and the Construction of States

The post-war international order was dominated by realist and neorealist orthodoxies predicated upon zero-sum assumptions regarding interstate relations and the need to maintain the dominance of Western hegemonies against the Communist threat. This period of peak US hegemony saw decolonization, self-determination and deve-lopment became key strategies in US containment policies. The concept of development played a key role in shaping North–South relations during the latter part of the twentieth century. While its roots stem from Enlightenment liberalism and Saint-Simonian ideology, President Truman's inaugural address on 20 January 1949 signalled the moment at which 'development' emerged as a global strategy for the United States[74] and 'underdevelopment' became the pivotal signifier for the largest part of the world. In fact it was at this point, Wolfgang Sachs suggests, that colonization's double mandate of economic profit and 'civilizing' the native races converged and 'development', which under the British Development Act of 1929 applied only to the exploitation of resources, became extended to people and societies.[75]

The concept of 'development', included at the last minute in Truman's address,[76] was centred on the concept of democratic 'fair dealing'. As an 'international effort' and a 'collective enterprise', development was based on an immense increase in production and an 'improved' use of the world's resources. The 'fair deal' model saw economic development as a single progressive movement by which all countries would in their own time and at their own speed 'catch up' to the economic level of the industrialized countries. It promised an end to the old imperialism that involved exploitation for profit and offered in its place the 'American Dream' through industrialization and production, made achievable for all via Walter Rostow's five-stage pathway to economic growth and modernization.[77] Politically, Rist suggests, the development paradigm enabled the United States to deploy an anti-colonial imperialism, within which 'development' became the new global hegemonic discourse.[78]

Having been divided up amongst the major colonial powers following the First World War, the world was now redivided within a new paradigm – one which, like colonialism, reclassified the world into new hierarchies of societies, and in which gross national product, or GNP, became the hallowed signifier of a country's attained level of civilization. In this Hegelesque reclassification, underdevelopment became an effective means of discrediting colonialism. The dichotomy between developed and underdeveloped now became part of a new universal paradigm within which new hierarchies were created and which provided a new legitimation for the possibility and then the necessity of intervention. US-backed aid strategies carried out in the name of liberal democracy focused on 'development' and state building in Western Europe, Asia and the Pacific as a bulwark against Communism and radical movements, and in the acquisition of access to resources. The creation of states became a central strategy in the creation of a democratic world order that was to be firmly grounded in US hegemony.

The construction of new states, particularly in Africa, coupled with the ideology of development as a universal paradigm, had unintended consequences. Hardt and Negri point out that New Deal/'fair deal' development ideology ignored the fact that the economics of 'developed' countries are determined more by their dominant position in the global system than by their internal structures or other quantitative factors.[79] Recognition of this point became pivotal to the theories of underdevelopment and dependency, which, emerging from South America and Africa during the 1960s, provided a counter-argument to the post-war modernization theories. The principle that developing countries should follow the same course that developed countries had travelled – by pursuing isolationist policies aimed at full economic autonomy – underpinned calls by Third World elites for a New International Economic Order (NIEO) in the early 1970s,[80] and became a compelling factor in monetarist responses.[81]

Subaltern Nations and the Ideology of Development

In their analysis of the transition to empire in the late twentieth century, Hardt and Negri point out differences in function between the concept of the nation[82] that developed as a response to colonial domination and the concept of the nation that developed in Europe in tandem with capitalist expansionism. In the case of 'subaltern nationalism', that is, the concept of nation wielded by the subordinate as a weapon for change, the nation has two primary and highly ambiguous functions. As a line of defence against domination by more powerful nations and other external ideological forces, the nation appears as progressive and is used as a concept with which to obstruct and defeat the occupying power. The concept of the nation also becomes an ideological tool by which to erect a defence against the dominant discourses of superiority, to affirm the dignity of the people, and to support the demand for independence and equality. In both situations, they emphasize, 'the nation is progressive strictly as a fortified line of defence against more powerful external forces'.[83] On the reverse side of this progressive image, this concept of the nation is also regressive, functioning as 'a dominating power that exerts equal and opposite internal oppression, resisting internal difference and opposition in the name of national identity, unity, and security'.[84] In many cases, they point out, the national unification of countries, as in the cases of Indonesia and China, has been prepared by the colonists. The same argument may be applied to African countries. Like the dominant countries, the subaltern nation denies and negates the multiplicity of identities and histories for the sake of national identity and homogeneity. Thus, Hardt and Negri suggest, the unifying function of the subaltern nation becomes a two-edged sword that is 'at once progressive and reactionary'.[85] In the case of Africa, liberation movements led by elites promoted the establishment of new political regimes based on the territorial boundaries prescribed under colonization. Now carried out with the cooperation of Western-educated elites in what was essentially a recolonization of indigenous peoples, as the new states sought to establish their authority within the frontiers established by the former colonial powers, the oppression of indigenous peoples in many cases increased.[86]

The conjunction of developmentalism with the increasing articulation and recognition of indigenous rights, and the protection of indigenous cultures and rights to land within international law frameworks, impacted on indigenous peoples in multiple ways. Discussing the ecological impact of changing modes of developmentalism, Sachs pinpoints the dissolution of cultures that were not built around a frenzy of accumulation as one of the most insidious effects of the development paradigm.[87] The identification of 'obstacles to development' and the implementation of education programmes aimed at overcoming cultural 'deficiencies' saw the deliberate and sustained targeting of collective social structures, local relations of exchange, and subsistence lifestyles and paradigms of self-sufficiency. Sachs points out that turning societies of the South into economic competitors required more than an injection of capital and the transfer of technology; it required a 'cultural transformation'. The resultant dislocation of cultural identities, language loss and cultural deprivation has been amply documented.[88] The functionality of this approach was well demonstrated by J. L. Sadie, writing in the *Economist* in 1960:

> Economic development of an underdeveloped people is not compatible with the maintenance of their traditional customs and mores. A break with the latter is prerequisite to economic progress. What is needed is a revolution in the totality of social, cultural and religious institutions and habits, and thus in their psychological attitude, their philosophy and way of life. What is, therefore, required amounts in reality to social disorganization. Unhappiness and discontentment in the sense of wanting more than is obtainable at any moment, is to be generated. The suffering and dislocation that may be caused in the process may be objectionable, but it

appears to be the price that has to be paid for economic development; the condition of economic progress.[89]

In the newly created states, indigenous peoples' traditional cognitive and social patterns, modes of governance and ontological world views were identified as 'obstacles to development' and at odds with those of an economically based society. Through the effective use of the tools of education and modernization, and in cooperation with Third World and indigenous elites, traditional social fabrics were disintegrated and reintegrated according to the Eurocentric model of modern societies. The South, Sachs points out, was thus precipitated into an increasing degradation of indigenous ways as the 'unfettered hegemony of Western productivism and accumulation' undermined the well-being of traditional and communally based societies.[90]

The drive for the development of resources and the resultant increased exploitation of indigenous lands and natural resources saw indigenous subjectivities reconstructed via state education programmes which targeted indigenous peoples in terms of productivity in the labour force and their assimilation into the dominant culture. The 'civilizing mission' ascribed to education having been largely dicredited, education now became the vehicle by which countries could achieve intellectual and eventually economic self-sufficiency. As Dale argued in 1982, it was during this phase that the technical-functionalist theory of education – concerned with demonstrating the correlation between levels of education and economic growth measured by *per capita* GNP – became popularized.[91] In this view, and driven by the findings of prominent educational psychologists such as David McLelland[92] and Alex Inkeles,[93] an essential role of education was the replacing of values of particularism, collectivity, ascription and diffuseness with the values of Western particularism – individualism, universalism, achievement and specificity.[94] Dale points out that while of itself education does not alter the relationship between developing and developed countries, what it does do is provide credentials, which, in the hands of elites, reinforce the power and status of already dominant groups. As he emphasizes, education is tied up with the production and reproduction of elites, the assertion and maintenance of capitalist ideologies, and the ultimate reproduction of the *status quo*. In Third World formations, this resulted in

> restricted and uneven capitalist development ... structured both by the
> reproductive requirements of the industrial capitalist mode of production

and by the possibilities for the continuing reproduction of the non-capitalist mode or its elements, embodied in particular divisions of labour. [95]

The impact of technical-functionalism theories of education on Maori in New Zealand has been identified and documented within numerous reports. Whilst the remedial measures it proposed were unashamedly assimilationist in nature, the 1960 Hunn Report signalled the enormity of the disparities in educational achievement between Maori and non-Maori New Zealanders. In the following decade, the increasing disparities across all social indices and educational achievement in particular, combined with the loss of cultural knowledge and language, became part of the catalyst for renewed Maori resistance to the assimilatory agenda.

The development of transformative strategies for the revitalizing of the language and cultural signifiers of 'being Maori', the revalidating of Maori ontologies and epistemologies, and the reclaiming of the right to Maori self-determination ultimately transformed the political landscape in New Zealand.

Notes

1 Gill, Stephen (1991) 'Historical materialism, Gramsci and international political economy', in Craig Murphy and Roger Tooze (eds.), *New International Political Economy*. Boulder, Colorado: Lynne Rienner, pp. 51–78.

2 In New Zealand, for instance, land that had been confiscated for 'the war effort' during the Second World War was retained by the government after the war and utilized for other purposes, including commercial development. During the 1960s, land taken under Public Works Acts for purposes that included emergency airfields during the war, in some instances, and state housing in other instances, was handed over to local councils. In one well-known case, land was given to the local golf club. In other cases it was subdivided for high-end residential use. These and other similar instances became the focus for Maori mobilization in the 1970s Maori land movement. For a detailed discussion, see Ranginui Walker (1990) *Ka Whawhai Tonu Matou. Struggle Without End*. Auckland: Penguin.

3 Cox, Robert W. (1996) [1989] 'Middlepowermanship, Japan and future world order', in Robert W. Cox (with Timothy Sinclair), *Approaches to World Order*. Cambridge: Cambridge University Press, p. 246.

4 Van der Pijl, Kees (1995) 'The second glorious revolution: globalizing elites and historical change', in Bjorn Hettne (ed.), *International Political Economy. Understanding Global Disorder*. London and Halifax, Nova Scotia: Zed Books, pp. 100–28.

5 Smith, Neil (2003) *American Empire. Roosevelt's Geographer and the Prelude to Globalization*. Berkeley, Los Angeles and London: University of California Press.

6 Prestowitz, Clyde (2003) *Rogue Nation. American Unilateralism and the Failure of Good Intentions*. New York: Basic Books, p. 211.

7 Smith (2003), p. 32.

8 Van der Pijl lists as early examples the governorship of the Royal Africa Company, the East India Company, and the Hudson Bay Company by members of the English royal family, including James, Duke of York and heir to the English throne, Prince

Rupert and the Duke of Marlborough.

9   Van der Pilj (1995), p. 109.

10 Shell, Jonathan (2003) *The Unconquerable World. Power, Nonviolence and the Will of the People*. New York: Metropolitan, p. 152.

11 For instance, the transferring of tens of thousands of settlers to North America by the Virginia Company and the Massachusetts Bay Company.

12 This notion is further taken up in Chapter 5.

13 Van der Pijl (1995), p. 121.

14 Held, David, McGrew, Anthony, Goldplatt, David and Jonathan Perraton (1999) *Global Transformations: Politics, Economics and Culture*. Stanford, CA: Stanford University Press, p. 43.

15 Geyer, M. and C. Bright (1995) 'World history in a global age', *American Historical Review*, 100, p. 1047, cited in Held *et al.* (1999).

16 Ferro, M. (1997) *Colonization: A Global History*. London: Routledge, cited in Held *et al.* (1999).

17 Smith (2003).

18 *Ibid.*

19 *Ibid.*, p. 196.

20 *Ibid.*, p. 117.

21 *Ibid.*, p. 374.

22 Cox (1996) [1989], p. 246.

23 See, for instance, Sellers, Mortimer (ed.) (1996) *The New World Order: Sovereignty, Human Rights, and the Self-Determination of Peoples*. Oxford: Berg.

24 Smith (2003), p. 375.

25 *Ibid.*

26 Kingsbury, Benedict and Adam Roberts (eds.) (1993) *United Nations, Divided World: the UN's Roles in International Relations* (second edition). Oxford: Clarendon Press; New York: Oxford University Press.

27 Wallerstein notes that at the 1945 San Francisco Conference there was much talk of the Big Three – the US, the Soviet Union and Britain – as permanent members of the Security Council, with China and France added as a sort of courtesy. Wallerstein, Immanuel (1988) 'The new world disorder: if the states collapse, can the nations be united?', in Albert J. Paolini, Anthony P. Jarvis, and Christian Reus-Smit (eds.), *Between Sovereignty and Global Governance: the United Nations, the State, and Civil Society*. Basingstoke: MacMillan Press; New York: St Martin's Press, p. 184.

28 *Ibid.*, p. 174.

29 Smith (2003), p. 349.

30 *Ibid.*, p. 353.

31 Minutes of political committee, P-52, 17 April 1943, NA NT 55, cited Smith, *ibid.*, p. 358.

32 Wallerstein (1988), pp. 172–3.

33 Tully, James (2000) 'The struggles of indigenous peoples for and of freedom', in Duncan Ivison, Paul Patton and Will Sanders (eds.), *Political Theory and the Rights of Indigenous Peoples*. Cambridge: Cambridge University Press, pp. 54–5.

34 One of many examples is that of the aboriginal nations of Australia, whose occupation of their lands for over 50,000 years culminated in the denial of the rights of citizenship to them by the colonizing power until 1967. To this day, the discriminatory nature of many Australian state policies and the uninhibited racism of many non-indigenous Australian citizens result in indigenous Australians suffering ongoing injustices at multiple levels.

35 See, for instance, Harvey, David (2003) *The New Imperialism*. Oxford: Oxford University Press.

36 Cox, Robert W. (1996) [1992] 'Multilateralism and world order', pp. 494–523.

37 Raminsky, Louis (1972) 'Canadian views – Louis Raminsky', in A. L. Keith Acheson, John F. Chant and Martin F. J. Prachowny (eds.), *Bretton Woods Revisited: Evaluations of the International Monetary Fund and the International Bank for Reconstruction and Development*. Papers delivered at a conference at Queen's University, Kingston, Canada, 2–3 June 1969, London: Macmillan, p. 47.

38 For a detailed account, see Dormael, Armand Van (1978) *Bretton Woods. Birth of a Monetary System*. London: Macmillan. Van Dormael's account is one of the few to describe in detail Germany's proposed economic order and the British response.

39 This position was strongly advocated by Hayek at the 1933 World Economic Conference in London. See Acheson, Chant and Prachowny (1972).

40 Shoup, L. H. and W. Minter (1980) 'Shaping a new world order: the Council for Foreign Relations' blueprint for world hegemony', in Holly Sklar (ed.), *Trilateralism. The Trilateral Commission and Elite Planning for World Management*. Boston: South End Press, pp. 135–56.

41 *Ibid.*, p. 138.

42 CFR Memorandum E-B43, 24 July 1941, to the US President and Department of State, cited *ibid.*, pp. 140–1.

43 Smith (2003), p. 381.

44 See Harvey (2003).

45 Cited Smith (2003), p. 350.

46 McMichael, Philip (1995) 'The new colonialism: global regulation and the restructuring of the interstate system', in David A. Smith and Josef Borocoz (eds.), *New World Order? Global Transformations in the Late Twentieth Century*. Westport. Conn: Greenwood Press, pp. 37–53.

47 Arrighi, Giovanni and Beverly J. Silver (1999) *Chaos and Governance in the Modern World System*. Minneapolis and London: University of Minnesota Press.

48 Rich, Bruce (1994) *Mortgaging the Earth. The World Bank, Environmental Impoverishment and the Crisis of Development*. London: Earthscan.

49 Eckes, Alfred J. Jr. (1975) *A Search for Solvency: Bretton Woods and the International Monetary System, 1941–1971*. Austin and London: University of Texas Press, p. 56.

50 Rich, B. (1994), p. 57; see Article III, Section 5 (b) and Article IV, Section 10.

51 See Saint-Simon, Claude-Henri (1976) 'Letters from an Inhabitant of Geneva to His Contemporaries' [1803] in *The Political Thought of Saint-Simon*. Oxford: Oxford University Press.

52 Saint-Simon, cited by Rich (1994), p. 215.

53 Hayek, F. A. (1952). *The Counter-Revolution of Science: Studies on the Abuse of Reason*. Indianapolis: Liberty Press, p. 164, cited by Rich (1994), p. 51.

54 *Ibid.*

55 *Proceedings and Documents of the United Nations Monetary and Financial Conference, Bretton Woods, New Hampshire, 1–22 July 1944*, Vol. 1, 79-83, cited in Van Dormael, Armand (1978) *Bretton Woods: Birth of a Monetary System*. New York: Homes & Meier Publishers, Inc.

56 Henry Morgenthau, closing address to the 1944 Bretton Woods Conference, cited in Chossudovsky, Michel (1998) 'Financial warfare', *Institute of Political Economy (IPE) Journal*, 18 (November), Manila, p. 11.

57 Rist, Gilbert (1999) *The History of Development. From Western Origins to Global Faith*. Cape Town: University of Cape Town Press, p. 69.

58 Hoeckman, Bernard M. (1997) 'Developing countries and the multilateral trading system after the Uruguay Round', in Roy Culpepper, Albert Berry and Frances Stewart (eds.), *Global Development. Fifty Years after Bretton Woods*. London: Macmillan. For a detailed study of the defeat by a US-based force of free trade interests and protectionists of all aspects of the proposed Havana Charter other than the GATT Agreement (1947) provided for in Article XVII of the Charter, see Gosovic,

Branislav (1972) *UNCTAD. Conflict and Compromise. The Third World's Quest for an Equitable World Economic Order through the United Nations.* Leiden: A. W. Sijthoff.

59 Whalley, John (1993) 'The Uruguay Round and the GATT. Whither the global system?' in Fred Bergsten and Marcus Nolan (eds.), *Pacific Dynamism and the International Economic System.* Washington: International Institute for Economics.

60 McCrae, Donald (1996) 'From sovereignty to jurisdiction: the implications for states of the WTO', in Mark Buchanan (ed.), *The Asia-Pacific Region and the Expanding Borders of the WTO: Implications, Challenges and Opportunities.* Victoria, BC: Centre for Asia-Pacific Initiatives, University of Victoria.

61 Rich (1994), p. 63.

62 According to Rich, access to the information in the Bank's files as well as to draft projects is prohibited also to the Board of Executive Directors and the Board of Governors, thus enshrining the top-down, secretive manner of the Bank's management and functions. The structural problematics of this power arrangement are cogently demonstrated by the fact that in 1993 the ten richest industrialized countries controlled 52 per cent of the decision-making vote of the World Bank. Exercised weakly when at all, the very limited accountability vested in the Bank continues to function solely through the locus of its Executive Board of Directors, to whom the powers of the Bank's governors (each of whom represents a member country) are devolved on a day-to-day basis.

63 Van der Pijl (1995), p. 122.

64 *Ibid.*, p. 123.

65 *Ibid.*

66 *Ibid.*, p. 34.

67 Foster, John Bellamy (1999) 'Contradictions in the universalism of capitalism', *Monthly Review*, 50 (11) (April), p. 33.

68 Cockett, Richard (1995) *Thinking the Unthinkable: Think-Tanks and the Economic Counter Revolution.* London: Harper Collins, cited in Foster (1999).

69 Hayek, cited by Harris, Ralph (1997) 'The plan to end planning', in *National Review*, 49 (16 June), pp. 23–4. (Lord Ralph Harris is founder-president of the Institute of Economic Affairs.)

70 Cited in Harris (1997).

71 Harris (1997), p. 24 .

72 Sklar (1980) points out that in many cases these organizations have overlapping membership.

73 Peters, Michael (1999) 'Neoliberalism', Encyclopaedia of Philosophy of Education, online at http://www.educao.pro.br/neoliberalism.htm, accessed 6 July 1999. Peters indicates that while the school favoured interventionist policies and was unconvinced regarding the efficiency of *laissez-faire* policies, it firmly rejected alternative paradigms such as Keynesian macroeconomics.

74 See Rist (1999); also Sachs, Wolfgang (1999) *Planet Dialectics. Explorations in Environment and Development.* London and New York: Zed Books, p. 199.

75 Sachs (1999), p. 4.

76 See Rist (1999), pp. 71–5.

77 Arrighi and Silver (1999), pp. 204–5.

78 Rist (1999), pp. 209–10.

79 Hardt, Michael and Antonio Negri (2000) *Empire.* Cambridge, MA: Harvard University Press, p. 282.

80 See Chapter 5 for a discussion of the New International Economic Order.

81 See Chapter 5, pp. 147–50.

82 The terms 'nation' and 'state' are frequently used interchangeably, as is the term 'nation state'. The notion that the two concepts coexist as identical units with identical boundaries is fundamental to neocolonial constructions of modern nation-

alism, which have been used with great effect to marginalize the indigenous occupants of colonized lands. For indigenous peoples for whom the notion of traditional indigenous nations is fundamental to their assertions of self-determination, Connor's definition of nations – as a group of people who believe that they are ancestrally related – is appropriate. Connor, Walker (1994) *Ethnonationalism : the Quest for Understanding*. Princeton, NJ: Princeton University Press, p. xi. Fenton and May note that the term 'ethnonations' is used to denote groups who define themselves as nations on the basis of ethnicity, and who are often referred to as 'nations without a state'. Fenton, Steve and Stephen May (eds.) (2002) *Ethnonational Identities*. New York: Palgrave Macmillan, p. 9.

83 Hardt and Negri (2000), p. 106.
84 *Ibid.*
85 *Ibid.*
86 Assies, Willem (1994) 'Self-determination and the "new partnership". The politics of indigenous peoples and states', in Willem J. Assies and A. J. Hoekema (eds.), *Indigenous Peoples' Experiences with Self-Government*. Copenhagen: IWGIA and the University of Amsterdam, p. 32.
87 Sachs, Wolfgang (1995) 'Global ecology and the shadow of "development"', in George Sessions (ed.), *Global Ecology for the Twenty-first Century. Readings on the Philosophy and Practice of the New Environmentalism*. Boston and London: Shambala, p. 430.
88 *Ibid.*
89 Sadie, J. L. (1960) 'The social anthropology of economic underdevelopment', *Economic Journal* (June) p. 302, cited in McIntosh, Alistair (2001) *Soil and Soul. People versus Corporate Power*. London: Aurum Press, p. 94.
90 Sachs (1999), p. 29.
91 Dale, Roger (1982) 'Learning to be … what? Shaping education in "developing societies"', in Hamza Alavi and Teodor Shanin (eds.), *Introduction to the Sociology of Developing Societies*. London: Macmillan.
92 McLelland, David C. (1961) *The Achieving Society*. New Jersey, London, Toronto and New York: Van Nostrand.
93 Inkeles, Alex (1964) *Becoming Modern. Individual Change in Six Developing Countries*. London: Heinemann Educational.
94 Dale (1982), p. 410.
95 *Ibid.*, p. 417.

CHAPTER 4

✳

Contested Sites

State Sovereignty and Indigenous Self-Determination

Chapter 2 provided an indigenous analysis of the development of international law and of the international world order of nation states. The main objective there was to examine the impact of the twin processes of modernity and capitalism on indigenous peoples and the concomitant undermining and removal of their status as equal and sovereign peoples. Here I take up the overall theme of the contested processes and ideologies of world order by focusing on the development of international human rights law, including the right to self-determination, in the context of the international order of sovereign nation states.

Amongst the significant developments of the latter part of the twentieth century was the movement towards decolonization and self-determination. This was expressed in a number of ways, most notably by the UN Decolonization Resolution of 1960 and the designation of a Decolonization Decade to bring the century to a close. The last three decades have seen a significant shift in the international norms regarding indigenous peoples. These shifts in international legal norms have stemmed mainly from activities undertaken within the framework of the United Nations system, in which non-governmental organizations have supported indigenous peoples' efforts to regain some form of self-determination. One of my objectives in this chapter is to demonstrate how this has occurred, particularly with regard to international human rights law.

Inevitably this also highlights critical areas of tension and contradiction that are mediated by indigenous peoples in their struggles for self-determination. One such area is the conceptualization of state sovereignty and self-determination in international law. Despite the important developments outlined here, international law in relation to concepts of equality, self-determination and human rights remains contested and contradictory. Economic interests and political agendas continue to intervene significantly in indigenous peoples' struggles for recognition and self-determination. These interventions are primarily played out in an ongoing contestation between the perceived sovereign rights of states and the rights of indigenous peoples. It is these controversial aspects that I explore here.

Indigenous peoples' resistance to the processes of colonialism and imperialism is far from new, having been ongoing since the earliest period of the Spanish invasion of the Americas. The activism of indigenous peoples in the twentieth century has been impelled by the same concerns. The most notable aspect of this latter period of activism has been the emergence of a strong and articulate global network of indigenous peoples that engages in multiple strategies to articulate indigenous peoples' concerns and reclaim their rights. The driving force has been the historical denial of the right of indigenous peoples to self-determination and their continued exclusion from representation as culturally and politically distinct peoples within the political world order of nation states. The strengthening of international networks of indigenous peoples since the 1970s has seen the emergence of a new 'politics of indigeneity' as a critical component in the affirmation of indigenous peoples' determination to reclaim their histories, their epistemologies and their political autonomy. Key strategies at both the global and local levels are political engagement and the development of counter-discourses.

The politicizing and counter-discourses of indigenous peoples, particularly during the latter half of the twentieth century, and the responses of international agencies, sit at the intersection of evolving international human rights law, the sovereignty of nation states, and ideologies of developmentalism. Important counter-discursive strategies by indigenous scholars and political theorists include the employment of Western political theories to challenge the legitimating ideologies of Western political thought. Other critical strategies include the reclaiming, rearticulation and validation of indigenous ways of knowing and being as the foundation for the development of a range of structures and institutions that reflect indigenous aspirations for self-determination and self-governance.

The first section of this chapter identifies the competing ideologies that shaped the evolution of the Universal Declaration of Human Rights and its covenants, and highlight the disjuncture between these two branches of international legal norms, particularly in relation to the human rights of indigenous peoples. Following this, I examine the effectiveness of changes in international mechanisms through which indigenous peoples seek representation and redress, along with the implications of the inherent tensions between the two sets of rights that are integral in the shaping of policy at the international level – the right of peoples to self-determination and the sovereign rights of states. It is my contention that despite advances in human rights law, international law – defined, as Tully points out, by and for states[1] – remains limited in the degree to which it can advance indigenous peoples' desires for self-determination, since the law prescribes and understands self-determination within a Western legal context.[2]

The final part of the chapter engages the development of counter-discursive practices by indigenous peoples at the international and local levels. The increasing recognition of indigenous cultural beliefs and world views within international legal norms is central to my discussion here. At both the local and international levels, the counter-discourses of indigenous peoples have been important strategies in resisting the imposition of Eurocentric agendas for the assimilation and integration of indigenous peoples within the framework of states. Most notably since the 1970s, these strategies of resistance have resulted in significant challenges to the legitimacy of colonizing states. These challenges are predicated upon the reassertion of indigenous sovereignty, of customary rights over their lands and territories, the development of a politics of indigeneity, and the rearticulation and recentring of indigenous knowledge forms and world views, particularly in the context of indigenous frameworks for education. As Chapter 6 demonstrates, these strategies have contributed towards the redefining of indigenous peoples–states relationships at the local level.

Contested State Sovereignty

In his useful discussion of the problematic of state sovereignty, Walker declares that the attempt to treat sovereignty as a matter of definition and legal principle encourages a certain amnesia about its historical and specific character.[3] As Foucault points out, from its inception the concept of state sovereignty was allied to the problem of government and the need to discipline populations in a manner that would maintain both their productivity and docility.[4] Ideologically, the concept of state sovereignty has been constructed differently at different times within Western political thought. In 1915, for instance, the

English jurist Harold Laski rejected the popular notion of absolute state sovereignty in declaring that

> The will of the state obtains pre-eminence over the will of other groups exactly to the point where it is interpreted with sufficient wisdom to obtain general acceptance, and no further ... in such a view sovereignty means no more than the ability to secure such consent.[5]

Lapidoth provides a useful explanation of the differentiation between internal and external forms of state sovereignty in contemporary international law. Internal sovereignty is the right and capacity of the state to exercise control within its own borders, a control that nevertheless requires in its exercise some degree of consent and legitimacy from society. This form of sovereignty is predicated on the principle that each state is free to pursue its own domestic affairs without outside interference from any other state or foreign law other than public international law. External or juridical sovereignty is based on the notion of the inviolability of states and is viewed in realist terms as a mechanism for enhancing international security. Significantly for human rights, external or juridical sovereignty is based on the 'principle of non-intervention', defined as 'the freedom to use force and the right to refuse to submit to dispute settlement by a third party that would be binding'.[6] The limitation on human rights that this principle imposes has given rise to considerable debate regarding its inviolability. Walker, for instance, argues that 'as a claim about ontological status', the status of state sovereignty 'is in considerable doubt'.[7] Coates and McHugh, who also question absolutist notions of state sovereignty, point out that the notion of sovereignty varies from country to country.[8]

These generalized rejections of the concept of absolute sovereignty have had little or no impact on indigenous peoples' experiences within nation states. Realist interpretations continue to define the sovereignty of states as 'an indivisible and all-embracing quality' that has 'led to several phenomena that considerably enhanced the freedom of action of the state'.[9] This pervasive view is reflected in a 1993 publication of the Council on Foreign Relations in which Gordon Gottlieb maintains that the meaning of sovereignty expressed by Robert Lansing as US Secretary of State in 1921 is frequently held to provide the authoritative criteria by which political sovereignty can be measured.[10] In Lansing's view, sovereignty consisted of two major elements – the power to compel obedience to the sovereign will and the possession of physical force superior to any other that makes such compulsion possible. This interpretation of state sovereignty as a political concept that has as much to do with power over people as over territories is notably expressed in contemporary recommendations regarding US foreign policy by neoliberal think tanks such as the Council for Foreign Relations and the Heritage Foundation. Many of the papers prepared by the Heritage Foundation posit sovereignty as the rationale for a range of foreign policy recommendations. Thus state sovereignty remains inextricably linked to the primary concepts of authority, territory and populations.

Self-Determination in International Law

Mystifying and ambiguous language has been a vehicle for the exclusion of indigenous peoples from representation and equality of rights in both local and global arenas. This is nowhere more evident than in the discursive construction of self-determination and decolonization in the context of international law. As a principle within international law, self-determination is nebulous, contradictory and frequently interpreted as being oppositional to other fundamental Western political concepts, state sovereignty in particular.

As an organizing principle of the new international order, human rights were given considerable attention at both the Dumbarton Oaks Conference in 1944 and the San Francisco Conference on International Organization in 1945.[11] Self-determination, on the other hand, was ignored until the Soviet proposal at San Francisco that 'self-determination of peoples' be included.[12] The adoption by the US, UK and France of self-determination as a principle and its incorporation into Articles 1(2) and 55 of the UN Charter was eventually effected only through the imposition of considerable pressure and, according to Thomas Musgrave, with considerable misgivings. In both cases, the right of peoples to self-determination is expressed in the context of 'developing friendly relations among nations' and the equal rights of peoples'.[13] Article 1(2) defines one of the fundamental purposes of the UN Charter as being '[t]o develop friendly relations among nations based on respect for the principle of equal rights and self-determination of peoples, and to take other appropriate measures to strengthen universal peace'. Article 55 includes 'the creation of conditions of stability and well-being which are necessary for peaceful and friendly relations among nations based on respect for the principle of equal rights and self-determination of peoples'. Crucially, internationally acceptable definitions of those 'nations' and 'peoples' to whom the right of self-determination accrues under these articles remains elusive to this day.

The core values that determine the principle of self-determination have been articulated in a number of important legal determinations. One such is the case of Namibia before the International Court of Justice (ICJ) in 1971. This case is significant for the fact that it was the first in which the ICJ actually pronounced on the issue of self-determination in its 1971 *Advisory Opinion on the Status of Namibia: Legal Consequences for States of the Continued Presence of South Africa in Namibia (South West Africa) notwithstanding Security Council Resolution 276 (1970)*. A German colony in the First World War, South West Africa (SWA) was placed under mandate by virtue of Article 22 of the League of Nations, with South Africa as the administrative power. Instead of placing SWA under the UN trusteeship system upon the dissolution of the League of Nations, South Africa took the position that the mandate had expired and that therefore South Africa was entitled to annex. Following the failure of South Africa to acknowledge UN Security Council resolutions calling on South Africa to withdraw, the Security Council sought a judgement from the Court concerning the legal consequences of the continued presence contrary to Security Council Resolution 276 (1970). In its 1950 Advisory Opinion, the Court declared the principles of non-annexation and the principle of 'sacred trust' to be of paramount importance.

In its 1971 Advisory Opinion, the Court held that as a result of developments in international law, the 'sacred trust' now extended to 'all countries whose peoples have not yet attained a full measure of self-government' (Article 73). The Court further declared that 'the ultimate objective of the sacred trust was the self-determination and independence of the peoples concerned'.[14] In this instance, the principle of equality was determined to be a central precept of self-determination. The Western Sahara case, heard by the ICJ in 1975, which saw the Court refuse to give weight to legal doctrines of *terra nullius*, also concerned the right to self-determination: in this case it was ruled that such a right was applicable to all non-self-governing territories.[15] These determinations clearly reinforce the principle that decolonization with self-determination is a moral and legal right that accrues to all peoples. The judgments of the ICJ, as Venne points out, whilst not recognized as a source of international law, carry considerable moral persuasion; yet, despite this, the actual process of granting self-determination continues to be bitterly struggled over, every inch of the way.[16]

Thomas Musgrave identifies the origins of political self-determination in the rise of national consciousness in Europe and the US in the eighteenth and nineteenth centuries.[17] In his account, the origins of the concept of self-determination are contextualized in terms of Enlightenment ideas of popular sovereignty and representative government such as those articulated by Locke and given expression in Western Europe and the US, in which ethnic issues were not taken into account. A different and much more ethnically oriented view of self-determination developed directly out of the rising national consciousness in Central and Eastern Europe during the nineteenth century. This view, Musgrave states, was 'much more strongly linked to ethnic and cultural factors'.[18] In the context of the diverse cultural and ethnic make-up of the states that emerged out of the Austro-Hungarian and Russian empires, issues of identity developed a high priority and, in Musgrave's account, became the focus of much German writing in the early nineteenth century.[19] The Central and Eastern European concept of nationalism gave rise to a considerably different interpretation of the meaning of self-determination, one based on collective rights and ethnic and cultural identity. The idea of self-governing nations determined on the basis of ethnic and linguistic criteria was seen as reaching fulfilment in the concept of 'true' nations as possessing an inherent national character, each with its own unique mission to fulfil. This view contrasted strongly with the notions of popular sovereignty, representative government and individual freedoms that characterized Britain, France and the US. The view of self-determination from Central and Eastern Europe, as including collective rights, in certain respects closely resembles that held by indigenous peoples – yet this view is broadly regarded in the Western world as exclusive and particularistic,[20] threatening the hard-won concept of individual rights.

Self-determination as a principle of international relations provided the justification for the break-up of the German, Austro-Hungarian and Ottoman empires and was the prescribing vehicle for the redivision of Europe.[21] With the conclusion of the First World War, self-determination as a principle of governance was developed and applied in the context of the decolonization of colonies and territories formerly under the control of the defeated powers. At the end of the Second World War, and despite the protests of some states, Western liberal democratic ideals linked with European nationalist aspirations saw 'self-determination of peoples' become enshrined in the UN Charter as a principle of international law.[22] This was contested.[23] The Committee discussing self-determination identified two views of self-determination in the debates. One was the notion that 'the principle corresponded closely to the will and desires of peoples everywhere and should be clearly enunciated in the Charter'; the second was that 'the principle conformed to the purpose of the Charter only in so far as it implied the right of self-government of peoples and not the right of secession'.[24] Rather than further defining the meaning, the Full Committee stated that the principles of equal rights and the self-determination of peoples were 'two complementary parts of one standard of conduct' with the 'free and genuine expression of the people' being an essential element.[25] Importantly, the actual definition of self-determination remained nebulous and contradictory and left unresolved the definition of 'peoples' to whom the right accrues.

The Post-Second World War Decolonization Programme

Self-determination as a principle of governance was brought to the forefront of Western political theorizing through the efforts of US President Woodrow Wilson. The League of Nations, in the construction of which Wilson played a primary role, embedded self-determination as a goal to be achieved through the decolonization of colonies and territories formerly under the control of the defeated powers. Led by US President Franklin Roosevelt and strongly opposed by British Prime Minister Winston Churchill, self-determination of colonized territories was strongly contested in the post-war planning during the Second World War. Nonetheless a policy of decolonization was established in those externally colonized territories in which a European settler population had not established dominance.[26] This policy was administered by the UN trusteeship system that extended to include the 'non-self-governing territories formerly under the dominion of the now vanquished powers'.[27] Opposition to this policy by hard-line elements within colonized territories saw the eruption of wars of independence. Self-determination movements driven largely by the Third World and Soviet bloc emerged as a key strategy in a war of position by Third World countries and nationalist liberation movements. The linking of self-determination with decolonization saw the emergence of 'a new political order for subject peoples'.[28]

The delegitimation of colonization was accompanied by a decade of debates over the determination of colonized territories and the territorial sovereignty of states. These culminated in the Declaration on the Granting of Independence to Colonial Countries and Peoples (1960)[29], better known as the Decolonization Resolution, and its accompanying Resolution 1541, which defined the meanings of 'colonial' country and 'non-self-governing territory'. The Decolonization Resolution reiterated the right of all peoples to self-determination by recognizing that 'the peoples of the world ardently desire the end of colonization in all its manifestations', and by proclaiming 'the necessity of bringing to a speedy and unconditional end colonialism in all its forms and manifestations'. However, in an attempt to guard against secessionist attempts, the Decolonization Resolution declared that

> Any attempt at the partial or total disruption of the national unity and the territorial integrity of a country is incompatible with the purposes and principles of the Charter of the United Nations.[30]

The key point here is that the contradictory nature of the language of the Decolonization Resolution enabled narrowly defined interpretations that ruled out classifying ethnic or cultural minorities within a state's territory as being 'non-self-governing entities'. The limits to which self-determination could be applied were further narrowed in the Resolution by what came to be known as the 'salt-water thesis' or the theory of 'salt-water colonialism'. This specifies that only those territories that can be considered 'geographically separate' and 'distinct ethnically and/or culturally from the country administering it' could be considered non-self-governing under Chapter XI of the UN Charter.[31] Resolution 1541 was therefore applied only to territories that had been externally colonized. These dual requirements became the criteria against which claims for self-determination were measured. In this manner, the decolonization programme could be applied only to those territories involved in what Wilmer calls the second pattern of colonization, that is, those countries in which colonizing immigrant populations did not become numerically dominant but in which European-educated indigenous elites frequently acted as agents of the colonizing power.[32]

Unquestionably, the inclusion of the right to self-determination as a general right of peoples in Article One of each of the human rights covenants widened the definition and application of the principle of self-determination beyond the classic decolonization context. Its applicability to the indigenous inhabitants of internally colonized territories, however, was even further limited by subsequent UN resolutions such as the 1970 Declaration on Principles of International Law Concerning Friendly Relations and Cooperation among States, which prohibited the disruption of a state's territorial integrity.[33]

Mortimer Sellers describes the restrictions that accompanied the evolution of self-determination into customary international law as a 'shift from self-determination as an exercisable right to self-determination as a privilege'.[34] As Anaya points out, rights to self-determination and decolonization within the context of international law were defined in accordance with contemporaneous law rather than attaching to groups defined by ethnicity or by historical accounts of sovereignty. The decolonization of selected mandated territories and the dissolution of the British Empire served US interests in two ways: by the creation of new states to further strengthen containment policies, and in opening up access to new markets. The demarcation between territories and peoples that were given entitlement to decolonization and those that were not was determined by multiple and overlapping agendas. These notably included states' concerns for their territorial sovereignty, and in particular their control over resources, their position within the international system, and the power relations between the two major world powers.

In this situation, the integration of indigenous peoples into the existing political structures of Western society was integral to the maintenance of the *status quo* within the world order of nation states, to the territorial integrity norms of the dominant powers and to the continuance of capitalist exploitation and expansion under the ideology of development. The prohibition on altering the frontiers established by the colonial powers through the process of decolonization meant that, while the number of independent states doubled following decolonization, the new states were a reinscribing of the same colonial boundaries, superimposed on indigenous peoples' traditional territories with total disregard for their existing political systems and nationhood. These new neocolonial states were integrated into the international system, with representation in the United Nations General Assembly. As new states sought to establish their authority within the frontiers established by the former colonial powers, the oppression of indigenous peoples in many cases increased. The declaration of the Decade of Decolonization (1990–2000), by the end of which all mandated territories and trusts were to have achieved self-determination, reflected the increasingly held view that the days of colonization were over. This mandate applied only to externally colonized territories. The decolonization of indigenous peoples' territories was not to be included in this process.

Developing International Human Rights Law

In the years following the Second World War, the Universal Declaration of Human Rights, together with its twin covenants, came to be regarded in the Western world as the foundation stone of liberal democracy. Tony Clarke and Maude Barlow note that the Declaration was central to the negotiation of protection for the industries, natural resources and agricultural products of developing countries.[35] Among the citizenship rights that nation state signatories were obliged to protect were social well-being and the right to employment. However, despite the discursive prominence accorded to human rights principles in the UN Charter itself, the subordinate position of human rights within the hierarchy of principles contained in the Charter reflected unresolved tensions between notions of state sovereignty and individual rights. Although prominent in the debates regarding the UN Charter, affirmation of rights to self-determination and decolonization both preceded the widespread acceptance by states of the legitimacy of human rights norms within the UN framework of international law.[36]

Farer and Gaer's analysis of the development of human rights legislation within the UN highlights the extreme ambivalence of states towards suggestions that human rights be reinforced through the UN system.[37] They point out that the inclusion of human rights in the Charter of the United Nations was due only to 'the effort of a few deeply committed delegates and the representatives of some 42 private organizations'.[38] Their account emphasizes the contestation between the dichotomies of state and individual sovereignty, and individual and collective rights that characterized the development of an international human rights framework in the aftermath of the Second World War. Tensions between the principle of state sovereignty and the notion of individual and collective human rights, whether or not aligned to self-determination in the original drafting of the Declaration of Human Rights in 1948, led to some principles being removed to create what were to become twin human rights covenants, the International Covenant on Economic, Social and Cultural Rights (ICESCR) and the International Covenant on Civil and Political Rights (ICCPR), and the Declaration's Optional Protocol.

The elaboration of the UN Declaration of Human Rights, a non-enforceable document, within documents that are legally enforceable in international law was contested by states throughout its development. The twenty-year span between the original drafting by the UN's Economic and Social Council (ECOSOC) of an International Bill of Rights and the 1966 voting in the UN General Assembly on the twin human rights covenants, and the further ten years before the required 35 votes were received for these covenants to become international law, evidenced the intensity of the struggle over individual human rights, self-determination and state sovereignty that involved states, non-governmental organizations and other groups in civil society.[39]

The legally binding obligations on signatory states that are contained in the covenants include certain minimum provisions for all 'peoples'. The first article of both covenants provides for the self-determination of peoples by virtue of which 'they freely determine their own political status and freely pursue their economic, social and cultural development' and destiny. In both instances, paragraph 2 of Article 1 includes the right of peoples to 'freely dispose of their own natural wealth and resources,' and not to be deprived of their means of existence. The covenants also share a prohibition against discrimination on the grounds of race, colour, sex, language, religion, political or other opinion, national or social origin, property, birth or other status. Like its companion, the International Covenant on Economic, Social and Cultural Rights elaborates and expands on the rights contained in the Universal Declaration; however, where the ICCPR requires states to give immediate effect to the rights recognized therein, the ICESCR exhorts states to initiate a programme of gradual implementation of recognition of the specific rights that it endorses. These rights, as Alfredsson notes, are not expressly linked to the right of self-determination.[40] Scott Davidson points out that this has given rise to the undermining of these rights by the arguments of some states that they are not absolute but depend upon economic factors.[41]

The ICCPR, which obligates participating states to allow individuals who are members of an ethnic, religious or linguistic minority 'to enjoy their own culture, to profess and practise their own religion or to use their own language', contains one mandatory and two optional provisions that enable the monitoring or supervision of signatory states by the UN Commission on Human Rights (UNCHR). The individual communication procedure contained in the First Optional

Protocol of the ICCPR – widely regarded as the most significant development in the universal human rights system – subject to certain provisos allows direct access to the UNCHR's Human Rights Committee to individuals who believe that any of their own rights as articulated within the Covenant have been violated. This Committee is described as an impartial international body with the power to determine whether or not a state has violated those human rights that are protected under the Covenant. To date, no communication brought to the Committee by an indigenous individual or group has enjoyed a successful outcome.

Despite its shaky beginnings in international law, the international human rights movement has been one of the most significant factors in the reshaping of international law, particularly in diminishing the individual–state dichotomy.[42] The eventual ratification of the two international human rights instruments opened up the possibility of support for other forms of self-determination within international law. Important as the international human rights mechanisms are, their functional ability to protect the human rights of groups and individuals within states' territories is severely limited by the state-centric paradigm of international law.[43] The evolution of human rights norms has in large measure facilitated indigenous peoples' participation in consultations within fora of the UNCHR as well as the employment of international legal mechanisms such as the Optional Protocol of the ICCPR. Since their entry into force in 1976, the covenants have provided indigenous peoples with a forum for the pursuit of justice within the international arena. To date these pursuits have been largely unsuccessful.

Indigenous peoples across the globe define their rights in terms of fundamental collective rights, yet there is no provision in the covenants for the acknowledgment and protection of collective rights within international law. Further, there is considerable resistance to the notion that collective rights should be provided for in international law. Kymlicka points out that some measures that define the special status of indigenous peoples, such as those in force in Canada, do not involve collectively exercised rights but in fact modify or differentially distribute individual rights. In fact, he notes, there seems to be enormous difficulty in accommodating the idea of collective rights within the moral ontology of liberalism.[44]

The difficulty for indigenous peoples is that although the human rights covenants and their protocols are one of the few possible avenues within the United Nations system available to indigenous peoples as a means of seeking redress, they apply in ways that mitigate against the fundamental collective rights of indigenous peoples.[45] The two key reasons for this are, first, the contested nature of state sovereignty and its interpretation within international law, and, second, the relatively recent shift from collective rights to the recognition of individual rights, a shift that in the main has occurred only since the Second World War.

State Sovereignty and the Right to Self-Determination

The discursive construction of indigenous peoples as 'minorities' or 'populations' within sovereign states enables injustices perpetuated upon indigenous peoples in both internally and externally colonized territories to be invisibilized within a general human rights discourse and functions to mask many of the injustices and atrocities perpetuated on groups and individuals.[46] The Vienna Declaration issued from the 1993 UN Conference on Human Rights and signed by 171 countries re-emphasized the notion of human rights as a universal concept. Nevertheless ideological power relations continue to dominate the way in which tensions between the notions of state sovereignty and human rights are played out. In this respect, Yongjin Zhang's discussion of human rights in the post-Cold War period highlights the increasing prominence accorded to human rights in the context of world peace and international security.[47] Military interventions authorized by the United Nations – as in the cases of Somalia (1991, 1992), Iraq (consistently since 1998) and Kosovo – are legitimated on the basis of their importance in preventing human rights abuses and disruption of the international order. Zhang points out that the challenges to state sovereignty represented by such interventions demonstrate the increasingly strategic role of human rights in international relations and a widening international consensus concerning the need for protection of and respect for human rights. Nevertheless, he notes, although the entrenchment of human rights within international law has to a limited extent compromised state sovereignty, it has not yet resulted in human rights being accorded a higher priority than the assertion of state sovereignty.

As Roberts and Kingsbury demonstrate, there are inherent contradictions between the two formative principles of justice and of non-intervention in the internal affairs of sovereign states. The refusal of the Australian government in 1999, for reasons of 'foreign policy and democracy', to allow a UNCHR investigation onto Australian soil to investigate its inhumane treatment of Aboriginal peoples, including its policy of mandatory imprisonment for petty crimes, highlighted the ongoing problematic between human rights, state sovereignty and international law.[48] The disjuncture between human rights rhetoric and practice by states was again underscored in respect of Australia's leadership in the human rights interventions in East Timor, initiated in response to enormous public pressure. The political economy underpinning protestations of state sovereignty and complicity in human rights abuses was further highlighted in the contradiction between this well-publicized intervention and twenty-five years of silent complicity in human rights abuses in East Timor, a lengthy period of social amnesia related to Australia's contractual arrangements with Indonesia and Canada to exploit what was believed to be a large reservoir of oil in the Timor Gap. In this light, the recently released evidence that Australia was fully informed by Indonesia three days before the attack on the Timorese town in Bilbo in October 1975, in which attack five Australian journalists were killed,[49] problematizes the integrity of states' foreign policy and the political economy underpinning compliance with international human rights norms by industrialized nation states. The geopolitical rationale was provided in the statement of the then US Ambassador to Indonesia: to wit, that American support of Indonesia's invasion of East Timor, an act that resulted in the deaths of over 200,000 indigenous Timorese people,[50] was viewed as essential in order to ensure that 'this vast stretch of territory representing Indonesia not fall into anti-American hands'.[51] In short, the tacit consent of US President Gerald Ford and US Secretary of State Henry Kissinger to the 1975 invasion of East Timor by Indonesia[52] demonstrates the prioritizing of political expediency over human rights.

Human Rights and Indigenous Self-Determination

The construction of indigenous peoples as 'populations' to be governed and controlled, and ultimately integrated into mainstream society, was inherent in an emerging body of international law articulated within new legal instruments. These frequently ambiguous legal instruments highlighted the inherently contradictory nature of international legal norms regarding indigenous peoples. In 1957 the only specialized agency of the UN to have passed any standards relating specifically to indigenous peoples, the ILO, adopted its Convention 107 on Indigenous and Tribal Populations as a measure for enhancing the assimilation and integration of indigenous peoples into the societies of states,[53] a goal in which education was to play a key role.[54] The Convention, which was binding on its 27 state signatories, was eventually revised in 1989 in an effort to remove its assimilatory nature. Despite its intent, however, ILO Convention 107 provided for limited recognition to 'indigenous peoples' collective and individual right of ownership over the lands that these populations traditionally occupy' and for compensation by the provision of 'land at least equal to that previously held by them' in the event of their removal 'without their free consent from their habitual territories'.[55] This right was nonetheless closely circumscribed through a provision by which indigenous traditional lands could be taken by states 'under national laws and regulations for reasons relating to national security and in the interests of national economic development'.[56] As in other international instruments, the overriding theme of Convention 107 was the 'progressive integration' of 'indigenous individuals into national societies and economies, thus legitimizing the gradual extinction of indigenous peoples as such'.[57] The characterization of indigenous peoples as 'populations' within the language of the Convention also underlined the denial of the unique character of indigenous peoples as an ongoing and distinct grouping within international law and within the world order of nation states.

Recognition within international law of indigenous peoples' human rights, like those of minority populations within states, has been a slowly evolving process. This was assisted in 1951 by the establishment by the Commission on Human Rights of a Sub-Commission on the Prevention of Discrimination and the Protection of Minorities. A twelve-year study by Special Rapporteur Miguel Alfonso-Martinez Cobo, which derived from a 1969 recommendation of the Sub-Commission, drew attention to the problem of discrimination by states against indigenous peoples. Key points made by the Cobo study included the right of indigenous peoples to self-identification and the special position of indigenous peoples within the society of nation states, a position deriving from their historical rights to their lands and from their rights to be different and to be considered as different.[58] In its 600 recommendations the Cobo Study included further studies on the issue of self-determination, in particular the right of indigenous nations and peoples to self-determination; the Declaration of Principles for the Defence of Indigenous Nations and Peoples of the Western Hemisphere (adopted at the 1977 International NGO Conference on Indigenous

Peoples); and a Study on Treaties Entered into by Indigenous Peoples, initiated in 1989 with the appointing of a Special Rapporteur.[59]

Studies undertaken by the Sub-Commission have been important in highlighting the conflicting language and principles pertaining to the right to self-determination of minorities as well as those of indigenous peoples. A review undertaken in 1974 by Special Rapporteur Hector Gros Espiell determined that international law denies minorties the right of self-determination that accrues to 'a specific type of community sharing a common desire to establish an entity that functioned to ensure a common future'.[60] Importantly, Espiell concluded that in the instance of states applying the right of territorial integrity to deny the right of peoples to determine their own futures, this should be viewed as a misapplication of the principle of self-determination.

Indigenous Peoples in the International Arena

Like many other indigenous peoples, Maori have made frequent efforts throughout the twentieth century to use international law as an instrument for recourse and justice. In 1996, the Maori delegation interceding at the UN Intercessional Working Group on the Draft Declaration on the Rights of Indigenous Peoples drew attention to the fact that, as early as 1924, Maori went to Geneva to seek protection of their human rights before the League of Nations. On that occasion, active lobbying by the New Zealand government saw the Maori delegation denied a voice in what was almost a reenactment of the response by Britain to the attempt by the Iroquois Confederacy to have their grievances heard at the League of Nations four years earlier.[61]

In 1977 a group of indigenous delegates from all over the world led by Irihapeti Murchie from New Zealand invaded a UN Sub-Commission hearing, demanding the right to be heard. Their action signalled to the world the heightened political movement and collective combination of indigenous peoples through the development of strong cross-national indigenous networks and organizations.[62] In many respects, this marked the beginning of major changes in the way in which international legal mechanisms dealt with the rights of indigenous peoples. In a petition to the Special Committee on Decolonization, Rudolph Ryser on behalf of the World Council of Indigenous Peoples (WCIP) pointed to what amounted to a 'conspiracy of silence regarding the condition of indigenous nations', detailing the colonial experiences of the Kanaks of New Caledonia, the Indigenous Nations of Canada and the Aboriginal Nations of Australia as examples of the colonization of sovereign indigenous nations.[63] Noting that both the UN and the League of Nations had been responsible for fostering colonial domination over indigenous peoples against their will, and for the denial of indigenous peoples' right to use and dispose of the wealth of their own natural resources, Ryser called for the re-examination of international conventions such as ILO Convention 107 that embodied the assimilatory ideologies of colonialism.

A major shift in the positioning of indigenous peoples' rights and aspirations in the international institutions of world order was signalled with the establishment in 1981 of a Working Group on Indigenous Populations (WGIP). Its two important mandates were the evolution of standards concerning the rights of indigenous peoples and the review of developments pertaining to the promotion and protection of human rights and fundamental freedoms of indigenous peoples. Among the most important legal mechanisms that have since emerged from the efforts of the WGIP are the revision of ILO Convention 107 in ILO Convention 169, and the UN Draft Declaration on the Rights of Indigenous Peoples.

Generally viewed as a significant step forward within the regime of indigenous rights and specifically anti-assimilationist in intent,[64] ILO Convention 169 broadly reflects a more positive view of indigenous peoples,[65] requiring participating states to develop measures to safeguard the 'persons, institutions, property, labour, cultures and environment'[66] of indigenous peoples. In a discussion of indigenous peoples and measures towards self-government, Willem Assies identifies ILO 169 as the first international instrument to recognize 'the right to collective ownership of land'.[67] Nevertheless, the 1989 revision of ILO Convention 107 was the subject of intense debate over meanings and interpretations between states and indigenous peoples. Among the most controversial aspects was the drafting of provisions for land rights, a controversy that Anaya contends ensued from 'resistance to efforts by indigenous peoples' representatives, worker delegates, and some governments, to attain specification of greater land and resource rights than that ultimately included in the convention'.[68] The strongest controversy, however, centred on the use of the term 'peoples'. Attempts to simultaneously expand indigenous peoples' rights and to allay states' fears of indigenous peoples forestalling national economic development or seceding resulted in the inclusion of 'peoples' instead of the term 'populations' preferred by the states within the text of ILO Convention 169. The use of 'peoples' was nonetheless carefully circumscribed by a clause that declared that '[t]he use of the term "peoples" in this convention shall not be construed as having any implications as regards the rights which may attach to the term in international law'.[69]

While ILO Convention 169 amends the assimilatory nature of its predecessor ILO Convention 107 and, for the first time, casts indigenous peoples in a non-hierarchical relationship with modernity, the contestation over the determination of indigenous peoples as 'peoples' within international law norms confirmed the views of some indigenous peoples that ILO Convention 169 ignored their legitimate aspirations for self-determination and continued to assert the authority of states.[70] In the view of Cree lawyer Sharon Venne, 'after twenty-two years of struggle only the language of assimilation has changed. Convention 169 is still assimilationist but far more destructive than its predecessor'.[71] From this perspective, advances made in protecting the rights of indigenous peoples within international law are offset by the inherent paternalism embedded in international legal instruments such as ILO Convention 169, which reaffirms the rights of nation states over the rights of indigenous peoples. Nonetheless, for other indigenous peoples whose ongoing experience is one of dislocation and genocide, these moves represent a significant improvement over their current conditions and are seen as representing at least a minimal level of legal recognition and protection within international law.

New Mechanisms in International Law

The final drafting in 1993 of the UN Draft Declaration on the Rights of Indigenous Peoples, following eight years of an unprecedented level of consultation between parties, the conclusion in 1999 of the Study on Treaties, Agreements and other Constructive Arrangements between States and Indigenous Peoples,[72] and the establishment in 2000 of a UN Permanent Forum on Indigenous Issues are all highly significant achievements in the advancement of indigenous rights within international law.

The UN Draft Declaration on the Rights of Indigenous Peoples represented the first UN instrument to develop standards concerning the rights of indigenous peoples with the direct participation of indigenous peoples in the drafting process, and was moved to the UNCHR for debate in 1995. At this point, moves by states to limit indigenous peoples' access to the negotiating process within the Inter-sessional Working Group established by the UNCHR to 'elaborate a draft resolution'[73] resulted in a marked decrease in indigenous peoples' participation, affecting hundreds of indigenous peoples and their organizations.[74] The inevitable result was a state-dominated review process. May ascribes this decrease in indigenous participation to the restrictive nature of the UNCHR, whose membership is limited to accredited non-governmental organizations.[75] Subsequent negotiations under the auspices of the Inter-sessional Working Group have been marked by contention between states and indigenous peoples concerning the principles, definitions and meanings of the articles of the Declaration. Particularly problematic are principles concerning the collective rights of indigenous peoples and the application of the terms 'peoples' and 'self-determination'.[76] Articles 3 and 31, both of which address the thorny issue of self-determination, have been particularly contested by states, which view any attempt to grant indigenous peoples self-determination as facilitating the possibility of secession. Provision in Article 29 for the protection of the cultural and intellectual property of indigenous peoples has caused similar consternation, as has the possibility that indigenous peoples should be entitled to recognition of their inherent group rights. To date, repeated efforts by the indigenous caucus to mediate these fears have failed to advance consensus around the key articles of the Draft Declaration in which these principles are articulated in any meaningful way.

As Anaya suggests, the development of these instruments signifies an increasing recognition within international norms of the need to address and protect the rights of indigenous peoples. The development of new international legal mechanisms for indigenous peoples involves the ongoing mediation of competing ideologies and aspirations of states and indigenous peoples. In this process, however, contestation over language and meaning in relation to indigenous peoples' 'lands' and 'territories' reflects the problematic relations of power and territorial control over resources that have historically defined the relationship between capitalism and the sovereign state.[77] As the preceding discussion has demonstrated, the term 'peoples' has become one of the most contested terms with regard to meaning within international law. Guaranteed in Article 1 of the United Nations Charter, the right of self-determination for all 'peoples' sees indigenous peoples discursively constructed as 'non'-peoples within international law. Anaya points out that while the linkage of the principle of self-determination to 'peoples' in international law articulates the collective and widely embracing nature of this principle, restrictive interpretations limit the scope of self-determination to narrowly defined communities that have sovereign rights entitlements. These interpretations, Anaya suggests, underpin the ongoing controversy over the definition of indigenous peoples as 'peoples' within international law. While indigenous peoples campaign strongly for the right to be recognized as 'peoples' within international law, particularly in the context of indigenous claims to nationhood, states continue to construct the term 'peoples' to imply the possibility of secession based on sovereign ethnic states, and equally strongly oppose its application to indigenous peoples within international legal mechanisms.

Recent decades have seen important remedial measures prescribed within international rights regimes that have significant implications for the political order.[78] The ideological shift from assimilation as the goal of states' relationships with indigenous peoples has seen the development of more explicit rights to cultural identity and practice. This was expressed by the 1985 Inter-American Commission on Human Rights when it declared that Article 27 of the ICCPR 'recognizes the right of ethnic groups to special protection on their use of their own language, for the practice of their own religion, and, in general, for all those characteristics necessary for the preservation of their cultural identity'. In some cases, this has been echoed at the local level. One such case is that of New Zealand, where the Waitangi Tribunal ruled in 1986 that, under the terms of the Treaty of Waitangi, the Maori language had a '*guaranteed* right to protection'.[79] In the context of legal identity, however, states' denial of the status of 'peoples' to indigenous peoples and the resultant denial of the right to equal and full participation in decision making, evidences the failure of international legal mechanisms to meet the needs of indigenous peoples.

From the perspective of many of the indigenous participants in these processes, the marginalization of indigenous peoples' participation in the consultation process and the refusal of states to recognize indigenous peoples' resolutions and decisions in regard to the UN Draft Declaration on the Rights of Indigenous Peoples confirm the statism embedded in international law and the exclusionary nature of practices that function to co-opt indigenous peoples' aspirations while maintaining them in a state of political colonization.[80] Decades of political activity and representations by indigenous peoples internationally

have seen significant changes of a positive nature in terms of indigenous peoples' representation and voice internationally, largely through
the fora of the United Nations. Nevertheless, as Tully contends,
international legal norms regarding indigenous peoples remain essentially state-centric,[81] characterized by tensions between the rhetoric of
individual and group rights, and the rights of indigenous peoples
versus the inherent sovereignty of states.

Throughout this period, which included the first Decade of
Colonization that aimed at the eradication of colonization by the year
2000, indigenous peoples have sought recognition of their right to
self-determination and decolonization. In the same period, states'
proposals to the Trusteeship Council have ranged from disbandment
of the Council – charged with overseeing the decolonization of
'Non-Self-Governing Territories'[82] – to the assertion of new mandates.
In 1995, referring to a recommendation advanced by the Secretary-
General in the previous year, the New Zealand representative openly
supported the Secretary-General's opinion that 'the Trusteeship should
be quietly put to sleep', a view contrasting with that of the Afghanistan
representative, who in the same consultation proposed that the Council
'be mandated to raise the Organization's awareness of genocide and
its prevention', and also with that of the representative of Malta, who
advanced the notion that Council 'take on the role of holding in trust
humanity's common heritage'.[83]

In 1996, the Indigenous Peoples of the Pacific Workshop affirmed
the role of indigenous peoples of the Pacific as protectors of the
oceans and other natural resources of the Pacific and, pointing to the
destruction of indigenous lands and natural resources and a raft of
other environmental and health concerns, called on the international
community to 'endorse the development of a process by which all
indigenous peoples can realize remedies for the historical and continuing denial of basic rights and meaningful choices, the right to self-
determination'.[84] With 17 non-self-governing territories still in
existence, of which 14 are small island nations in the Pacific, failure to
achieve the goal of the eradication of colonization by the year 2000
saw the declaration of a Second International Decade for the Eradication of Colonization.[85] The strong degree of US opposition to this
resolution demonstrates the ongoing tension between the right of
peoples to self-determination and the right of states to control the
natural resources within their territory.

An important case in point is that of Hawai'i. Illegally invaded and
annexed by the US in 1893, Hawai'i was placed on the UN List of

Non-Self-Governing Territories in 1946. In 1959 when the US enacted a law for incorporating Hawai'i as a state of the US, the US government failed to identify the indigenous Kanak Maoli people as colonized people eligible for decolonization, instead promoting voting by the non-Kanak Maoli majority; failed to present all options for self-determination, including independence; and, according to Kekuni Blaisdell, misrepresented the plebiscite results to the UN. As a result, and in the face of strong objections from the Kanak Maoli people, Hawai'i was removed from the list of non-self-governing countries. Despite US President Bill Clinton having tendered an official apology to the indigenous Kanak Maoli people on behalf of the US government in 1993, this situation continues to be in dispute. Having now been granted 'internal independence', Hawai'i remains a state of the US and continues to function as a vital strategic US base within the Pacific. [86]

Indigenous Sovereignty and Developmentalism

The particular nature of the relationship of indigenous peoples to their traditional lands and territories has been increasingly recognized within international instruments, particularly those concerning indigenous peoples' 'right to development'.[87] Among the more significant of these instruments are the 1948 UN Declaration of Human Rights, the American Convention on Human Rights, the 1986 UN Declaration on the Right to Development, and ILO Convention 169. Numerous investigative reports affirm the commonalities and specificities of the fundamental spiritual, philosophical, social and political values and principles that are at the root of indigenous peoples' social, cultural, economic and political existence. UN Special Rapporteur Cobo described this relationship and the 'profound sense of deprivation experienced by indigenous populations when the land to which they, as peoples, have been bound for thousands of years is taken away from them' in his final report on the lengthy ten-year Study of the Problem of Discrimination against Indigenous Populations. He noted:

> for indigenous populations, land does not represent simply a possession or means of production. It is not a commodity that can be appropriated, but a physical element that must be enjoyed freely. It is also essential to understand the special and profoundly spiritual relationship of indigenous peoples with Mother Earth as basic to their existence and to all their beliefs, customs, traditions and culture.[88]

These principles were reiterated in the final working paper of the report of Special Rapporteur Erica-Irene A. Daes on indigenous peoples and their relationship to land.[89] The final report of her three-year investigation included a commentary by Professor James Sakje Henderson, who stated:

> The Aboriginal vision of property was ecological space that creates our consciousness, not an ideological construct or fungible resource .... Their vision is of different realms enfolded into a sacred space .... It is fundamental to their identity, personality and humanity ... [the] notion of self does not end with their flesh, but continues with the reaches of their senses into the land.[90]

The stewardship function articulated by indigenous peoples as their specific and unique role is frequently interpreted as an obligation to hold and protect the land in order to pass its guardianship to future generations. This view has been strongly articulated by Maori. The Waitangi Tribunal, reporting on its findings in the Manukau Claim report, noted the following expression of the Maori concept of land ownership:

> They own no more than a right to use and enjoy the fruits of the land and water. They hold them in trust for their children, and their children's children after them. They cannot sell or destroy the rights of future beneficiaries but have a duty to pass them on in at least as good a condition as when they received them.[91]

Benedict Kingsbury's exploration of the intersection of international law and the Treaty of Waitangi that in 1840 formalized the relationship between the indigenous peoples of New Zealand and the British Crown, highlights an emerging conjunction between indigenous peoples' rights to traditional lands and territories and the 'right to development' that became a significant aspect of international norms discourses pertaining to indigenous peoples during the 1980s.[92] An important outcome of the international activism of indigenous peoples has been the recognition in international law that the customary rights of indigenous peoples were unextinguished by treaties of secession unless specifically stated otherwise by the indigenous occupants. This has shaped states' responses to indigenous peoples' demands for self-determination in significant ways. Situated at the intersection of emerging new forms of liberalism and the recognition that the overtly colonizing dynamics of assimilation and integration that had underpinned indigenous peoples' relationships with

states could no longer continue in the same form, the counter discourses and resistance strategies of indigenous peoples impacted on
the reshaping of international human rights instruments and on the
development of new forms of engagement at the national and international level. Kingsbury sees this as influenced by the development
of international human rights law as well as by the increased international and national legal activity concerning indigenous peoples.

A series of regional 'Meetings of Experts on Ethnodevelopment
and Ethnocide' over the period 1981–3 sought to articulate standards
for indigenous peoples' participation and control over their own
development, defining ethnodevelopment as:

> the extension and consolidation of the range of its own culture, through
> strengthening the independent decision-making capacity of a culturally
> distinct society to direct its own development and exercise self-determi-
> nation, at whatever level, which implies an equitable and independent
> share of power. This means that the ethnic group is a political and admin-
> istrative unit, with authority over its own territory and decision-making
> powers within the confines of the development project, in a process of
> increasing autonomy and self-management.[93]

The restructuring of indigenous rights within a discourse of development was given impetus by what Kingsbury describes as 'a written
statement of some significance'[94] delivered by one of the five
members of the UN Working Group on Indigenous Populations at
the 1987 session of the Working Group. In a comment regarding the
obligations of states to 'adopt special measures in favour of groups in
order to create conditions suitable for their development' Professor
Danilo Turk suggested that indigenous peoples' requests for 'autonomy' could be usefully interpreted as an 'instrument necessary for
their development and the development of their members, as well as
the state as a whole'.[95] In Turk's view, such development-oriented
interpretations of the rights of groups could 'be helpful in the present
efforts for further elaboration of international standards relating to
these groups'. According to Turk, '[t]he usefulness of the idea of the
right to development in the context of such groups is that it places the
accent of their claim on development rather than political status as
such'. By this means, he suggests, autonomy would be reinterpreted,
'not as an end in itself or a first step to political independence but
rather as an instrument necessary for their development and for the
development of the state as a whole'.[96] Whilst undoubtedly well-
intentioned, these efforts can be interpreted as the co-optation of

indigenous aspirations of sovereignty and aboriginal land rights through discursive reinterpretations within ideological frameworks predicated upon the same liberal economic rationalizations that underpinned the reconfiguring of the state.

Due in large measure to the international activity of indigenous peoples and their supporters, undeniable changes in international legal norms have in many cases highlighted existing tension between states and indigenous peoples, much of which coalesces around what are frequently seen as conflicting interpretations of state sovereignty and indigenous self-determination. Advances in recognition of indigenous peoples' rights to their culture, to their land and to a measure of self-determination are severely mitigated by ongoing situations. Daes includes in these the failure of states to accord appropriate legal status, juridical capacity and other legal rights, failure to demarcate indigenous lands and territories, the failure of states to enforce or implement laws protecting indigenous lands, the removal and relocation of indigenous peoples, state assumption of trust titles, management of sacred and cultural sites by governments, failure to protect the integrity of the environment of indigenous lands and territories, and contemporary measures to enact the juridical extinguishment of aboriginal rights regarding land and resources, and the abrogation of treaties.[97]

These conflicting interpretations and situations have given rise to a wide range of strategies and responses adopted by both indigenous peoples and the colonizer states. Challenges to the legitimacy of the exercise of sovereignty by the state have been expressed both through protest and through the articulation of aboriginal sovereignty. Critical strategies by indigenous peoples include the articulation of indigenous histories and cultural and social values as unique characteristics, which, according to international legal instruments, must be acknowledged and protected. Within the local arena, the recognition afforded to indigenous peoples' rights to their own cultural, political, economic and social rights is increasingly expressed in remedial measures pertaining to the loss of land and other rights over centuries of exploitation and, frequently, imperial rule. In Chapter 6 we shall see that, like many other indigenous peoples actively engaged in both the international and local arenas, Maori have pursued the restoration of collective and inherent indigenous rights regarding land, identity, political voice and the insurrection of subjugated knowledge through multiple venues.

Notes

1 Tully, James (2000) 'The struggles of indigenous peoples for and of freedom', in Duncan Ivison, Paul Patton and Will Sanders (eds.), *Political Theory and the Rights of Indigenous Peoples*. Cambridge: Cambridge University Press, pp. 36–59.

2 Cf. Kymlicka, Will (1989) *Liberalism, Community, and Culture*. Oxford: Clarendon Press; New York: Oxford University Press; Fenton, Steve and Stephen May (eds.) (2002) *Ethnonational Identities*. New York: Palgrave Macmillan.

3 Walker, R. B. J. (1993) *Inside/Outside: International Relations as Political Theory*. Cambridge: Cambridge University Press, p. 166.

4 Foucault, Michel (1991) 'Governmentality', in Graham Burchell, Colin Gordon and Peter Miller (eds.), *The Foucault Effect. Studies in Governmentality*. Chicago: The University of Chicago Press, pp. 87–104.

5 Laski, Harold (1924) 'Letter 1: September 26', in M. D. Howe (ed.) (1953) *Holmes–Laski Letters: the Correspondence of Mr Justice Holmes and Harold J. Laski, 1916–1935* (two volumes). Cambridge, MA: Harvard University Press, cited in Lapidoth, Ruth (1992) 'Sovereignty in transition', *Journal of International Affairs*, 45 (2) (Winter), p. 334.

6 Lapidoth (1992), p. 331.

7 Walker, R. B. J. (1995) 'From international relations to world politics', in A. Joseph, Anthony P. Jarvis and Albert J. Paolini (eds.), *The State in Transition: Reimagining Political Space*. Boulder, Colorado and London: Lynne Rienner, p. 27.

8 Coates, Ken S. and P. G. McHugh (1998) *Living Relationships. The Treaty of Waitangi in the New Millennium*. Wellington: Victoria University Press.

9 Lapidoth (1992), p. 331.

10 Gottlieb, Gideon (1993) *Nation Against State: a New Approach to Ethnic Conflicts and the Decline of Sovereignty*. New York: Council for Foreign Relations Press.

11 At the 1944 international conference held at Dumbarton Oaks, Washington, representatives of the US, Britain, Soviet Union and China drew up proposals that served as a basis for the Charter of the UN, formulated at the San Francisco Conference the following year. At the Dumbarton Oaks Conference, the main focus was to establish measures to assure the maintenance of international peace and security, hence one of its main achievements was the planning of the UN Security Council.

12 In the context of the zero-sum game in the lead up to and during the period of the Cold War, many of the proposals and resolutions in relation to self-determination were put forward for propaganda advantage rather than for realization.

13 Charter of the United Nations, 26 June 1945.

14 See Musgrave, Thomas D. (1997) *Self-Determination and National Minorities*. Oxford and New York: Oxford University Press, pp. 80–5.

15 International Court of Justice (1975) *Western Sahara Advisory Opinion of 16 October 1975*. The Hague: ICJ Reports, p. 12.

16 Venne, Sharon (1998) *Our Elders Understand Our Rights: Evolving International Law Regarding Indigenous People*. Penticton, BC: Theytus Books, p. 86. See also Anaya, S. James (1996) *Indigenous Peoples in International Law*. New York: Oxford University Press, p. 84; Musgrave (1997), pp. 85–6.

17 Musgrave (1997).

18 *Ibid.*, p. 2.

19 An important author in this period was Johann Gottfried von Herder, whose notion of the *volk* as a community of people with shared blood ties, language, culture, religion and customs – regarded by Herder as a 'natural' unit – became incorporated into the notion of the 'nation' that prevailed in some areas of Europe.

20 Cf. Musgrave (1997), p. 6.

21 Anaya (1996); see also Musgrave (1997); Sellers, Mortimer (1996) (ed.) *The New*

World Order: Sovereignty, Human Rights, and the Self-determination of Peoples. Oxford: Berg.

22 Anaya (1996).

23 Musgrave (1997).

24 Cited Musgrave, *ibid.*, p. 64; See also Murphy, Alexander B. (1996) 'The sovereign state system as political-territorial ideal: historical and contemporary considerations', in Thomas J. Biersteker and Cynthia Weber (eds.), *State Sovereignty as a Social Construct.* Cambridge: Cambridge University Press, pp. 81–120.

25 *Ibid.*

26 Cf. the salt water thesis.

27 Wilmer, Franke (1993) *The Indigenous Voice in World Politics. Since Time Immemorial.* Newbury Park, London and New Delhi: Sage, p. 188.

28 Anaya (1996), p. 76.

29 Adopted by UN General Assembly Resolution 1514 (XV) of 14 December 1960.

30 UN General Assembly Resolution 1514 (XV), 6.

31 Sellers states that this limitation is generally applied to protect the rights of other groups who may be affected by the exercise of the right to self-determination, pointing to the issue of territorial integrity as another specific limitation on the right of self-determination. This stems from the Declaration on Principles of International Law, which states that the right of self-determination shall not 'be construed as authorizing or encouraging any action which would dismember or impair, totally or in part, the territorial integrity or political unity of sovereign and independent states'. However the ability to apply this limitation is confined to those states that are themselves 'in compliance with the principle of equal rights and self-determination of peoples ... and thus possessed of a government representing the whole people belonging to the territory without distinction as to race, creed or colour.' See Sellers (1996), p. 17.

32 Wilmer (1993), p. 96.

33 Tully (2000), pp. 55–6.

34 Sellers (1997), p. 37.

35 Clarke, Tony and Maude Barlow (1997) *MAI. The Multilateral Agreement on Investment and the Threat to Canadian Sovereignty.* Toronto: Stoddart Publishing.

36 Hannum, Hurst (1996) in Donald Clark and Robert Williamson (eds.), *Self-Determination. International Perspectives.* Basingstoke: McMillan, p. 32.

37 Farer, Tom J. and Felice Gaer (1993) 'The UN and human rights: at the end of the beginning', in Adam Roberts and Benedict Kingsbury (eds.), *United Nations, Divided World: the UN's Roles in International Relations.* Oxford: Clarendon Press; New York: Oxford University Press, pp. 240–96.

38 *Ibid.*, p. 245.

39 The fundamental principle of self-determination enunciated in the first Article of both covenants, which declares the right of 'all peoples': to self-determination by virtue of which 'they freely determine their political status and freely pursue their economic, social and cultural development', was strongly debated. India, for instance, attempted to limit it to peoples under foreign domination and not to sovereign independent states or to a section of people or nation, a restriction to which France, Germany and the Netherlands strongly objected. See Musgrave (1997), pp. 97–8. Nevertheless Article 1 of both covenants makes explicit the link between human rights law and self-determination. Entered into force in 1976, these two treaties have to date been ratified by approximately two thirds of the members of the United Nations and more than eighty states.

40 Alfreddson, Gudmundur (1996) 'Different forms of and claims to the right of self-determination', in Clark and Williamson (1996).

41 Davidson, Scott (2000) *Human Rights.* Buckingham: Open University Press, p. 89.

42 Anaya (1996), pp. 39–71.

43 Cf. Musgrave (1997).

44 Kymlicka (1989), p. 139.

45 Sinclair, Moana (2000). '*Mana Motuhake*: International Law and Indigenous Peoples' Rights'. Unpublished LLM thesis, School of Law, University of Auckland.

46 Robert and Kingsbury (1993).

47 Zhang, Yongjin (1997). 'Human rights and the post-cold war international society', in Rorden Wilkinson (ed.), *Culture, Ethnicity and Human Rights*. Auckland: New Zealand Institute of International Affairs, pp. 39–54.

48 Brace, Bob (2000) *Guardian*, 31 July 2000; see also UN Human Rights Committee Press Release HR/CT580 21 July 2000 regarding the Committee's report on mandatory sentencing of Aboriginals in Australia.

49 Hopkins, Andrea (2000) 'Special report: Australia and East Timor', *Guardian*, 13 September 2000, online (accessed 14 September 2000) at
http://www.guardianunlimited.co.uk/Print/ 0,3858,4062928,00.html

50 Milbank, Dana (2002) 'East Timor invasion got US go-ahead', *Washington Post*, 7 December 2001, online (accessed January 2002) at
http://www.globalpolicy.org/security/issues/etimor/2001/1206kissinger.htm
Also Robie, David (1989) *Blood on Their Banner. Nationalist Struggles in the South Pacific*. Leichardt, New South Wales: Pluto Press.

51 Milbank (2002); See also Chomsky, Noam (1999) *The Umbrella of US Power. The Universal Declaration of Human Rights and the Contradictions of US Policy*. New York: Seven Stories Press, pp. 39–40; Chomsky, Noam (2000) *Rogue States. The Rule of Force in World Affairs*. Cambridge, MA: South End Press, pp. 51–61.

52 Evidenced in recently declassified documents of the US State Department posted on the website of the National Security Archive at George Washington University.

53 ILO Convention 107, Article 2 (1); cf. ILO Convention 169.

54 *Ibid.*, Article 6; Article 22 (1).

55 *Ibid.*, Article 11.

56 *Ibid.*, Article 12.

57 Berman (1988), ILO Revision, supra note 10 at 49, cited in Venne (1998), p. 97.

58 Cobo, Martinez (1986) *The Cobo Report. Study of the Problem of Discrimination Against Indigenous Populations* E/CN.4/Sub.2/1986/7/Add.4 (Vol. 5 of the final report), paras 368–77.

59 UN Economic and Social Council Resolution 1988/77, 24 May 1989.

60 Espiell, Hector Gros (1980) *The Right to Self-Determination. Implementation of United Nations Resolutions*. New York: United Nations, 1980. E/CN.4/Sub.2/405/Rev.1.

61 For a discussion of this event, see Titley, E. Brian (1986) *A Narrow Vision – Duncan Campbell Scott and the Administration of Indian Affairs in Canada*. Vancouver: University of British Columbia Press, pp. 120–3; see also Wilmer (1993), p. 3.

62 These include the World Council of Indigenous Peoples (WCIP), the International Indian Treaty Council, the South Pacific Regional Council, and the Inuit Circumpolar Conference.

63 Ryser, Rudolph (1981) Remarks before the Sub-Committee on Petitions, Information, and Assistance of the World Council of Indigenous Peoples, President Jose Carlos Morales, by Special Assistant Rudolph C. Ryser, New York City, 24 June 1981, Centre for World Indigenous Studies, Fourth World Documentation Project (accessed March 1997) at
http://www.halcyon.co./pub/FWDP/International/decolon.txt

64 Assies, Willem J. (1994) 'Self-determination and the "new partnership": the politics of indigenous peoples and states', in Willem J. Assies and A. J. Hoekema (eds.), *Indigenous Peoples' Experiences with Self-Government*. Copenhagen: IWGIA and the University of Amsterdam, p. 40.

65 Cf. Fenton and May (2002), pp. 1–20.
66 ILO Convention 169, Article 4.
67 Assies (1994), p. 39.
68 Anaya (1996), p. 120, note 85.
69 Cited in Assies (1994), p. 40.
70 In 1988 the International Labour Office Committee on the Revision of Convention 107 recommended the inclusion of the statement that: 'The [indigenous and tribal peoples] concerned should have the right to decide their own priorities for development as it affects their lives, beliefs, territories, institutions and spiritual well-being.' This statement was not however, included in the final version.
71 Cf. Venne (1998); also reports distributed online through networks such as *Netwarriors*, at http:// www.hookele.com/netwarriors/
72 E/CN.4/Sub.2/1999/20.
73 E/CN.4/1995/l/62. The draft resolution called for the CHR to establish an Open-ended Inter-sessional Working Group for the 'sole purpose of elaborating a draft declaration as contained in the annex of the resolution 1994/45 of 26 August 1994, entitled 'Draft United Nations Declaration on the Rights of Indigenous Peoples' for consideration and adoption by the General Assembly within the International Decade of the World's Indigenous People.
74 Venne (1998), p. 157.
75 May, Stephen (2001) *Language and Minority Rights: Ethnicity, Nationalism, and the Politics of Language.* Harlow and New York: Longman, p. 277.
76 See Report of the Working Group on Indigenous Populations on its Fourteenth Session (E/CN.4/Sub.2/1996/32.
77 As Anaya notes, the mandate system of the League of Nations provided for the resources of indigenous peoples to be 'held in trust' by the dominant powers.
78 *Ibid.*, p. 87.
79 May, Stephen (2002) 'Indigenous rights and the politics of self-determination: the case of *New Zealand*', in Fenton and May (2002), p. 292 (italics in original).
80 Morris, Glen T. (1992) 'International law and politics. Toward a right to self-determination for indigenous peoples', in M. Annette Jaimes (ed.), *The State of Native America: Genocide, Colonization and Resistance.* South End Press, 1992, reproduced by the Fourth World Documentation project, accessed 12 March 2002 at http://www.halycon.com/pub/FWDP/International/int.txt
81 See Tully (2000), p. 55.
82 See, for instance, the Permanent Representative of Malaysia, speaking on the Trusteeship Council at the Special Committee on the Charter of the United Nations and on Strengthening the Role of the Organization, UN Press Release L/2755, 28 February 1996.
83 UN Press Release CA/9008, 21 November 1995.
84 Draft Resolution on Decolonization for Indigenous Peoples of the Pacific. Indigenous Peoples of the Pacific Workshop, 2–6 September 1996, Suva, Fiji, accessed 3 October 1997 at http://www.halcyon.com/pub/FWDP/International/int_econ.txt
85 Report of the Special Committee on the Situation with regard to the Implementation of the Granting of Independence to Colonial Countries and Peoples for the year 2000. UN General Assembly Official Records 55th Session Supplement No. 23 (A/55/23), New York: United Nations, 2001.
86 See Apology Resolution. US Public Law 103–150, 103rd Congress, Joint Resolution, 23 November 1993 (S. J. Res. 19). See also Kekuni Blaisdell (2002) *Kanaka Maoli Self-Determination and Reinscription of Ka Pae' Aina (Hawai'i) on the UN List of Non-Self-Governing Territories.* Accessed 22 June 2002 at http://www.inmotionmagazine.com/nga2.html

87 For a detailed discussion of the elaboration of international legal norms concerning indigenous rights to their lands and territories, see Anaya (1996), pp. 104–7.

88 Cobo, Martinez (1983) *Study of the Problem of Discrimination Against Indigenous Populations*. UN Doc E/CN.4/Sub.2/1983/21/Add.8, p. 67.

89 Daes, Erica-Irene (2000) *Indigenous Peoples and their Relationship to Land*. Final working paper prepared by Special Rapporteur Erica-Irene Daes, E/CN.4/Sub/2/2000/25.

90 Henderson, James (Sakej) Youngblood *et al.* (1999). *Aboriginal Tenure in the Constitution of Canada*. Carswell Thomas Professional Publishing, cited in *ibid.*, p. 42.

91 Kingsbury (1989), p. 147.

92 *Ibid.*

93 Article 3, Declaration of San Jose, 11 December 1981, cited *ibid.*, p. 141; also reproduced in UN Doc. E/CN.4/Sub.2/1986/7.

94 Kingsbury (1989), p. 140.

95 Turk, Danilo (1987) Statement at the Fifth Session of the Working Group on Indigenous Populations, UN Doc E/Cn.4/Sub.2/1987/22, cited in *ibid.*

96 Turk (1987), cited in Kingsbury (1989), p. 141.

97 Daes (2000), pp. 13–25.

❀

CHAPTER 5

Global Hegemony and the Construction of World Government

This chapter takes up the theme of the construction of the modern world order. Here the primary focus is the transformation of the hegemonic liberal international order into a new imperialist forma-tion during the second half of the twentieth century. The unravelling of the set of post-war political and economic arrangements is widely regarded as the point at which globalization in its current form emerged[1] and provides the context for my exploration in this chapter. Cox has argued that the phenomenon of globalization is less the result of the conscious will of an identifiable group than the cumulative effect of the actions of many groups, corporate bodies and states.[2] Whilst I acknowledge the nature of globalization as resulting from what Jessop calls 'a multi-scalar, multi-temporal, and multi-centric series of processes operating in specific structural contexts',[3] the central argument that I develop here is that underlying these processes – and, more particularly, the ways in which they are theorized and understood within dominant orthodoxies – is a set of ontological and epistemological assumptions. The roots of these assumptions lie in a rationalist-positivist model of being associated with particular forms of liberalism.

I begin this chapter with a brief examination of the competing ideologies and policy responses that shaped the transition from international liberalism to a transnational hegemony in which states have diminished sovereignty and, like the Bretton Woods institu-tions, have become accountable to what is nebulously referred to as 'the global economy'.[4] Following the work of Gill, Peters and others, I argue that since the onset of the global economic crisis of the 1970s, ideologies of world order have been increasingly dominated by a form of neoliberalism which, while transatlantic in its operations, is locatable within a particular historical/philosophical context. In drawing on arguments that the assertion of neoliberalism as both the dominant set of ideologies and a specific form of governmentality underpinning the construction of a global economic order has been consciously driven by particular interest groups, I acknowledge Cox's point that while these interest groups share similar aims and ideals, they do not necessarily act as a unified body. Both Cox and Jessop have both pointed out that the competing interests of these groups are frequently a source of internal conflict and instability within the world order system. Cox argues that the consequences of these processes, while forming an interrelated pattern, also contain within them inherent contradictions that threaten the persistence of this emerging structural whole. These contradictions, he maintains, should be carefully studied in order to work for the eventual replacement of the emerging formation. During the 1970s, these differing ideological responses were reflected in the responses of groups to Third World calls for a New International Economic Order and perceptions of declining US hegemony.

In the aftermath of the economic crisis of the 1970s and given further impetus by the collapse of the Eastern Bloc at the end of the 1980s, notions of US decline occupied the centre stage in international relations theorizing of the emerging new world order. The result of this embedded limited conceptualization of hegemony was a political myopia about the nature of the reconfigurations of neoliberal capitalism occurring at that point in time.[5] In assuming the decline of US hegemony, the notion of a post-hegemonic or non-hegemonic world order was taken for granted. Since then, a series of militarist interventions, most notably in the Middle East, have given rise to fresh conceptualizations of American hegemony or dominance. Many of these are articulated around notions of either a first or a second 'American Century'.

My contention is that during the latter half of the twentieth century, the locus of hegemony shifted from the level of the state to the global arena. Here it is represented by a particular form of global governance that operates at the convergence of the interests of global capital and the specific form of liberalism widely referred to as neoliberalism. In this I am informed by Cox's explanation of international hegemony as 'an order within a world economy with a dominant mode of production that penetrates into all countries and links into other subordinate modes of production'.[6] Arrighi extends this to elaborate the collective nature of world hegemony in which 'the leadership that defines hegemony rests on the capacity of the dominant group to present itself and be perceived as, the bearer of a general interest'.[7] The breakdown of this ability leads eventually to hegemonic crisis and systemic chaos. Out of this comes the possibility for the forging of new hegemonies through the emergence of 'a new complex of governmental and business agencies endowed with greater system-level organizational capabilities than those of the preceding hegemonic complex'.[8] As Harvey pertinently shows, however, the way the power of the hegemon is expressed is through a continuously shifting balance 'between coercion and consensus'. This is well demonstrated in the shifting of the locus of hegemonic power in the last 30 years of the previous century.

The emergence from relative obscurity of a network of trans-national forces, most notably during the 1970s and 1980s, can be seen as a shift in the locus of hegemony from a dominant state to a global historic bloc consisting of a broad alliance of transnational financial and capital interests, international organizations and institutions. During the final decades of the twentieth century, this alliance of financial interests was notably influential in the assertion of new forms of interventionism aimed at the recapture of contender states and the reconstruction of world order around the interests of finance and capital. These interventions have taken the form of what has been referred to as both financial and militaristic forms of warfare. As we have seen, the function of US militarism has become more overtly directed towards the political and strategic reconfiguration of the global system in ways that establish and maintain the dominance of US-based financial interests whilst attempting to maintain the discursively constructed role of the US as global protector of Western democracy articulated through discourses of freedom and justice. Despite the shift in hegemony from the local to the global, the hegemonic function of the US within the emergent global system became more overt during this period, particularly in relation to its role as protector and facilitator of the activities of transnational capital.

The Third World Challenge to Transatlantic Fordism

Van der Pijl suggests that the alliance of Third World countries and the non-aligned movement in the Cold War period represented the most serious challenge to the Lockean heartland of transatlantic capitalism by a Hobbesian contender state formation in recent times.[9]

The origin of this revolutionary movement was the Bandung Conference of the representatives of 29 Asian and African nations in April 1955. This conference marked the birth of the 'Third World', the signing of the Non-Aligned Pact and the emergence of collective demands in the fields of decolonization and development by Third World countries. As the newly emerging counter-hegemonic bloc of Third World and non-aligned states sought to manoeuvre international economic policy towards supporting Third World development and autonomy, a paradigmatic shift occurred in the nature of the resolutions passed within the UN General Assembly. Ideologies of development and underdevelopment became a site of struggle between the industrialized nations of the North and those known as the 'Third World' countries.

Influenced by the prevailing development economics theories, Western-educated Third World elites viewed development as economic development that would enable their autonomy from the North, and sought strategies to rectify the causes of underdevelopment rather than simply ameliorate its effects. These included calls for a New International Economic Order, the development of an agency within the UN that would concentrate on Third World development, and attempts to limit the adverse effects of multinational activities in developing countries through binding international restrictions in the form of a Code of Conduct for Multinationals. The UN Decade of Development, initiated in 1961, was an integral aspect of these strategies. It was also the catalyst for intense debates regarding the nature, purpose and functioning of the world economy.

The shocks of the Chinese Cultural Revolution of 1967 and the student protests of May 1968 were harbingers of the turbulent decade of the 1970s that ultimately saw the transformation of world order. Increased social protest throughout the Western world, combined with a series of political and economic crises, many of which were interrelated, impelled and facilitated these transformations. The anti-war movement, the defeat of US foreign policy in the Vietnam War, the ballooning of US budget deficits and the subsequent dismantling by the US of the gold standard on which the Bretton Woods fixed exchange system was predicated, the hiking of oil prices through collusion by then US President Nixon with the Organization of Petroleum-Exporting Countries (OPEC) that preceded financial deregulation, the black civil rights movement, the conscientization and international movement of indigenous peoples, and, finally, demands by developing countries for a New International Economic

Order, all provided the context for new theoretical analyses that articulated declining US hegemony. They also provided the political and economic space for a reformulation of the structures of world order. Throughout the 1960s and 1970s, the need for development assistance for the Group of 77 Developing Countries (G77) dominated calls for new UN agencies such as the United Nations Conference on Trade and Development (UNCTAD). Within a decade these had been overtaken by monetarist calls for reform driven by the North, and the United States had re-established its position of dominance within the United Nations. The monetarist interventions that followed the apparent collapse of the international economic system and the role of debt in the economic and political crisis of the 1970s included the reassertion of the structural power of capital and the restructuring of production.

Branislav Gosovic's 1971 study of the development of UNCTAD details the unequal relations engendered by GATT and the struggles of Third World countries to achieve some measure of equity within the world economic order through the United Nations.[10] Developing countries saw GATT as biased in favour of the rich countries and actively working in opposition to their own efforts to achieve growth through trade. While the principles of GATT were purported to provide an equal footing for member countries, developing countries contended that in practice GATT further impoverished poorer countries – a view, Gosovic reports, that found little response in the North. Also contentious was the lack of a suitable organization able to dedicate itself to issues of Third World trade and development. Established in 1964 as a response to this situation, UNCTAD rapidly became a site of conflicting interests and contested power relations. As it became the favoured platform of the G77, Northern countries actively sought to undermine UNCTAD's ability to function effectively, arguing that its functions replicated those of GATT.

During what was designated as the Second Development Decade, 'collective self-reliance' and the need for a New International Economic Order became the two key principles advanced by developing and non-aligned countries. These principles represented a profound ideological threat to transnational capital interests. The 1970 declaration of collective self-reliance as the key principle for developing countries[11] was the first stage in Third World planning for the control of trade and development and a more equitable redistribution of the wealth and benefits of global capital. In 1974, the Declaration on the Establishment of a New International Economic

Order (NIEO),[12] together with a Programme of Action, was rapidly followed by the adoption of the Charter of Economic Rights and Duties of States[13] that urged 'radically new economic and political responsibilities on states'.[14] The extension of the debate to the role of multinational and transnational corporations saw the establishment in 1972 of an eminent persons' group[15] charged with preparing recommendations for international action on multinational corporations.[16]

Proposals for a compulsory mechanism to regulate the behaviour of transnational corporations developed from within three arenas. The UN, under pressure from developing countries, took the lead in crusading for a comprehensive, legally binding international code of conduct. The European Community's initiative was undertaken under pressure from the European Trade Union Confederation, while the Organization for Economic Cooperation and Development (OECD) acted in a retaliatory fashion to pre-empt these endeavours. In the UN, work on international mechanisms to regulate the conduct of multinational and transnational corporations took place within ECOSOC, the ILO and UNCTAD. A newly created Commission and a Centre on Transnational Corporations (CTC) was charged with drawing up recommendations that would provide the basis for a code of conduct dealing with transnational corporations.[17] In keeping with the objectives of the 1974 Charter of Economic Rights and Duties of States, the original proposals for the code of conduct produced in 1975 contained provisions that called on multinational corporations to respect national sovereignty, to refrain from interfering in international political affairs and to respect the economic objectives of developing countries – proposals that were strongly opposed by the Reagan administration of the United States.

The Counter-Response by Industrialized Countries

John Robinson argues that economic stagnation in the mid-1970s was responsible for the shift from debate to negotiation regarding multinationals. As the principal negotiating forum for the substantive drafting of the UN Code of Conduct for Multinationals, the replacement of the ECOSOC-appointed Commission by a 'so-called intergovernmental working group on a code of conduct' appointed in 1977 and 'chaired by a "progressive" from an industrialized country', signalled an important change in the direction of UN policy.[18] Adopted in November 1977, the ILO Declaration of Principles concerning Multinational Enterprises and Social Policy aimed at controlling the impact of transnational and multinational corporate activity on employment and industrial relations in the developing countries, was the first international agreement on multinational corporations (MNCs) produced and adopted by a United Nations agency. In what Robinson describes as 'a rapid, rich world response to the threatened emergence of a much tougher, legally binding code of conduct being negotiated by the United Nations in New York'[19] and heavily influenced by the Reagan Administration in the US, the ILO's Code of Conduct for Multinationals and the proposed UN Code of Conduct for Multinationals were pre-empted by the 1976 voluntary code of conduct sponsored by the OECD. This move saw the 1976 OECD Guidelines for Multinationals become the model to be copied for use by the UN as well as for sectoral arrangements on the transfer of technology and restricted business practices affecting multinationals being developed within UNCTAD. The outcome was the negotiation of a much more flexible and non-binding arrangement that was far removed from the Code of Conduct originally envisaged by both trade unions and the G77 group of countries. The resultant Guidelines became, in Robinson's terms, essentially an 'Industrial Relations Code for the Disinvestor'.[20]

The negotiation processes between the countries of the North and South that took place in response to the South's demands for revised international policies engendered wide-ranging debates regarding the actual and desirable basic structure of world economic relations.[21] Cox's analysis of the ideological perspectives represented in the literature on the New International Economic Order provides a comprehensive summary of the processes and competing demands involved in the debates it engendered.[22] Cox summarizes these in terms of five networks of ideological perspectives.[23] These were (1) the monopolistic liberalism represented in the reports of the Trilateral Commission; (2) a social democratic variant that argued for more generous adjustments without disturbing the existing hegemony; (3) a network of Third World intellectuals and elites who in varying ways rejected the development model of the West and advanced alternative models, and who saw social and political revolution as a necessary condition for development in the Third World; (4) a range of neo-mercantilist perspectives; and (5) a historical materialist approach with the main focus on production.

The similar views of the future world economy entertained in what Cox describes as the establishment and social democratic perspectives – in terms of a dualistic approach to national economies and the continuing role of multinational or transnational corporations – contrasted with their differing views about the future institutional framework of the world economy. In Cox's view, 'Reshaping the International Order' (RIO), a report prepared by a committee of the Club of Rome – advocating regulation of multinational companies within some form of corporatist international framework – was representative of the social democratic perspective. Centred around such slogans as 'decentralized planetary sovereignty', it envisaged a world economic order based upon comprehensive planning on a global scale under the aegis of the United Nations. However, the 'piecemeal functionalism' approach advocated in the report of the Trilateral Commission, Cox claims, positioned the IMF, the World Bank and GATT as the central pivots of the world economic framework.[24] In the context of global politics, these reports represent the two faces of global hegemony, sharing 'the same fundamental assumptions about the progressive nature of world capitalism', a new international division of labour, and 'an international welfare programme to be carried out by the poor themselves'.[25]

Cox's analysis of broad groups of responses to the calls for a New International Economic Order completely excludes indigenous responses.[26] It does, however, draw out important competing ideologies and contradictions identifiable in the processes of globalization. While neo-mercantilists argued from the perspective of the defence of American power, the interests of transnational capital sought the vision of a 'reunified Trilateral world as the anchor of a liberal world economy'[27] to displace the notion of 'a pentagonal organization of world power' that was the prevailing ideology of the Kissinger–Nixon administration, as well as that of George Bush Snr.

The Emergence of Neoliberalism

The convergence of the series of political and economic crises and the political and economic challenge issued by the alliance of the Third World and non-aligned countries saw a strong, focused response occur at the corresponding convergence of new forms of classical economics articulated by neoliberalist organic intellectuals and new neoliberal lobby groups. This phase of economic imperialism and its dispersal through neoliberal organizations and think tanks[28] was the driving force for the transformation of the post-Second World War structure of nation states and transatlantic Keynesian-Fordism into a borderless economic order underpinned by Schumpeterian workfareism and free market ideologies. One of the most influential neoliberal networks, the Trilateral Commission, like other influential bodies such as the US Heritage Foundation and more recently, the World Economic Forum (WEF), has exerted considerable influence on the shaping of US domestic policy. Launched at a Bilderberg meeting in 1971 with the support of David Rockefeller, chairman of the Chase Manhattan Bank,[29] the Trilateral Commission is identified by Gill as 'the quintessential political forum of the transnational elites'.[30] One of its immediate aims was the reversal of protectionist US policies perceived as threatening to undermine the free movement of international capital essential to the internationalization of production and accumulation.[31] Although initially focused on political strategies, as van der Pijl shows, the Trilateral Commission ultimately played a key role in realigning American monetary policy to the neoliberal agenda. The Heritage Foundation, which shares much of its membership with the Mont Pelerin Society, has also helped to guide the insertion of neoliberal policy within the foreign policy of the US.[32]

The most significant variable in the emergence of globalization as the new politico/economic structure of world order is that of the intersection of neoliberalism and governmentality. Michael Peters offers an interpretation of neoliberalism as a form of governmentality that is helpful in understanding the nature of the shift towards a redefinition of the meaning of governance. In his examination of historical relationships between American neoliberalism, the Chicago School and human capital theory, Peters examines the intersection between neoliberalism and governmentality, and the mechanisms by which power is exercised.[33] What is distinctive about these forms of neoliberalism is that rather than being 'a simple and naïve return to past principles', there are 'major differences between past and present forms of liberalism'. A central feature of neoliberalism in its varying forms is its restyling of basic principles in ways that accommodate new exigencies. Common to these various forms is the application of the 'competitive, optimizing market relations' principle towards both the limiting of government intervention and 'rationalizing government itself'.[34]

In presenting the emergence of neoclassical economics Peters illuminates the role of mainstream academics in the processes by which the NIEO strategies of the Third World were reversed and monetarist policies inserted in their place. It was during this period that the influence and application of the Chicago School's renaissance of neoclassical economics was extended into other areas 'traditionally regarded as the prerogative of other fields, such as political science, legal theory, history and sociology'.[35] Opposed to Keynesian economics, the Chicago School strongly advocated monetarist policies that provided theoretical and empirical legitimacy to the undermining and rolling back of interventionist policies.[36] In the 1970s, the neoclassical economics advanced within the Chicago School signalled a new phase in the application of economics to the wide gamut of human experience. Particularly significant was the influence of neoclassical economics on development theory. Aligned with neoclassical economics were 'New Economic History' and movements such as 'Law and Economics' as well as the 'New Institutionalism' which, as cited by Peters, refers to:

> the collection of schools of thought that seek to explain political, historical, economic and social institutions such as government, law, markets, firms, social conventions, the family, etc. in terms of neoclassical economic theory.[37]

William Robinson's comprehensive study of US hegemony and interventionism in the establishment of the global economic order details the evolution of modernization and political development theory into an intellectual movement that functioned to legitimate new forms of political interventionism. This intellectual movement, Robinson contends, was 'parallel to and deeply interpenetrated with US policy', contributing 'important theoretical and practical elements to the development of a new political intervention' legitimized by the emergence of a new generation of democratization theory.[38] In Robinson's analysis, the theoretical evolution from development theory to democratization theory 'parallels the reconfiguration of US–Third World and North–South relations over the past few decades'.[39] Like post-Second World War institutions, the institutions of the emergent global order were proposed, designed and widely promoted under the aegis of the international hegemonic bloc, in this case comprised of neoliberal academics, organizations and think tanks.

Remoulding World Order

The beginning of a paradigmatic shift in the structural framework of world order and the parameters of democracy was signalled in a systematic series of reports undertaken in the late 1970s, primarily by the Council for Foreign Relations and the Trilateral Commission, which sought to design the elements of a new world order. The first and most controversial report by the Trilateral Commission, *The Crisis of Democracy, 1975,*[40] raised questions about the ongoing validity of political democracy, the legitimacy of the state, and the future of economic conditions.

The section of the report authored by Samuel Huntington argued that state legitimacy was being dangerously undermined. Huntington's contention that the development of an 'adversary culture' among 'intellectuals and related groups' represented a threat to democracy as potentially serious as 'those posed in the past by aristocratic cliques, fascist governments and communist parties'[41] has echoes of the exclusionary notions of democracy that underpinned the development of the Lockean nation states. Other specified 'threats to democracy' included a shift in values towards 'private satisfaction, leisure and the need for belonging and fulfilment' which, Huntington argued, limited the ability of democratic governments to 'mobilize their citizens and impose discipline and sacrifice' for the 'achievement of social and political goals', and finally, an 'intrinsic challenge to the viability of democratic government'.[42] A breakdown of traditional means of social control, a delegitimation of political and other forms of authority and an overload of demands on governments were seen as contributors to the undermining of democracy, thus signalling the need for longer-term, more broadly formulated purposes and priorities for a greater coherence of policy.

The popular notion of democracy was itself perceived as a danger to state legitimacy. Rather than being self-sustaining or self-limiting, Huntington argued, popular democracy, if unchecked by some outside agency, may give rise to forces that 'will undermine democracy itself'. Thus, the 'governability of democracy' was presented as a 'vital and indeed urgent issue in the trilateral societies'.[43] The report advocated the limiting of democracy as a necessary means for the reassertion of social control within the trilateral countries, and specifically, within the US. Thus conceptualized, 'limited democracy' legitimated new forms of political intervention and consensual domination as occurred in key countries in Central and South America, in which the preservation of coercive military apparatuses in the 1980s and early 1990s acted as a deterrent to demands for popular democracy.

The Reconstitution of Democracy

Robinson's comprehensive analysis of the shift from coercive to consensual forms of political domination identifies a radical revision of the concept of democracy and a shift from the institutional and classic definition of Parsonian-Schumpeterian democracy to a polyarchic version developed largely within US academia and promoted within elite circles and the reports of neoliberal think tanks.[44] In this account, the remoulding of the concept of popular democracy from a 'fully participatory form of politics' to a 'strategic weapon in the limiting of popular participation and the reshaping of countries' policies and institutions to the support of the US agenda for transnational capital', was developed and promoted through a converging consensus that occurred at the conjunction of social science and liberalist think tanks and organizations.

Following Gramsci's concept of organic intellectuals as 'experts in legitimation', Robinson describes the function of organic intellectuals as 'providing the theoretical understanding of historical processes and of structure necessary for dominant groups to engage in the social practice of domination and for the construction of hegemony as a fit between power, ideas and institutions'.[45] Importantly, Robinson argues, organic intellectuals also 'make essential practical and technological contributions to society'.[46] From this perspective, the reports of the Trilateral Commission can be properly seen as 'the reflection by organic intellectuals upon structure in order to orient policy'.

The decline in the notion of popular democracy took place concomitantly with the conflation of polyarchy and the staple definition of democracy in both 'democratization' and 'democracy promotion' discourses and literature. From the 1980s, popular democracy was suppressed in both theory and practice as promoting polyarchy and neoliberal restructuring became 'a singular process in US foreign policy'.[47] As a means of legitimating existing inequalities, Robinson explains, 'polyarchy as a distinct form of elite rule is more effective than authoritarianism and in the 1980s became the hegemony within social, scientific, political and mass public discourse'.[48] Underpinning the contradictions between polyarchy and popular democracy are contested social orders reflected in antagonistic notions of the democratic society. Thus, while the locus of power in both models is civil society, in polyarchy the state is the domain of the dominant classes, while the popular classes are incorporated into civil society under the hegemony of the elite – which is the formula for the exercise of consensual domination.[49]

Popular democracy, on the other hand,

> involves participatory mechanisms for popular sectors to subordinate and utilize the state in pursuit of their interests, with mobilization in civil society as the principal form in which political power is exercised.

Whereas under popular democracy society is governed by the 'logic of the majority', under polyarchy 'sovereignty is exercised by dominant minorities, but under conditions of hegemony', here defined as consensual domination.[50] In this sense, 'polyarchy plays a legitimating function for an increasingly cohesive transnational elite that seeks to legitimate its rule by establishing formal democratic institutions',[51] thus becoming 'the emergent global political structure of the emergent global economy'.[52]

As outlined by former US Secretary of State George Schultz, the actual content of 'democracy promotion' within civil society itself targeted five overlapping areas – 'leadership training', 'education' defined as inculcating 'the principles and practice of democracy and … the character and values of the United States in the education systems of other nations', 'strengthening the institutions of democracy', 'conveying ideas and information', and the 'development of personal and institutional ties'.[53] In this new intervention programme, Robinson explains, linkage building between two sets of relations – those between intra-elites and those between dominant and sub-ordinate groups – are critical components of the development of consensus-building processes among elites in targeted countries and for the construction of elite hegemony.

The shift from the concept of popular democracy as a fully participatory form of politics, to the notion of 'limited democracy' expressed in the reports of the Trilateral Commission, and the 'democracy promotion' articulated by US foreign policy makers, can be read at two levels. In the Foucauldian sense, the shift to limited democracy and a tightening of control over populations represents a new technology of domination and the subduing of populations. In another sense, 'democracy' became the vehicle for the insertion of new discursive hegemonies that were reflected in political discourses regarding world order. The Commission's report advocated strategies for the 'limiting' of democracy as a means of the reassertion of control over populations within the trilateral or 'core' countries. As a key instrument of US foreign policy, the promotion of limited forms of democracy was a major component in the reassertion of the North over those countries that van der Pijl refers to as 'Hobbesian contenders', those who sought to maintain and develop their own economic autonomy. The convergence of US military interventionism and the limiting of democracy saw the toppling of governments, some of them democratically elected, in Iran, Guatemala, the Middle East, Indonesia, Vietnam, Cambodia, Brazil, Greece, East Timor, Nicaragua, Iraq, Chile, Afghanistan and elsewhere.

The emergence of overtly neoliberal forms of governance was marked by the election of Margaret Thatcher in Britain in 1979 and of Ronald Reagan in the US in 1980. Despite disjunctures between factions, such as the tendency toward protectionism on the part of some neoconservatives, the consensus that emerged in the strategic centres of US power had established an unequivocal hegemony in the US by the mid-1980s, so that from the beginning of the second period of the Reagan administration in 1984 core US economic and foreign policy responded to the agenda of the transnational elite.[54] This broad consensus included the notion that, in playing a leadership role for the transnational elite, it was necessary for the US to develop policies to reconstruct the international order.[55] Critical to this agenda was the development of a broad new range of political, military and economic programmes that would place revolutionary and nationalist forces in the Third World and the Soviet Union on the defensive. This new 'reassertionism' included the necessity to assist with the adjustment of the US itself to the emergent global economy and society. Thus the fiscal and monetary policies developed within the Reagan administration sought to attune US economic policy to the new mode of global accumulation and capital.

Reform of the International System

The shift in the definition and operation of democracy from that of popular democracy as the participatory form of politics to its application as a strategic weapon in the limiting of popular participation and the reshaping of national politics and institutions to the support of the agenda for transnational capital, took place alongside the construction of the new international system of world order and the re-emergence of the US as an aggressive, dominating world power. During this period, the reports of both the Council on Foreign

Relations and the closely related Trilateral Commission, that included the Council for Foreign Relation's *1980s Project* and the Commission's report *Towards a Renovated International System,* converged around calls for a 'moderate international order' comprising a global economic environment in which barriers to the free movement of capital, goods and technology would be removed, and the transfer to the South of labour-intensive phases of production within a new international division of labour in which multinational corporations played an integral role. These reports called for reform of the international institutions of world order, the renovation of the international system, and a new regime for the oceans.[56] Important directives articulated within these reports were the need for a new international institution to govern foreign direct investment and multinational enterprise, the need for rules limiting the ability of governments to appropriate for national purposes 'a disproportionate share of the benefits generated by FDI', and the reform of existing international institutions including the GATT and the IMF. Significantly, the report also called for a shift in economic management by officials in the largest countries towards managing a single world economy. This move was mirrored in a shift in international relations discourses advocating increasing interdependence between nations.

In its functionalist response to international issues, the Trilateral Commission report on the renovation of the international system echoed the liberalist ideologies that comprised the historical foundation of the capitalist world order. The elitist nature of the proposed restructured international order was clearly identifiable in proposals for identifying and bringing 'selected newcomers into the inner circles of international decision making' as part of a response to the demands for a New International Economic Order.[57] This 'inner circle' consisting of an 'informal core group' was located at the centre of a series of 'concentric circles' through which initiatives agreed in a consultation process with states would be implemented through new and existing international institutions. Based on a 'series of circles of participation', final decision making regarding policies would rest in the hands of an 'inner group', amongst whom there would be 'close collaboration and coordination of policies'.[58] Piecemeal functionalism, which Gardener described as being able to 'produce some remarkable concessions of sovereignty that could not be achieved on an across-the-board basis',[59] became the preferred approach to managing what was viewed as 'the steady expansion and tightening of the web of interdependence'.[60] In theoretical terms, at the fore-front of this development within international relations theorizing was Keohane's concept of a network of linkages consisting largely of business and civil society organizations that operated on a global scale and centred upon the world economy.

This phase of expansion saw the internationalization of production accompanied by the proliferation of multinational corporations that functioned as conduits for new forms of finance capital. Operating through multilateral institutions, these regimes encompassed a wide range of intervention measures, including financial, military, intelligence and communication measures. Multilateralism thus became 'an instrument for institutionalizing the core–periphery structure of domination'.[61] In the same period, the GATT regime of seven rounds of trade negotiations saw the number of countries included in the negotiations progressively rise. The 1967–70 Kennedy Round of negotiations included more than eighty countries. By the conclusion of the Uruguay Round in 1993, almost all countries in the world were included.[62] Based on the four main principles of non-discrimination (the 'most favoured nation' principle), reciprocity, transparency, and fairness, these multilateral negotiations saw a vast reduction in tariffs and other trade barriers, thus significantly liberalizing trade. Alongside the GATT regime, an expanding network of bilateral and multilateral economic agreements fostered the expansion of a global free trade order while simultaneously tightening the web of economic interdependence for developed and eventually, developing countries, or so it was promised.

Discourses of Limits

The link between international regimes and structural power delineated by Keohane in the 1970s is identifiable in the functionalist response to the conscientizing and competing environmental discourses generated by the publication of Rachel Carson's *Silent Spring*.[63] Contextualized within the framework of the energy crisis and the Cold War, the competing environmental discourses of this period laid the framework for the increasing commodification of what Habermas termed 'the lifeworld' and thus played an important role in the development of new imperialist discourses. John S. Dryzek usefully provides an analysis of the environmental discourses that emerged in the 1970s in response to the notion of environmental crisis.[64] Prior to the period of 1960 to 1979, he suggests, environmental discourses were largely shaped around promethean-based discourses of an unlimited confidence in the ability of humans and their technologies to solve any problem presented to them, including environmental issues. The emergence of the ecology movement signalled by the 1972 UN Conference on the Human Environment held at Stockholm drew the attention of the world to the dangers of pollution, the exhaustion of natural resources and the problems of desertification. Accompanied by the Report of the Club of Rome,[65] a series of UN-sponsored conferences on the problems of population, human settlements, water, food, desertification, renewable energy, science and technology[66] detailed concerns about the short supply of resources, and especially non-renewable resources, as a result of economic and industrial growth, promulgating what Dryzek calls a 'survivalist response' that advocated strong government control.

The discourse of 'limits' promoted in Trilateral Commission reports saw agency as invested only in elites whose coordinated action would control access to the global commons. The objective was to regulate a diminishing supply through a series of multilateral agreements. These agreements included the 1967 Treaty of Principles Governing the Use of Outer Space, the 1978 MARPOL convention on ship pollution, the 1979 Agreement Governing Activities of States on the Moon and the 1982 United Nations Convention on the Law of the Sea, plus a raft of regional sea agreements regarding cooperation and the control of pollution. The proliferation of conventions and treaties during the 1970s and 1980s, aimed at regulating the international waters and marine pollution, signalled the increasing institutionalization of regimes governing the 'global commons'. In Dryzek's view, the Malthusian nature of these agreements reached their zenith in the 1992 Convention on Climate Change. In this Convention, the rearticulation of concerns regarding global warming that had been identified as early as the nineteenth century and reiterated in the UN Conferences of 1972 and 1979[67] was framed within a discourse of population expansion and the degradation of the environmental commons. The discursive shift towards an economic rationalist approach to environmental crises became apparent in the 1987 Montreal negotiations that were dominated by the US and European Community and led by the American multinational chemical manufacturer Du Pont. This shift saw privatization of the 'commons' advocated on the basis of neoliberal self-interest.[68] Under this market-led approach carbon sink credits in one area of the globe could be traded against pollution credits in another area. Thus it could be argued that the privatization of the commons would provide opportunities from which all would benefit.

The establishment of wide-ranging environmental regimes aimed at meeting international targets – including conventions on biodiversity, greenhouse emissions, rainforests and arrangements for the transfer of technology from the North for environmental purposes – was a major goal of the 1992 UN Environmental Programme (UNEP) 'Earth Summit' at Rio de Janeiro. The Convention on Biological Diversity (CBD) that was initiated at the Summit and was the first major international document to recognize the contribution of indigenous and traditional communities towards the maintenance of biological diversity,[69] calls upon states to 'respect, preserve and maintain knowledge, innovations and practices of practices' pertaining to 'conservation and sustainable use of biodiversity'[70] of such communities and to 'promote the wider application … of such knowledge, innovations and practices'. It also advocates the encouragement of the 'equitable sharing of the benefits arising from the utilization of such knowledge, innovations and practices'.[71]

Article 8(j) of the CBD requires that states enter into multilateral or bilateral agreements with indigenous nations in its territory. One of the problems with this, as Ryser notes, is how to administer such a requirement with indigenous peoples and territories who are located across more than one state. Hence Ryser argues that, 'having originated during the 1970s as a 'major effort by people of goodwill to establish international protections for the world's diverse biological and other beings', despite its convoluted words suggesting otherwise, the CBD has the sole purpose of dividing and commercializing Fourth World nations'.[72] The tenor of his argument is reflected in Sachs's view that the Rio project enshrined the relaunching of 'development' as the solution to environmental crises by 'invoking its significance throughout the document wherever possible'.[73] The outcome, he states, was the inauguration of environmentalism as 'the highest state of developmentalism'.[74]

Bretton Woods Institutions and the Disciplining of States

An important aspect of these processes has been a shift from the 'development regime' of transatlantic post-Fordism to a universal 'debt regime'[75] carried out, as Harvey puts it, by neoliberal forms of imperialism. The reconfiguring of the state in developing countries through a process of 'accumulation by dispossession'[76] was achieved by means of the restructuring of debt and loan conditionalities through circular schemes that saw the economic and political resources of previously colonized countries again come under the control of Anglo-American-based financial interests. Through policies involving the provision of new loans to repay previous debts, billions of dollars were recycled through the same group of 19 creditor countries known as the Paris Club, thus further impoverishing the debtor countries while enriching the Paris Club members, who were able to buy debtor nations' state assets at bargain basement rates. The dismantling of state institutions and the privatizing of publicly owned goods provided markets for the expansion of creditors' capital. The effect of these 'new forms of economic and political domination'[77] was the internationalization of macroeconomic policy under the control of powerful financial and political interests on whose behalf the Bretton Woods institutions now act. In Chossudovsky's words,

> Macro-economic management plays a central role in the emergence of a new global economic order: the reforms 'regulate' the process of capitalist accumulation at a world level. This is not, however, a 'free' market system: while supported by neoliberal discourse, the so-called 'structural adjustment programme' sponsored by the Bretton Woods institutions constitutes a new interventionist programme.[78]

In both developing and developed countries the transformation of state structures into variants of the neoliberal form of competitive states has coincided with changes in the productive powers and the balance of social and financial forces throughout the interstate system. During the period of the 1970s, states in developing countries were concurrently the objects of disciplinary strategies exercised through the agency of international institutions and the vehicle for the restructuring of national economies and the redisciplining of populations through the imposition of stringent economic reforms. Applied differently in developing and, at a later stage, developed countries, economic strategies centred round structural adjustment programmes were aimed at establishing free market economic regimes that functioned to support the economic interests of finance and capital. In Third World countries, the structural adjustment programme of the 1980s decimated the national economies and livelihoods of Third

World, pastorally based countries such as Somalia, which prior to the 1970s was self-sufficient in food. In Vietnam, repeated devaluing of currency, IMF-led demands for the repayments of debts incurred to support the US war effort, the liquidation of state enterprises and the transfer of Vietnam's industrial base to foreign-owned interests directly contributed to the decimation of Vietnam's economy and the destruction of the state. The increasingly larger share of export earnings earmarked for debt servicing, coupled with imposed rescheduling, restructuring and debt-conversion schemes, meant that by the mid-1980s 'developing countries had become net exporters of capital in favour of the rich countries.'[79]

Structural adjustment programmes were extended throughout Eastern Europe, South-east Asia and the Far East in the 1980s. Documented in a 1984 US National Security Decision Directive (NSDD 133) and released in a declassified and censored version in 1992 (NSDD 54), Washington's objective in regard to Eastern Europe included 'expanded efforts to promote a "quiet revolution" while integrating the countries of Eastern Europe into a market-oriented economy'.[80] The IMF Standby Agreement resulted in the collapse of real wages by 41 per cent, plus an inflation figure in excess of 70 per cent in 1990.[81] In Croatia, by 1991 inflation was 140 per cent, in 1992 it was 937 per cent, and in 1993 reached 1,134 per cent. Out of an industrial workforce of approximately 2.7 million, more than 600,000 workers were laid off in a period of less than two years and over 1,100 firms were either steered into bankruptcy or liquidated.

According to World Bank figures Serbia, Bosnia-Herzegovina, Macedonia and Kosovo suffered the largest numbers of bankruptcies and lay-offs.[82] Discourse-bound media accounts of long-held ethnic rivalries and divisions obscured from the public gaze the realities of a carefully constructed economic and political war against the federation of Yugoslavia. The imposition of the combined policies of debt servicing and loan conditionalities that had bankrupted Third World countries and cemented their indebtedness to Western financiers and international institutions during the 1970s and 1980s effectively ensured Bosnia's total dependence upon Western capitalism. At the same time, the territorial partitioning of Bosnia-Herzegovina through the Dayton Accord ensured that deposits of oil and coal found on the slopes of the Dinarides Thrust, and under exploration by Amoco (the Chicago-based oil company), as well as reportedly 'substantial petroleum fields in the Serb-held part of Croatia' are protected on behalf of Western economic interests.[83] The carefully orchestrated, deep-seated economic crisis precipitated civil war and provided a rationale for US-led military intervention. The prize was the control of a region rich in oil and minerals.[84]

Chossudovsky declares that in contributing towards the destabilizing of national currencies and ruining the economies of developing countries, structural adjustment programmes have contradicted the stated intentions of the 1944 Bretton Woods agreement.[85] In OECD countries, debt played an important role in the development of consensus around neoliberal policies. In the 1990s the extension of forms of structural adjustment to OECD countries, including North America and Western Europe, as well as to the countries of the former Soviet Bloc, completed the process Chossudovsky calls the 'globalization of poverty'. The organizations that emerged during this period shared in common a broad set of ten ideological principles. Summarized by economist John Williamson as the 'Washington Consensus', these principles represented a consensus between the 'political' Washington of the US Congress and Administration and the 'technocratic' Washington of the IMF, World Bank and think tanks. They comprised fiscal discipline, the redirecting of public expenditure, tax reform, financial liberalization, the adoption of a single, competitive exchange rate, trade liberalization, elimination of barriers to foreign direct investment, privatization of state enterprises, deregulation of market entry and competition, ensuring property rights.[86]

The development of these principles as guidelines for countries either wishing or required[87] to reform their economies had an enormous influence on the economic policies of countries in debt. Key actors were the Bretton Woods institutions following their recapture by Northern-based capital interests; new international organizations such as the OECD and the G7 Group of countries; regional organizations such as the European Union and the Asia-Pacific Economic Cooperation (APEC); and regional trade and economic agreements such as the North American Free Trade Association (NAFTA).[88] The debates generated around the 'Washington Consensus' model of economic reform became a catalyst for renewed calls for reform of the international institutions. Within a few years, these principles had been denounced, notably by Joseph Stiglitz, former Chief Economist at the World Bank. Nonetheless, throughout the 1990s, the same principles continued to be applied as loan conditionalities to debt-ridden countries.[89]

Undermining the United Nations

In an examination of the transformation of the political space occupied by the UN, Camilleri questions the nature of that space not only in terms of the state sovereignty (and non-intervention)– human rights dichotomy but also in terms of mandate, representation and role within the structures of global governance.[90] Another question might concern who occupies the political space of the international agencies of the UN when, as in the case of Bosnia, the condemnation of the countries involved in the attack on Bosnia by the International Court of Justice results in the United States' refusal to acknowledge the jurisdiction of the Court?[91] Or, in the case of Somalia and the Iraq–Kuwait conflict noted by Camilleri, the decision of the UN to sanction the use of force functioned to sub-ordinate the international organization to 'the strategic imperatives of the US'?[92] If, as Richard Falk argues in his examination of the need for UN reform,[93] the UN is an extension of the state system and therefore inevitably must reflect the problems inherent within the system, or if, as Wallerstein argues, the crisis of the UN is a reflection of the larger crisis of the world system,[94] what is the nature and impact of that crisis as it pertains to the UN?

An important phase of the redefining of the institutions of inter-national order during the 1980s was signalled by an increasing tendency on the part of industrialized countries, and in particular the US, to reject the United Nations as a vehicle for international action and the resolution of international affairs.[95] Conspicuously led by the US Congress and driven by influential neoliberal lobby groups, this quasi-withdrawal by the US from UN commitments during the late 1970s and 1980s was a response to the view that the peripheral countries were using their majority in the UN assemblies in ways contrary to the interests of the world economy.[96] The transformation of the United Nations from supporter of Third World development to partner of transnational corporations and agent of global capitalism involved the deliberate manipulation of UN indebtedness and an overt undermining of its authority on several fronts. While payment of dues to the UN by member states has not been devoid of problems from the beginning, in the late 1970s the United States began a process of systematic and deliberate withholding of dues as a coercive strategy. Whereas the US had previously been a strong supporter of the payment of member countries' dues as a legal treaty obligation, by 1979 calls for tighter control over UN spending, especially on policies with which the US government and Congress members did not agree, had accelerated.[97] During the period of the Reagan administration, hostility towards the UN from within the US Congress markedly increased under the influence of right-wing conservative groups. The influence of organizations such as the Heritage Foundation, vociferous throughout the 1980s in its demands for UN reform, the subsequent continued withholding of United States dues and the downsizing of the UN General Assembly saw the United Nations come under increasing pressure. By 1985, the UN had been forced to curtail its spending by 10 per cent and drastically reduce staff.

US Congress efforts at reforming the United Nations during this period took the form of both legislative and executive action. One example of the latter was the withdrawal of the United States from the United Nations Educational, Scientific and Cultural Organization (UNESCO) in 1984. By the end of the 1980s, the UN crisis had reached extreme proportions. Contributing factors were the rejection of the United Nations as a vehicle for international action and the shift toward unilateral action by industrialized countries, in particular the US, and combined collective action by industrial powers facilitated by transnational networks. By 1990, US dues to the United Nations totalled over 70 per cent of the total arrears owed to the United Nations, over US$1 billion of which were peacekeeping dues.[98] Throughout the 1990s, reformist discourses that undermined the legitimacy and validity of the United Nations gained greater currency with the assertion of neoliberal economic policies and the reconfiguration of the United Nations role. The appointment of Boutros Boutros-Ghali as UN Secretary-General in 1992 was instrumental in redefining the meaning of sovereignty and in restructuring the institutions of the UN. One of the first targets of his series of reforms was the Centre on Transnational Corporations. In his first year, Ghali removed its director, its organizational autonomy and most of its budget. The following year the CTC was replaced with UNCTAD, which was given a mandate to work with transnational corporations in stimulating flows of foreign investment to developing countries.[99] In the same period, development aid was transformed into 'technical assistance' and work on disarmament that had been an important priority was downgraded. As United Nations indebtedness grew, its ability to maintain its peacekeeping operations diminished.

The prelude to the fiftieth anniversary of the United Nations in 1995 provided the environment for renewed attacks on the United

Nations, again led by the US. On the eve of the fiftieth anniversary, the UN Withdrawal Act called for the withdrawal of the United States from the UN by the year 2000, arguing that it no longer served the national interests of the United States. In a move reminiscent of the McCarthy period when the US installed an office at the UN to check on US citizens working there, legislation passed by the US Congress in 1997 demanded the establishment of an Inspector-General at the UN to ensure that dues going to the UN were utilized in a manner that met the approval of the US. Echoing the Foreign Relations Authorization Act, Fiscal Years 1994 and 1995,[100] it also required that the UN accept a vastly reduced figure for US dues.

In the face of a gathering momentum of protests against the rising tide of economic liberalism within the UN from non-governmental organizations and the group of developing countries, strong US pressures within the UN General Assembly, combined with the severity of the UN economic crisis, dictated the passing of resolutions that advocated UN social and economic reform and much closer liaison with the Bretton Woods institutions. While developing countries supported the strengthening of the UN and the retention of UNCTAD, the United States called for the removal of all responsibility for economic development from ECOSOC, the closure of UN agencies such as UNCTAD on the grounds of inefficiency and duplication of effort, and the reservation of responsibility for the world's economic and social policies to the Bretton Woods institutions and the World Trade Organization (WTO).[101]

The undermining of the UN delinked aid to Third World countries from the Bretton Woods institutions, paved the way for US-led demands for reform of the UN and the undermining of the UN Security Council, and laid the groundwork for a new partnership between the institutions of the UN and some of the world's most powerful transnational business interests. Springboarded by the accelerating economic crisis of the UN, by a series of International Chamber of Commerce-sponsored consultations between the UN and transnational business, and by the intensified dialogue between the UN and the Bretton Woods institutions, and formally proposed by the UN Secretary-General at the World Economic Forum in Davos in January 1999, the UN Global Compact included amongst its founding members transnational corporations with controversial records in respect of indigenous peoples, labour rights and the environment.[102] This new linkage between global capital and the United Nations was a significant development in the establishment of a global constitution for world order. In the words of UN Secretary-General Kofi Annan, the Compact represented the uniting of 'the power of the market with universal ideals'.[103] By signing up to environmental and labour-friendly non-enforceable declarations, members of the Global Compact receive the right to use a specially designed UN logo, thus implying UN approval of their business values, policies and practices. This embedding of the social in the economic at the level of the highest international institution elevated the hegemony of the market over human rights to a new level.

The Shift to Global Imperialism

The shift in the accountability of the Bretton Woods institutions from the UN to global capital that occurred in the 1980s and 1990s was the culmination of a process that included the deliberate defunding and weakening of the UN in response to the shift in the balance of power within the UN General Assembly and the privatization of assets throughout the developing and much of the developed world. The driving impetus was the transition from Keynesian economics to Hayekian neoliberalism and the emergence of a new global class of transnational elites. From the mid-1960s, finance and militarism became increasingly intertwined as the two main coercive strategies for enforcing compliance with the exigencies of a globalizing world economy.[104] Following the severing of the dollar from the gold standard, US military power and its role in the world were increasingly enmeshed in the negotiations among the treasuries and central banks of the chief industrialized powers. The increase in US budget deficits during the 1970s, managed by increased borrowing from foreign societies, culminated in the US achieving the position of the world's biggest debtor nation by 1987 (some US$400 billion). Unlike other debtor nations who have been forced to submit to 'structural adjustment programmes', however, military force and financial coercion enabled the US to maintain its position of dominance.

By the beginning of the 1990s, the emergent global order was one in which militarist interventions coupled with the reconstitution of democracy provided the strategic and political underpinnings for a new global constitutionalism. Signalled by US President George Bush Senior's declaration of a 'New World Order', a dramatic acceleration in the promotion of polyarchy was accompanied by an overt increase in militarist interventionism that frequently occurred despite strong world opinion and protest. The unleashing of the pressures of international finance on a heavily indebted Third World and the promotion of US-backed revolutionary destabilizing movements in Central America culminating in acts of direct aggression against the oil state of Kuwait, an act described by Cox as an object lesson to the Third World of the consequences of acting in ways contrary to the interests of the global economy.[105] Facilitated by the deliberate destabilizing of strategic countries, the promotion of 'democracy' by the defenders of the 'free world' legitimated a series of military interventions during the 1990s that successfully brought Eastern Europe under the control of the core industrial countries, and regions containing massive oil reserves under the guardianship of US peacekeepers. Dominating the redefined relationships were discourses of security underpinned by a shift from the common road of universal civilization to global apartheid, as represented by the statistical gulf between the loss of life of 115 American soldiers and over 100,000 Iraqis. As Sachs tellingly observes, the concept of young, 'emerging' nations full of potential and for whom a golden future was assured now gave way to the concept of Third World countries as breeders of violence and terrorism.[106] It also, Cox points out, brought transparency regarding the change in the direction of global politics and the shift from the hegemonic system that had been in place since the 1970s.[107] At the same time, the Third World became further acquainted with the perils of defying the power guarding the global economy.

Many analysts viewed the 1991 US military intervention in Iraq and the announcement of a 'New World Order' by George Bush Snr as marking the final act in a century of strategic moves to embed coercive US imperialism at the heart of the global order. In an action redolent of the rejection by the US of the 1986 International Court of Justice decision against America's support of military actions by the so-called 'Contras' against the government of Nicaragua, the US-led invasion of Iraq in 2003 signalled the final rejection of the role and function of the UN in its role as mediator and coordinator in what had been seen as a liberal international order. Harvey suggests that although ostensibly about the removal of yet another dictator in the name of freedom and democracy, the invasion provided a useful domestic diversion from the fact of America's current account crisis that saw it become the world's biggest debtor nation of all time.[108] What it most certainly did do was position American strategic bases and US-based transnational corporations in the centre of the world's primary oil-producing region and the most geopolitically strategic position in the globe. With its roots in a series of geopolitical manoeuvres that from 1945 onwards sought control of the Middle East, the ratcheting up of US militarism in the Middle East signalled a new phase of global dominance in which military might needs no other justification beyond American geo-economic and strategic interest.

By the mid-1990s, the imposition of monetarist reform programmes had successfully recolonized the Third World, Russia's threat to the industrial dominance of the US had been disabled by the imposition of structural adjustment and the sell-off of Russia's industry, and the East Asian threat to the economic dominance of the United States had been successfully routed. The Federation of Yugoslavia had been dismantled and land containing potentially large reservoirs of oil on the borders of Bosnia had been brought under US control through militaristic North Atlantic Treaty Organization (NATO) exercises under the direction of the US. Efforts to restrict the influence of transnational corporations on international politics and national interests had been overturned in favour of international arrangements that protected the economic interests of transnational capital above those of countries and citizens whose labour had been transformed into a 'standing reserve'.

The shift from the bipolar world of the Cold War, at the end of which the world might well have expected a reduction in US standing armies around the globe, saw the emergence of new forms of domination. In this period, the locus of hegemony shifted from a dominant state to a global cabal of financiers, industrialists and neoliberal intellectuals on whose behalf new modalities of militarist and financial intervention were developed and 'democracy' became synonymous with the needs of capital and finance. The vehicle for this transition was the US state itself. The emergence of new neoconservative think tanks, notably including the Washington-based Project for a New American Century (PNAC), saw a remarkable increase in the level of US military presence around the globe. As expressed in the PNAC document 'Rebuilding America's Defences: Strategies, Forces and Resources for a New Century', 'America's strategic goal used to be containment of the Soviet Union; today the task is to preserve an international security environment conducive to American interests and ideals.'

'The irreducible bottom line of US grand strategy during the 1990s', Bacevich writes, was that '[f]aced with opposition and under duress, the United States would do whatever was necessary to achieve its purposes'.[109] The goal of full spectrum dominance was to become the key strategy towards achieving that goal. During this period and particularly during the 1996 World Economic Forum meeting in Davos, the anti-globalization movement began to emerge in full strength.

Notes

1   Dale, Roger (1999) 'Globalization: a new world for comparative education?', in M. Jurgen Schweimer (ed.), *Discourse on Comparative Education*. Bern: Peter Lang, p. 3.
2   Cox, Robert W. (1996) [1992a] 'Global perestroika', in Robert W. Cox (with Timothy J. Sinclair), *Approaches to World Order*. Cambridge: Cambridge University Press, p. 296.
3   Jessop, Bob (1999) 'Reflections on globalization and its (il)logics' (draft), the Department of Sociology, Lancaster University, online at http://www/comp.lancaster.ac.uk?sociology/soc013rj.htmpl
4   Cox (1996) [1992a], p. 298.
5   Richards, Gareth Api (1999) 'Challenging Asia–Europe relations from below?' *Journal of the Asia Pacific Economy*, 4 (1), pp. 146–70.
6   Cox (1996) [1983] 'Gramsci, hegemony and international relations', p. 137.
7   Arrighi, Giovanni and Beverly J. Silver (1999) *Chaos and Governance in the Modern World System*. Minneapolis and London: University of Minnesota Press, p. 26.
8   *Ibid.*, p. 34.
9   Van der Pijl, Kees (1995) 'The second glorious revolution: globalizing elites and historical change', in Bjorn Hettne (ed.), *International Political Economy. Understanding Global Disorder*. London and Halifax, Nova Scotia: Zed Books, pp. 100–28.
10 Gosovic, Branislav (1972) *UNCTAD. Conflict and Compromise. The Third World's Quest for an Equitable World Economic Order through the United Nations*. Leiden: A. W. Sijthoff.
11 The Third Non-Aligned Nations Summit Conference meeting in Lusaka, Zambia, 8–10 September 1970.
12 UN General Assembly Resolution 3281 (XXIX) adopted 12 December 1974.
13 *Ibid.*
14 Robinson, John (1983) *Multinationals and Political Control*. New York: St Martins Press, p. 165.
15 UN Economic and Social Council Resolution 1721 (L.III) adopted 28 July 1972.
16 Robinson (1983), p. 164.
17 UN Economic and Social Council Resolution 1913 (LVII), adopted 5 December 1974.
18 Robinson (1983), p. 165.
19 *Ibid.*, p. 151.
20 *Ibid.*, p. 152.
21 Cox (1996) [1979] 'Ideologies and the New International Economic Order', pp. 377–8.
22 *Ibid.*, pp. 376–419.
23 *Ibid.*
24 *Ibid.*, p. 394–5.
25 *Ibid.*, p. 397.

26 The declaration of the World Council of Indigenous Peoples (WCIP) Northwest Regional Conference on the Emerging International Economic Order was a response to increasing demands on the natural resources and raw materials of the indigenous nations within newly created and developing nation states. See 'The New International Economic Order: Promise or Peril for the Indigenous Peoples of the World?' Northwest Conference on the Emerging International Economic Order, Plenary Session, 30 March 1979.

27 Cox (1996) [1979], p. 383. See also Frieden, Jeff (1980) 'Economics and politics in the 1970s', in H. Sklar (ed.), *Trilateralism. The Trilateral Commission and Elite Planning for World Management*. Boston: South End Press, p. 66.

28 In particular, the Trilateral Commission, the Heritage Foundation, and the Council for Foreign Relations.

29 Van der Pijl describes the Chase Manhattan Bank as 'the most central firm in the international network of interlocking directorates in that period'. Van der Pijl (1995), p. 123. The Bilderberg group, so named after the hotel in Holland where the group's first meeting was held in 1954, is an elite coterie of Western thinkers and power brokers, comprising some of the West's chief political movers, business leaders, bankers, industrialists and strategic thinkers. It celebrated its 50th anniversary at its annual meeting in 2004 – held, like all Bilderberg get-togethers, behind strictly closed doors.

30 Gill, Stephen (1991) 'Historical materialism, Gramsci and international political economy', in Craig Murphy and Roger Tooze (eds.), *New International Political Economy*. Colorado: Lynne Rienner, pp. 51–78.

31 Cf. Sklar (1980).

32 The Heritage Foundation describes itself on its website as 'a think tank – whose mission is to formulate and promote conservative public policies based on the principles of free enterprise, limited government, individual freedom, traditional American values, and a strong national defence'.

33 Peters, Michael (2001) 'Foucault and governmentality: understanding the neoliberal paradigm of educational policy'. AERA Symposium, New Zealand Association for Research in Education. AERA Conference, Seattle.

34 Burchell, D. (1997) '"Liberalism" and government: political philosophy and the Liberal Art of Rule' in C. O'Farrell (ed.), *Foucault: the Legacy*. Brisbane: Queensland University of Technology, cited *ibid*.

35 Peters (2001). See also Chapter 4, this book.

36 *Ibid*.

37 http://cepa.newschool.edu/het/schools/newinst.htm, cited Peters (2001).

38 Robinson, William I. (1996) *Promoting Polyarchy. Globalization, US Intervention, and Hegemony*. Cambridge: Cambridge University Press, p. 42.

39 *Ibid*., p. 44.

40 Crozier, Michael, Huntington, Samuel and Joji Watanuku (1975), *The Crisis of Democracy. Task Force Report No. 8*, New York: New York University Press.

41 Text of Introductory Chapter, http://www.trilateral.org.projwork/tfrsums/ tfr08.htm

42 *Ibid*.

43 *Ibid*.

44 Robinson explains that polyarchy, a structural-functionalist concept developed by US academic Robert Dahl, refers to 'a system by which a small group actually rules and mass participation in decision making is confined to leadership choice in elections carefully managed by competing elites'. Robinson (1996), p. 49.

45 *Ibid*.

46 *Ibid*., p. 42.

47 *Ibid*., pp. 55, 62.

48 *Ibid.*, p. 52.
49 *Ibid.*, p. 58.
50 *Ibid.*, p. 60.
51 *Ibid.*, pp. 60-61.
52 *Ibid.*, p. 40.
53 'Project Democracy' statement before the Sub-Committee on International Operations of the House Foreign Affairs Committee, 23 February 1983, cited *ibid.*, pp. 107–8.
54 Gill, Stephen (1991) *American Hegemony and the Trilateral Commission.* Cambridge: Cambridge University Press.
55 Robinson (1996), pp. 77–8.
56 These proposals were first signalled by Gardener, Richard (1974) 'The hard road to world order', *Foreign Affairs*, April, Council for Foreign Affairs.
57 *Ibid.*, pp. 34–8, 41–2.
58 *Ibid.* See also Bergsten, Fred, Berthoin, Georges and Kinhide Mushakoji (1976) *The Reform of International Institutions. Task Force Report No. 11,* New York: The Trilateral Commission, text of summary of report accessed 22 September 2001 at http://www.trilateral.org/projwork/tfrsums/tfr11.htm
59 *Ibid.*
60 Cooper, Richard, Kaiser, Karl and Masataka Kosaka (1977) *Towards a Renovated International System.* Task Force Report No. 14. New York: The Trilateral Commission.
61 Cox, R. W. (1996) [1992b] 'Multilateralism and world order', p. 511.
62 Held, David, McGrew, Anthony, Goldplatt, David and Jonathan Perraton (1999) *Global Transformations: Politics, Economics and Culture.* Stanford, CA: Stanford University Press, p. 164.
63 Rachel Carson's *The Silent Spring,* published in 1962, detailed the devastating impact of pesticides and other toxic material on the environment: it generated a great deal of debate. George Sessions, however, points out that biological scientists had been actively concerned with the deteriorating state of the world since at least the mid-1950s. Sessions, George (ed.) (1995) *Deep Ecology for the Twenty-First Century. Readings on the Philosophy and Practice of the New Environmentalism.* Boston and London: Shambala, p. 87.
64 Dryzek, John S. (1997) *The Politics of the Earth. Environmental Discourses.* Oxford: Oxford University Press, p. 20.
65 Meadows, Donella H., Dennis, L., Randers, Jorgen and William H. Behrens (III) (1972) *The Limits to Growth.* New York: Universe Books.
66 Sachs, Wolfgang (1999) *Planet Dialectics. Explorations in Environment and Development.* London and New York: Zed Books, p. 57.
67 Concerns about the impact of global warming were first articulated in work by both Tower and the Swedish meteorologist Arheius in the late nineteenth century. See Goldplatt, David (1995) 'Liberal democracy and the globalization of environmental risks', in Daniel Archibugi and David Held (eds.), *Cosmopolitan Democracy. An Agenda for a New World Order.* Cambridge: MA: Polity Press, pp. 87–9.
68 Dryzek (1997), pp. 108–11.
69 Posey, Darrell Adison (2001) 'Intellectual property rights and the sacred balance: some spiritual consequences from the commercialization of traditional resources', in John A. Grim (ed.), *Indigenous Traditions and Ecology. The Interbeing of Cosmology and Community.* Cambridge, MA: Harvard University Press, p. 12.
70 UN Convention on Biodiversity, Article 8(j).
71 *Ibid.*
72 Ryser, R. (1999) 'Biodiversity convention threatens fourth world nations with

extinction', *Fourth World Eye*, 2 (July), online newsletter, Centre for World Indigenous Studies, accessed 1999 at http://www.cwis.org/fweye-2.html

73 Sachs (1999), p. 27.

74 *Ibid.*

75 McMichael, Philip (1995) 'The new colonialism: global regulation and the restructuring of the interstate system', in David A. Smith and Joszef Borocz (eds.), *New World Order? Global Transformations in the Late Twentieth Century*. Westport, CT: Greenwood Press, pp. 37–53.

76 Harvey, David (2003) *The New Imperialism*. Oxford: Oxford University Press, p. 184.

77 Chossudovsky, Michel (1997) *The Globalization of Poverty. Impacts of IMF and World Bank Reforms*. Manila: Institute of Political Economy and Penang: Third World Network, p. 37.

78 *Ibid.*, p. 15.

79 *Ibid.*, p. 51.

80 Gervasi, Sean (1993) 'Germany, US and the Yugoslav Crisis', *Covert Action Quarterly*, 43 (Winter 1992–3), cited in Chossudovsky (1997), p. 244.

81 *The Banker*, January 1995, cited Chossudovsky (1997), p. 246.

82 World Bank (1983) *Yugoslavia, Industrial Restructuring, Study, Overview and Issues for Restructuring*, cited Chossudovsky (1997), p. 249.

83 *The San Francisco Chronicle*, 28 August 1995, cited Chossudovsky (1997), p. 250.

84 Chossudovsky (1997), pp. 243–63. This has particular salience in the context of post-war Iraq: the war on Iraq was legitimated by discourses of weapons of mass destruction, which, tellingly, have since failed to materialize, despite the efforts of hundreds of inspectors and military weapons seekers.

85 See Chossudovsky, M. (1998) 'Global poverty in the late twentieth century', *Journal of International Affairs*, 52 (1) (Fall).

86 See Williamson, John (1993) 'Democracy and the Washington Consensus', *World Development*, 21 (8), pp. 1329–36.

87 These principles of economic reform became a prerequisite for IMF/World Bank loans to developing countries.

88 Dale, Roger (1999) 'Specifying globalization effects on national policy: a focus on the mechanisms', *Journal of Education Policy*, 14 (1), pp. 1–18.

89 For a discussion of contestations around the Washington Consensus, see Naim, Moises (1999) 'Fads and fashion in economic reforms: Washington consensus or Washington confusion?', *Foreign Policy Magazine*, 26 October.

90 Camilleri, Joseph (1998) 'The UN's place in the era of globalization: a four-dimensional perspective', in Albert J Paolini, Anthony P. Jarvis and Christian Reus-Smit (eds.), *Between Sovereignty and Global Governance: the United Nations, the State, and Civil Society*. Basingstoke: MacMillan Press and New York: St Martin's Press.

91 A key issue here is that the decisions of the Court are binding only when countries agree to accept them. For a thoughtful review of the powers of the ICJ, see Roberts, Ken (1995) 'Second-guessing the Security Council. The International Court of Justice and its powers of judicial review', *Peace International Law Review* (Spring).

92 *Ibid.*, p. 336.

93 Falk, Richard (1998) 'The outlook for UN reform: necessary but impossible', in Paolini, Jarvis and Reus-Smit (eds.), pp. 296–311.

94 Wallerstein, I. (1998) 'The new world disorder: if the states collapse, can the nations be united?' in Paolini, Jarvis and Reus-Smit (eds.), pp. 171–85.

95 Cf. Cox (1996) [1992b], p. 497.

96 *Ibid.*, p. 512.

97 Global Policy Forum (1998) 'Background and history of the UN financial crisis', accessed 6 December 1998 at
http://www.igc.org/globalpolicy/finance/chronol.hist.htm

98 Global Policy Forum (1998) 'US percentage share of the total regular budget arrears: 1975–1995', accessed 6 December 1998 at
http://www.igc.org/globalpolicy/finance/tables/tab.htm

99 Gosovic (1972).

100 'Legislation on Foreign Relations through 1996', PL 103–236 [HR 2333], Sec. 401, US House of Representatives and US Senate, 103rd Congress, 2nd Session, pp. 1766–76, cited in Schaefer, Brett D. (1997) *The United Nations Reform Act of 1997. A Step in the Right Direction.* The Heritage Foundation, Document No. 241, 18 July 1997, online at http://www.heritage.org/

101 Khor, Martin (1996) 'A greater need for the UN in a liberalizing global world'. Third World Network, accessed 17 November 1998 at
http://www.globalpolicy.org/socecon/un/ khor.htm

102 In particular, Nike, Rio Tinto, Placer Dome, Novartis, Aventis, Shell Group.

103 Annan, Kofi (1999) Speech to the World Economic Forum at Davos, January, accessed 13 June 2000 at http://65.214.34/30/un/gc/unweb.nsf/

104 *Ibid.*

105 Cox (1996) [1991] 'Structural issues of governance', p. 239.

106 Sachs (1999).

107 Cox (1996), p. 33.

108 Harvey (2003), p. 14.

109 Bacevich, Andrew (2002) *American Empire. The Realities and Consequences of American Diplomacy.* Cambridge, MA and London: Harvard University Press.

❊

CHAPTER 6

Globalization, Regionalism
and the Neoliberal State

Local Engagement in New Zealand

The transformation of the state's functions into variants of the neoliberal form of competitive states in both developing and developed countries coincided with changes in the productive powers and the balance of social and financial forces throughout the interstate system. As we saw in the previous chapter, whilst having occurred most notably within developing countries, these structural changes have also had an impact on OECD countries. One of the spatio-economic characteristics of globalization is the changing role of the state in relation to new formations of regionalization. One perspective of new forms of regionalism that has been advanced by critical political economists is in terms of the second phase of Polyani's 'double movement' – the protective response by civil society to the over-expansion of the market (Polanyi's first phase) such as occurred in the nineteenth century. Hettne, for instance, sees new forms of regionalism as a 'bottom–up' response by states to the dominance of market models imposed from the top.[1] In this case, new regionalism is seen as enabling wider participation at the base. This perspective of contemporary forms of regionalism as a non-hegemonic, bottom–up movement reflects two neomercantilist assumptions that in my view are problematic.

The first assumption is that states commonly act in the best interests of civil society; the second is that the ending of the Cold War signalled a non- or post-hegemonic era. In the context of the arguments developed in the previous chapter, I follow Mittleman's assertion that, 'against the background of US hegemony, regionalism in its various formats is an important feature of hegemonic geo-politics'.[2] As a number of authors have noted, territorial power formations, whether seemingly benign or otherwise, are an important arena for the playing out of geopolitical struggles for power and hegemony. Harvey points out that while the rise of sub-imperial formations in Europe and East- South-east Asia defined territorial spheres of influence, these spheres were often overlapping and interpenetrating rather than exclusive. The triadic regional formation with North America at the apex is not, he suggests, necessarily stable. Seen against the backdrop of the Eurasian geo-political struggle for dominance, fluctuations in economic power and the frequently destabilizing influence of militarism combine to produce an environment that is decidedly fragile. Another arena of struggle is that between the European Union and the US. Harvey suggests that the increasing integration of the EU offers the potential for an integrated economy that is as least on a par with that of the US.

Changes to the role and functions of the nation state have important consequences in the context of a globalized world order and the aspirations of indigenous peoples. These consequences are far from uniform, being shaped by the regional and national specificities that define indigenous peoples' historical experience and contemporary engagement with the nation state. Attempts at constructive engage-ment with states on the part of indigenous peoples in internally colonized territories include efforts to negotiate forms of shared governance framed around the principle of shared sovereignty. In many cases, where treaties entered into on a 'nation to nation' basis determined in principle although not in practice the parameters of colonial settlement, indigenous peoples' demands for juridical recognition of indigenous customary rights and sovereignty over their lands and resources have given rise to new or renegotiated treaties between states and indigenous nations and a redefining of the parameters of relationships between states and indigenous peoples. In other cases, pre-existing treaties are acknowledged and addressed (although not without protracted struggle and contention) through negotiated settlements involving land, resources and financial compensation.

Framed within discourses of restitution and reconciliation, these settlements are construed as providing indigenous peoples with the means of self-development and the re-establishment of a level of social and economic, if not juridical, autonomy. From another per-spective, the settlement of treaty claims by the bestowal of financial compensation and the return of some natural resources has the more prosaic purpose of removing hindrances to and opening up opportunities for foreign investment. The co-optation of tribal elites within a Western paradigm of corporatization and commodification plays a crucial role here. In cases where, as in externally colonized territories such as Australia, Canada and New Zealand, relationships between indigenous peoples and states were reassessed and structures for more participatory forms of governance negotiated, the increasing influence of new forms of liberalism had a prescribing influence that shaped these relationships in frequently problematic ways. In the neoliberal climate of the reconstruction of civil society, the undermining of collectivity has aroused growing concern. This undermining is manifested, for example, in the reshaping of indigenous identities and the construction of corporate institutions as pseudo-traditional social and cultural institutions. Within this neocolonial framework, indigenous knowledge forms are subjected to commodification, on one hand, and, on the other, devaluation and marginalization through reductionist reconstructions.

I begin this chapter with an examination of regionalism as a site of contested power relations. Drawing on Mittleman's analysis of two forms of regionalism, as outlined in the Introduction to this book, the thrust of my argument is that regionalism has emerged as a site of struggle for global hegemony. I look at this from two perspectives: (1) the transnational shaping of the European Union into what Robert Cooper, formerly British Prime Minister Tony Blair's senior foreign policy adviser, calls the postmodern state, and (2) the transformation in the Pacific (now commonly referred to as 'Asia-Pacific') from strategic exploitation disguised as benevolent aid to undisguised economic hegemony in the form of APEC and free trade agreements. Although I have not included in my analysis any acknowledgement of what Jessop refers to as the diffusion of the post-war American model of relations of production or the expansion into Europe of foreign (primarily American) capital,[3] any full discussion of regionalization surely requires this dimension. My main focus here, however, is the transformation of the structures of the state through the processes of globalization as manifested, in this case, by regionalization in the Pacific.

In the previous chapter, I noted that the transformation of state economies in developing countries occurred alongside militarist interventions. In industrialized countries, including New Zealand, the transformation of the state has similarly occurred alongside new coercive technologies. In place of militarism, however, these technologies are discernible in new forms of surveillance and discursively driven reconstitutions of the self. Here I examine aspects of the changing role and function of the nation state in the context of the transformation of the state in New Zealand from a Keynesian welfare model to one of the most liberalized forms of the neoliberal competitive state and the impact on Maori endeavours towards self-determination. Thus in the second half of the chapter the focus is on contemporary relationships between states and indigenous peoples at the local level. Two sets of examples provide a means for examining some of the inherent tensions that accrue from state-imposed treaty settlement processes. An analysis of the Nisga'a Nation's treaty settlement in British Columbia by James Tully highlights some of the tensions and contradictions faced by many indigenous peoples in mediating forms of self-determination with the occupying states. In New Zealand, the Ngai Tahu treaty settlement provides an opportunity to explore some of the contested issues in the context of negotiations between the state and the indigenous elite. Questions highlighted here concern the nature of indigenous peoples' aspirations for representation and redress, the interpretation of sovereignty as an indigenous discourse, and the impact of the commodifying impulse played out in the reshaping of indigenous identities and in the construction of corporate institutions as traditional social and cultural institutions.

Two key themes underpin my discussion in the final section. First, utilizing Smith's cyclical model of conscientization, resistance and co-optation as the basis for incremental change[4] and Alfred's exploration of traditional notions of indigenous sovereignty and their interpretation today,[5] I contend that attempts to co-opt indigenous struggles for self-determination within the Western ideological framework of developmentalism can best be understood in terms of new forms of colonization. Second, I draw attention to alternative models that emerge out of traditional principles and practices. These principles, I contend, have the potential to be embedded as motifs for a transformative approach to global order.

New Regionalism and the Postmodern State

There is, of course, nothing new in the modern concept of regionalism. As Mittleman observes, territorial autarchies begin to emerge in the 1930s.[6] In the 'old' regionalism model such as that which developed after the Second World War in the Asia-Pacific region, the world was seen as divided into military blocs that are 'sometimes competing, sometimes aligned'.[7] This form of regionalism, created by the superpowers in the bipolar context, is characterized as an imposed, top-down model. In the Asia–Pacific, it gave rise to a number of organizations, many of which were centred round the UN vision of regionalism as a means of promoting mechanisms for the management and settlement of regional disputes and conflicts. A contemporary example of this is NATO.

The 1970s, Mittleman states, saw the delinking of Third World countries and the development of forms of collective self-reliance among developing and non-aligned states. The response was the development of neoliberal forms of regionalism in which the ability of states to control their own trade was heavily diminished. Mittleman contrasts two main forms of neoliberal regionalism – an extroverted model that opens to market forces and an inward-looking model such as has developed in Europe. It is this closed, inward-looking model that has given rise to what has been termed Fortress Europe. It has also given rise to a new nomenclature – the postmodern state and a new form of empire.

In the foreword to Cooper's *The Postmodern State and the World Order*, foreign policy analysts Tom Bentley and Mark Leonard assert that the end of the Cold War in 1989, which was followed in 1990 by George Bush Senior's declaration of a 'New World Order', gave way to a 'widespread sense of disorder fuelled by ethnic warfare, resurgent nationalism, and disintegration'.[8] This declaration of disorder, conflict and disintegration cleverly prepares us for understanding empire as the only rational response to chaos. Cooper himself declares that there is no new world order but a new triadic division of the existing order. For Cooper, the ending of the Cold War signalled a point of transformation of a magnitude similar to the emergence of the state system marked by the signing of the Peace of Westphalia in 1647. Thus 1989 marked the end of the balance-of-power system in Europe and the beginning of a radically new postmodern structure in which, according to Cooper, nationalism gives way to internationalism, and in which the freedom of the individual has finally triumphed over the will of the collective. In this view, the kind of the world we have depends on the kind of states that compose it.[9] 'A postmodern world requires a postmodern state',[10] which, for Cooper, embodies the ideals of openness and transnational cooperation and is 'the ultimate consequence of the open society'.[11] The ultimate end product of this process is 'the freedom of the individual; first protected by the state and later protected from the state'.[12]

Cooper's triadic division of the world comprises a premodern zone of chaos, a zone of danger consisting of the modern world of the classical nationalist state system, and the postmodern 'zone of safety' represented by the European Union (EU) model described as 'the most developed example of a postmodern system'.[13] The important characteristics of this system of postmodern order are mutual interference in traditionally domestic affairs coupled with mutual surveillance, the breaking down of the distinction between domestic and foreign affairs, the growing irrelevance of borders, and the rejection of force for dispute solving. Added to this is the relinquishment of state sovereignty in favour of regional cooperation with regard to security arrangements.[14] Cooper's view of the postmodern state focuses largely on issues of order and security. Transnational cooperation and openness pertain largely to security arrangements. Postmodern states are marked by an absence of war but only among themselves, as Cooper tellingly warns against dropping their guard against the dangers of the modern or the chaos of the premodern zones. Thus in Europe, at least, regionalized governance, in which nation-state sovereignty has been superseded by regional sovereignty, has become elevated to a new, more highly developed form of state in which the defence of regional borders against the nationalisms of those less developed is paramount. Fortress Europe indeed! However Europe is somewhat less isolationist than Cooper would have it. As Bacevich points out, bilateral arrangements between EU member nations and the application of neoliberal economics, combined with America's position at the head of NATO and the military presence of 100,000 troops across Europe, contribute to America's aim of ensuring, if not dominance, at least hegemony in the region. The 100,000 US troops stationed in East Asia play a similar role in maintaining American hegemony in the Asia-Pacific.

Regionalism and Hegemony in the Asia-Pacific

Where the constant redrawing of Europe's maps has been driven by political struggles between empires, between Church and civil society, and between competing states, the Pacific has been the site of multiple deterritorializations and reterritorializations through successive waves of colonization. The Pacific was the last area in the world to be drawn into the capitalist system. Demographically vast and complex, there is little consensus among political economists about the geographical delineation of the region recently discursively constructed as 'Asia-Pacific'. For the indigenous peoples who have traded their way across its vast expanses for literally thousands of years, the Pacific is defined by the boundaries of Te Moana-nui-a-Kiwa – the great ocean of Kiwa, the famous adventurer/explorer ancestral figure. For many, it is the originating point of *whakapapa* or genealogy; for others it is also the location of a 'sacred triangle' encompassing Easter Island, Hawai'i, and New Zealand.

As Mack and Ravenhill observe, regions are 'inevitably the constructs of analysts and decision makers'.[15] In the eighteenth century, the Pacific was identified by the imperial powers as an area of immense strategic importance and unlimited natural wealth. Announcing the US 'Open Door' policy of nineteenth-century American imperialism, American diplomat Alfred Knopf declared that 'our largest trade henceforth will be with Asia'. 'The Pacific', he stated, 'is our ocean. The Power that rules the Pacific ... is the Power that rules the world. And with the Philippines, that Power is and will forever be the American Republic.'[16] The site of countless waves of invasion, appropriation and dispossession, the Pacific continues to have strategic importance for its military bases and as a testing site and storage base for nuclear warfare, to the irreversible detriment of its peoples and lagoons. Peters, Green and Fitzsimons observe that the region referred to as the Asia-Pacific is made up of highly disparate socio-politico-cultural-economic entities, yet within the plethora of literature concerning the Asia-Pacific region that has emerged during the 1990s, these disparities are seldom mentioned. In this equation, the smaller island countries of the South Pacific section of the 'Pacific Rim' disappear like the proverbial 'hole in the doughnut'. In this sense, Asia-Pacific is identifiable as a discursive construct predicated primarily on economic and strategic interests.

Mark and Ravenhill note that during the Cold War decades the Asia-Pacific region developed as a major site on which the ideological and strategic rivalries joined battle. During this period, US hegemonic interests played a significant role in artificially constructing a hugely disparate geographic area into a singular region, albeit one based largely on economic interest, while simultaneously buttressing Asia-Pacific security arrangements against the spread of Asian Communism. American aid monies and military spending in the Asia-Pacific region played a major role in the expansion of the Japanese and other South-east Asian economies. Bilateral arrangements between the US and countries such as Japan, Malaysia,

Singapore, Taiwan and Korea, all of whom were recipients of US aid monies during the Cold War period. As Richard Stubbs asserts, while the most obvious consequence of these strategies was the trans-formation of the region's economies, another significant consequence was the expansion of the institutional state and its buttressing against the demands of weakened civil societies, in particular labour, social groups and left-wing movements.[17]

By the 1970s, a 'relatively strong state' with a 'reasonably competent bureaucracy capable of shaping and implementing economic policy' was common to many of the Asia-Pacific countries, which were thus well positioned to implement economic reforms based on US-driven ideologies.[18] During the 1980s, the reduction of US strategic involvement in the region and the expansion of Japanese activity into East Asia, combined with increased participation in regional and international organizations such as the Association of South-east Asian Nations (ASEAN) and the UN, saw the rise of Japan as a major economic and strategic power. By 1989 Japan had become the largest donor of foreign economic aid and by 1990 it was the second-largest economy in the world.[19] Camilleri states that despite the fact that Japan's position within the world economy was far from hegemonic, the threat of a possible Japanese-led trading bloc emerging in East Asia was a powerful trigger for US policies in the Asia-Pacific region aimed at protecting US economic dominance and containing the possibility of an East Asian threat. The long-running US trade deficit with several East Asian economies was not the least significant of these considerations.

In the 1990s, the Asia-Pacific again became a site of struggle for economic dominance and a strategic vehicle for the assertion of US-based ideologies of the free market and global capitalism. As an example of new regionalism, APEC itself was initially seen as largely ineffectual in terms of the global economic system. This changed with the much vaunted success stories of Asia's 'tiger economies', coupled with the highly publicized Leaders' Meeting in Seattle in 1993, at which the principle of open regionalism was first articulated within APEC. Almost overnight the Asia-Pacific area came to be seen as the most significant economic region in the world. As epithets such as the 'Pacific Century' 'and the 'Asian miracle' did the rounds, definitions of the Asia-Pacific region shape-changed as rapidly as the Asian economies grew. As fears of a 'fortress trading bloc' in Europe strengthened, APEC came to be promoted as a model of open regionalism. From its somewhat quiet beginnings in 1989, the

Association became, at least in the short term, a leader on the global economic stage.

In the context of a decade or more of economic and social turmoil, experienced particularly since the withdrawal from British markets and the increase in trade and immigration from Asia, the evolution of the Asia-Pacific region into the 'centre of gravity of world commerce'[20] was influential in the reshaping of New Zealand's cultural identity as well as its economic policies. The meteoric rise of the Asian economies saw New Zealand follow Australia's lead in realigning its economic objectives towards Asia. In an endeavour to cast Australia and New Zealand as Asia-allied nations, the Pacific became the 'Asia-Pacific' and the continued exploitation of the indigenous Pacific nations became even further submerged beneath the rhetoric of economic development. The collapse of Asian economies in 1997 led to the entrenchment of resistance by indigenous peoples and NGOs, many of whom saw APEC as a key instrument of the furtherance of economic globalization within the region. The indigenous caucus's challenge to APEC governments to withdraw from the negotiations regarding the Multilateral Agreement on Investment (MAI), the unequivocal opposition expressed to the APEC processes and the resultant increased plundering and pillage of indigenous resources and rights, together with the marginalization of environmental and human rights agreements,[21] were reiterated by an even greater number of indigenous participants at the APEC People's Summit in Kuala Lumpur the following year. Strongly articulated through these voices of opposition was the urgent need to rethink the premises upon which the new global order is predicated.

Transforming the Keynesian Welfare State: Neoliberalism in New Zealand

Since the mid-1980s, New Zealand has been in the forefront of the elimination of tariffs and other protective measures amongst OECD countries. In the GATT negotiations, Kelsey notes, New Zealand instigated the fewest protectionist measures, whereas the initiating country, the United States, inserted carefully calculated protection for its own industries while reaping the benefits of less astute bargaining from other countries.[22] During OECD negotiations on the MAI,[23] the New Zealand government was in the forefront of opposition to the inclusion of environmental or cultural protections within the text of the draft. In the 1990s, the New Zealand national government not only lowered its tariffs faster than any other of the APEC countries but also led moves to fast-track remaining tariffs in significant areas such as forestry and fishing. In a critique of New Zealand's position regarding APEC,[24] Rosenberg writes that

> having faithfully adopted the APEC agenda on foreign investment, New Zealand is now by far the most dependent on foreign investment of any in the OECD.[25] That has killed employment opportunities. Though overseas companies own half to two-thirds of the commercial economy, they provide less than one job in five, and the number of jobs they have offered has grown much more slowly than the expansion of those companies.[26] The current account deficit is largely due to the escalating dividends and interest paid to the owners of foreign investment in New Zealand. The investment has been overwhelmingly takeover – over 40 per cent is privatization alone.[27]

While the World Bank, the *Economist*, the OECD and others praised New Zealand as an example to the rest of the world – the country that had put into effect the most rapid and far-reaching programme of deregulation, privatization, cuts in tax rates and some categories of government expenditure – statistical evidence provides documented confirmation that the New Zealand experience of 15 years of structural adjustment was an unmitigated social disaster with virtually no economic gain other than for a very small and elite minority.[28]

The policy revolution that between 1984 and 1991 transformed New Zealand from what economist Tim Hazeldine suggests was 'probably the most, to now the least, regulated of the mature capitalist economies'[29] has been thoroughly documented, widely discussed and hotly contended. The transformation of health, welfare and education into quasi-markets was underpinned by principles that were strongly articulated in Treasury briefing papers to the incoming Labour government in 1984. Following the external crises of the Western capitalist world and an internal crisis aggravated by the loss of a guaranteed export market, the rise in New Zealand's overseas debt (as was the case with all other countries in the developed world at the time) provided the context and a pseudo-justification for what became essentially a bargain-basement sale of almost all publicly owned assets of the state.[30] Kelsey notes that although the Treasury's analysis of the economy in the 1984 pre-election briefing papers showed that the sharp recession of 1983 had ended with some improvement in employment and annual economic growth back up above 5 per cent, the Treasury recommendations played a key role in the economic reforms that swept New Zealand from 1984 onwards.

The downsizing of the state was a key aspect of economic restructuring and included the corporatization and sale of state services – initiated in December 1986 with the State-Owned Enterprises Act and the corporatization of nine state-owned corporations that bought their assets from the government at an agreed market price.[31] Legitimated by discourses of inefficiency, privilege, and the transformation of the national debt to a potential two billion dollars surplus – which, as Kelsey notes, did not in fact eventuate – the remaining years of the Labour government saw almost all possible state activity of potential commercial value transformed into the property of a state-owned corporate enterprise.[32] The corporatization of state services facilitated the potential for their procurement by overseas investors. As occurred in other economically restructured countries, the sale of state-owned enterprises was directly responsible for the loss of thousands of jobs. These reforms saw the transformation of New Zealand from a country with a tradition of social democracy, communitarian ideals, an interventionist welfare state, reasonably high employment and a relative absence of extremes in wealth distribution, to a country with a record overseas debt (in 1999 New Zealand's overseas debt had increased by NZ$5 billion from the previous year),[33] enormous disparities between the haves and the have-nots, and the highest suicide figures since the depression period of the 1930s.[34] Despite this, as Kelsey points out, the fundamentals of the policy revolution were taken as given and unchallengeable, to be embedded for the future.[35]

The quasi-marketization of health, education and welfare, and the devolution of state responsibility for health, education and welfare to quasi-markets, represented a fundamental ideological shift. The welfarism that saw the introduction of the first old age pensions in 1893 became transformed into a neoliberal state in which citizens have been reduced to 'autonomous choosers' of services, and the notion of the welfare state has been reconstructed as 'an overpowering, controlling, limiting institution'.[36] Notably, however, provision of welfare had always been selectively provided. For many years, just as Maori returned servicemen were denied the allocations of land granted to non-Maori returning servicemen, so Maori were denied the welfare entitlements granted to non-Maori. The embedded inequities that made New Zealand fall so far short of the racially harmonious and equitable image that it portrayed meant that the impact on Maori of the shift towards minimalist government was severe.

The outcomes of this shift included the loss of social, health, postal and education services to many rural areas, growing unemployment, a rapidly expanding increase in the disparity between the wealthy and the impoverished, and significant increases in foreign ownership and in the influence of high finance over domestic policy. In the final weeks of the national government in 1999, the liberalization of the rules governing foreign investment and the level at which Overseas Investment Commission (OIC) approval is required by foreign investors underwent a radical change. The raising of the threshold at which non-land investments require consent from NZ$10 million to NZ$50 million, coupled with the addition of three new categories to the exemptions from consents, including the acquisition of forestry rights and forestry cutting rights, the acquisition of easements that confer rights to transmit or convey essential services, and the addition of new powers in fishing to the OIC – all without public debate – confirmed the strong commitment to trade and investment liberalization by the outgoing national government and a minimalist commitment to the institutions of democracy.

Some commentators have noted the strong influence of the neoliberal advocates from within right-wing think tanks in this regard, particularly the fact that during this period, at least three of New Zealand's Members of Parliament were active members of the Mont Pelerin Society, a fact that influenced New Zealand's hosting of a Mont Pelerin Society Conference in 1989.[37] Maria Humphries describes how discursive constructions of New Zealand's 'economic crisis', launched at the 1984 Economic Summit and reiterated in a regularly rehearsed litany of economic crisis indicators, coupled with the presentation of 'management of quality' as a panacea, played a major role in co-opting New Zealand society into these reforms and creating the climate for change.[38] An important result was what she describes as a 'unitarist ambience' of adversity and a workplace commitment to new measures of productivity and surveillance. Humphries concludes that, in this manner, 'the voluntary subjection of employees to techniques of work(er) control and the extent of their assimilation into assumptions that serve global capital, involves employees in their own redefinition'.

Aligned with the ideological shift in the nature of education and knowledge, the impact of the internationalization of education strengthened the transformation and commodification of knowledge and the further marginalization of non-marketable pedagogies and epistemologies. In 1998, the report by the Ministry of Maori Development, Te Puni Kokiri, highlighted the increase in the gap between Maori and non-Maori across a wide range of health, welfare and educational indices. In 1999 New Zealand's overseas debt of NZ$102 billion (an increase of NZ$5 billion from the previous year) and trade deficit (almost NZ$1.5 billion for the year ended May 1999) reached record highs.[39] Rather than diminishing, the wide disparity in education achievement levels between Maori and non-Maori within mainstream education remained at a level that during the 1970s was one of the main catalysts for the development of Maori resistance initiatives in education, the other being the enormity of language and culture loss.

Indigenous Resistance and the Response of the Neoliberal State

By 1997, there were multiple and compelling reasons that drove many Maori to oppose the imposition of a multilateral agreement described by Pierre Bourdieu as the most recent in a series of 'political measures [in the case of the MAI ... designed to protect foreign corporations and their investments from national states] that aim to call into question any and all collective structures that could serve as a an obstacle to the pure market'.[40] The MAI represented the latest development in a plethora of economic and trade agreements aimed at liberalization of the economy and the removal of trade protections. Initiated as the result of lobbying by the US Council for International Business and others, the MAI draft was developed by the Office of the US Trade Representative and the State Department[41] and negotiated between 1995 and 1998.

Responding to the leaking of the draft text of the MAI and propelled by an initial discussion paper by Kelsey, Maori were in the forefront of the strong and widespread opposition to the MAI, the rapidity of which was undoubtedly impelled by the New Zealand experience of the neoliberal reforms. The unanimous rejection of the MAI by Maori in seven regional state-sponsored consultations and the wide dissemination of this rejection through radio and television constituted a useful learning experience for government officials.[42] As Kelsey notes in her comprehensive discussion of the MAI and APEC,[43] the New Zealand government did not make the same mistake when hosting the APEC Leaders Meeting in Auckland in 1999, but preempted Maori objections by determined efforts to coopt Maori leadership into the processes for this meeting. While, as Kelsey reports, some Maori remained unconvinced of the economic benefits that would accrue from the removal of tariffs and subsidies, success was sufficiently high to dissipate plans for an indigenous peoples' forum as part of an NGO Summit. An important point highlighted by this example is the role of indigenous elites in occupying the political vacuum between indigenous peoples and the neoliberal state.

It was the resurgence of Maori activism across multiple arenas in the late 1970s and early 1980s, Fleras and Spoonley suggest, that was directly responsible for a raft of state initiatives aimed at the reincorporation of Maori within what was rapidly becoming a neoliberal state. In their view, the main driving force for this response by the state was the recognition that unless new relationships were developed with Maori and a way found for key aspects of their demands to be met, the challenge by Maori to the legitimacy of the Crown would not only undermine investment confidence, but actively inhibit the ability of the state to carry out its business. This view gained further credence from Treasury recommendations to the incoming government in 1999 that advocated the conclusion of all treaty settlements by the year 2010. Indigenous elites and their cooperative association with the state have been a defining influence in these processes. As we saw in Chapter 4, one of the tensions and contradictions accompanying these developments is the neoliberal reinterpretation of indigenous self-determination as economic development. Negotiated largely between the Crown and tribal Maori elites, treaty settlements have been posited as a means of providing Maori with the possibility of economic development and a measure of self-determination. However more often than not, the contested nature of treaty settlements mitigates against that very possibility.

As one of the main resistance strategies of indigenous peoples, the principles and practice of sovereignty and self-determination have been problematized by some indigenous authors who question the appropriateness of these Western constructs in the development of resistance strategies for indigenous peoples. The reframing of indigenous sovereignty within a Western economic paradigm of developmentalism has raised questions regarding the origin and interpretation of the concept of sovereignty, the reconstruction of traditional political structures and the determination of new collective frameworks. It has also raised questions about the relevance of traditional indigenous values that are most often seen as antithetical to discourses of expansion and accumulation. A number of mainstream analyses examine the impact of contested treaty settlement processes on the state and on relationships between the state and indigenous peoples. In one such analysis, despite some problematics, the treaty claims process is viewed as enabling historical claims to be comprehensively addressed and 'put behind us'.[44] While Fleras and Spoonley acknowledge the potential for 'true partnership' between Maori and non-Maori, they view the confrontational and divisive nature of a 'double-edged' claims process as subordinating Maori rights and aspirations to 'national interests'.[45] In many cases, contestations are played out in the struggle between corporate entities established in conjunction with the Crown and purporting to represent tribal groupings, and sub-tribes who comprised the traditional political, social, cultural and economic entities of Maori society and are frequently invisibilized or disenfranchised in the claims process.[46] Again, at issue here is the penetration of elite power blocs into the functioning of the state and the role of the state in the re-ordering of self-identities.

Reconstructing Indigenous Subjectivities

Manuhia Barcham's Derridean analysis of two treaty claims in New Zealand, both of which had far-reaching consequences, highlights the state's role in the reconstruction of Maori identities based on a political agenda of accommodating the interests of particular groups that are determined on the basis of prior identity.[47] Barcham notes that legislative attempts to recognize treaty-based partnerships between the Crown and Maori have erroneously assumed the tribe as the fundamental political structure of Maori traditional society. A contemporary mythology that has since been given some credence within certain tribally based treaty claims, the claim that Maori signatories to the Treaty of Waitangi did so on behalf of tribes, has become embedded in a raft of government policy and legislation that, although designed to accommodate Maori as the treaty-based partner of the Crown, has effectively excluded non-tribally based Maori and Maori organizations from redress and claims-based allocation of assets. As discussed by Barcham and also Fleras and Spoonley, the issue of who could be recognized as a tribe became a major point of contestation. In one well-publicized case involving contemporary urban structures, the exclusion of non-traditionally determined tribes from allocation rights resulted in the irony of, first, a High Court of the Crown and, second, the Privy Council in England being asked to determine what constituted a tribe in legal terms.

Barcham's useful critique of this structuralist approach to addressing Maori historical grievances is based on the assumption by the state that Maori cultural identity is static, an assumption that arises out of the privileging of identity over difference and that excludes recognition of the processes of 'becoming'. As he sees it, the majority of theoretical and empirical work concerning Fourth World peoples is predicated on the assumption of a 'timeless, essentialized conception of identity',[48] a concept containing inherent tensions that are manifested in the arena of indigenous rights. In this regard, Barcham points to the impact of early census taking as well as endeavours by early Maori scholars to produce for posterity archival accounts of Maori culture and history. These efforts, he argues, have unwittingly been responsible for the objectification and reconstitution of particular forms of Maori social tradition and organization through an internal as well as external process of ascription. The result is the 'exclusion and delegitimation of associational forms of Maori organization' and 'the reification of certain neotraditional Maori organizational forms to the extent where they have come to constitute the definitional means by which Maori are identified as "authentically" indigenous'.[49] While he argues that, like all other constructions of identity, indigeneity is 'socially constructed and historically contingent', Barcham's analysis of the assumption of a 'natural', essentialized indigeneity overlooks the invisibilizing, even obliterating of the multiplicity of Maori histories by the state's privileging of certain interests over others.

One of the problematics of the treaty settlement process as a means of simultaneously settling grievances and removing barriers to foreign investment is that of mandate and representation. Another is the suppression of histories and the invisibilizing of particular genealogies that has been an inherent feature of colonization.[50] Webster's discussion of 'poststructural' tribes provides a useful example of this issue as he points to the contested tribal identities that characterized nineteenth-century negotiations regarding land reservations for the First Nations peoples of North America.[51] As Webster notes, in many cases tribal identities were lost or denied legal recognition because of legal fluctuations coupled with removal legislation and relocations. A parallel can be drawn between the difficulties experienced by

Waitaha in achieving government recognition and the experiences of some First Nations peoples. In one account, a 1976 federal court case in which the Mashpee Wampanoag Tribal Council sued for possession of approx 16,000 hectares of land, led to a trial aimed at determining 'whether the group calling itself the Mashpee tribe was in fact an Indian tribe and the same tribe that in the mid-nineteenth century had lost its lands through a series of contested legislative acts'.[52] The federal court's finding was that the Mashpee had not constituted a tribe since 1790, a finding that Webster interprets as an alignment of the understanding of culture and the notion of a 'tribe' with control over resources. The trial process highlighted the fluidity of Mashpee cultural formations and shifting identities across and between a continuum of historically determined spaces.

In his critique of the inherent ambiguity of the notion of a tribe, Webster points to critical analyses that view the development of the notion of a tribe as 'as 'political and territorial entities [that] were a product of colonization, especially mercantile trade'.[53] Similar views have been expressed regarding Maori social and political organization. The uncritically accepted assumption of traditional Maori social formations as 'centralized', 'hierarchically nested' and 'ordered in a parallel manner'[54] has recently been challenged by anthropologists, jurists and historians, including Maori. From his own analysis of historical evidence, Maori Land Court Judge Eddie Durie concluded that 'tribes' as well as a class of hereditary 'chiefs' emerged in the context of early contacts through industry and trade, musket wars, missionary activities, land alienation and confiscations.[55] This is supported in Waitaha oral traditions of the pre-contact period that describe a loosely organized, flat, non-hierarchical organizational structure.

Webster traces government policies that legislated the vesting of tribally owned assets in statutory trust boards, critiquing the government's intention to force Maori to compete among themselves for limited resources. Graham Smith sees these as part of a legislative process that is responsible for the development of new tribal formations;[56] the 'cultural tribe', a traditional formation comprising a genealogically based coalition of smaller sub-groups, the 'state tribe', the 'urban tribe' and the 'corporate tribe'. The 'state tribe' developed in the 1980s from moves by the government to devolve to Maori responsibility for a range of social provisions, plus conditionalities imposed by the Crown for the receipt of settlement assets.[57] The subject of emotionally charged debate, High Court battles and Privy Council appeals, urban tribal formations are constructed around the social, economic and cultural consequences of dislocation. Smith asserts that this model has given rise to a form of 'brown welfarism' in which Maori develop welfare models for Maori, thus buying into the hegemony of 'doing good' for their people whilst maintaining the *status quo*. The emergence in the 1990s of Maori business entities built around compensatory treaty settlement packages and the development of business interests as a form of self-determination, gave rise to the 'corporate tribe' represented, Smith writes, by imposing buildings, highly paid economic consultancies, and the trade of assets. In these processes, Taiaiake Alfred argues, indigenous peoples become participants in the 'consumptive commercial mentality shaped by state corporatism that has so damaged both earth and human relationships around the globe'.[58]

Alfred argues for the structural reform of indigenous communities, involving the recovery of traditional systems of governance.[59] The critical characteristic of this model is the recovery of a different notion of power, one that supported 'respectful regimes of mutual coexistence'.[60] Like Smith and other indigenous critics, Alfred contends that the extinction of aboriginal customary rights through treaty settlements in which land is exchanged for money, which are driven by market-based ideologies, and in which such land as remains within indigenous ownership becomes subject to the imposition of state legislation, represents another form of assimilation by the state. Conducted in tandem with the construction of indigenous self-determination as economic development, the treaty settlement process is located at the intersection of the territorial notions of state sovereignty and the recognition of unextinguished aboriginal title over traditional lands and territories. Tully explains the legal ramifications of this point. He states that the contradiction between legal aboriginal rights of collective use and occupation and the inability to unilaterally extinguish these rights without appropriate legislation gave rise to two major official strategies of incorporation by states: assimilation by legislative action or accommodation legitimated by policies and theories of multiculturalism.[61]

Two landmark treaty settlements, both of which were passed into legislation in 1998, exemplify the tensions, contradictions and co-optation inherent within the treaty settlement process between nation states and indigenous peoples. These two settlements are the context against which I examine the nature and impact of the current process. First, Tully's analysis of the Nisga'a Nation's treaty settlement concluded in 1998 in British Columbia critiques the resolution model based on the ceding of customary rights in exchange for a finite settlement and certain legal and civil rights. Second, contested aspects of the Ngai Tahu treaty settlement seen by some commentators as, 'in many respects ... a model for achieving the objectives of Maori injured by Crown actions in breach of Treaty principles, and of the Treaty of Waitangi Act in trying to meet their claims',[62] provide a context in which to examine some of these issues in New Zealand. Finally, I follow Alfred and other indigenous writers in arguing for an alternative model of socio-political order based on traditional values and world views.

The Nisga'a Treaty Settlement: Extinguished Rights

The treaty negotiated between representatives of the Nisga'a Nation of Northern British Columbia and the Supreme Court of Canada arose from the assertion during the 1970s of the right of the Nisga'a Nation to collectively use and occupy their traditional lands. In its preamble, the treaty settlement document declares its objective to be the reconciliation of the prior presence of aboriginal peoples and the assertion of sovereignty by the Crown. It also defines the undefined distinctive aboriginal rights that are held by the Nisga'a Nation under section 35 of the 1982 Constitution Act. Concluded in 1998 after twenty years of official negotiations and over one hundred years of struggle by the Nisga'a Nation, the resultant treaty provided for the full incorporation of the Nisga'a people into Canadian society. In return for a voluntary relinquishment of 93 per cent of their traditional territories, the right not to pay taxes, and a compensatory settlement sum of approximately NZ$200 million or roughly NZ$11 per person, the Nisga'a Nation were granted aboriginal title in the form of an estate in fee simple with certain proprietary rights over the remaining 7 per cent, some rights with respect to trapping, wildlife and migratory birds outside this area, and the right to pay taxes and receive citizenship entitlements to training. In return, the Federal government of British Columbia achieved the complete extinction of aboriginal title over 28,751 square kilometres of Nisga'a traditional territories and accrued more than NZ$1 billion of foreign investment that had been waiting in the wings.[63]

The negotiation of a limited, Western-style self-government for the Nisga'a Nation simultaneously affirmed the dependent status of aboriginal peoples and provided the context for a reconceptualization of aboriginal sovereignty underpinned by the commodification of resources and human capital theory. The rights stipulated in the Nisga'a treaty represent the 'full and final' settlement of aboriginal rights concerning the Nisga'a people, not only in terms of Section 35 of the constitution but also with regard to any other aboriginal rights that might accrue now or in the future from any other source. As Tully states, although the wording of the treaty refers to 'release' rather than the traditional 'extinguishment', the legal effect is the same. Applauded by the federal and provincial governments as a milestone in the resolution of aboriginal rights, the Nisga'a case, Tully contends, represents the first in the history of Turtle Island (the US) in which an indigenous people (as represented by 61 per cent of the eligible voters) voluntarily relinquished their indigenous rights and status. In what Tully describes as 'the first success of strategies of extinguishment and incorporation by agreement', in addition to surrendering over 90 per cent of their territory, they agreed to the transformation of their status to one of 'a distinctive minority with group rights within Canada'.[64]

The Ngai Tahu Treaty Settlement: Contested Histories, Reconstructed Identities

The Ngai Tahu Treaty Claim provides an important example of the divisive nature of a competitive settlement process. The Ngai Tahu claim was predicated upon a historical grievance ensuing from what Harry Evison describes as a repeated contractual failure by the Crown to meet its obligations within the improperly negotiated terms of a nineteenth-century purchase of most of the South Island of New Zealand.[65] Concluded with the passing into legislation of the Ngai Tahu Settlement Act (1999), the Ngai Tahu claim was contested from both within and without the Ngai Tahu tribe. Driving this contestation were issues of identity, histories and Maori social and political structures.

Kymlicka refers to the defence of one group's claims by rendering invisible another group as a 'serious mistake in both theory and practice'.[66] The passage of the Ngai Tahu Act 1996 led to the assimilation within a corporate model of three identifiably distinct South Island tribal groups – Ngai Tahu, Kati Mamoe and Waitaha – the latter two of which had occupied South Island well before Ngai Tahu, in the case of Waitaha by a long period of time.[67] The passing of the Act at midnight in a largely deserted House of Parliament and in the face of widespread opposition by those whom it purported to represent presaged the ideological tensions that would inevitably accrue. The assimilatory nature of the claim process was rejected by both Waitaha and Kati Mamoe tribal leaders, who viewed the legislation as a denial of the right to their own unique identities and cultural practices guaranteed in the Declaration of Human Rights and its covenants, as well as a pre-empting of claims made on their own behalf. New genealogies of knowledge that were constructed for the successful completion of the Ngai Tahu settlement functioned in Foucauldian terms[68] as an empirical unitary body of conceptual understanding that acted to disqualify and delegitimate those very bodies of genealogical histories that had been appropriated to ensure the successful conclusion of the Ngai Tahu settlement.

The contestation over Waitaha claims to be descendants of the original Waitaha Nation in the South Island of New Zealand[69] was in many respects a replay of the historical Maori Land Court process in which Maori claims to land were validated on the evidence of those who were able to travel to the Court, a procedure that frequently saw certain families and other sub-groups disenfranchised through a simple act of omission.[70] To achieve a large 'full and final settlement' to a corporate body, the histories of earlier tribal groups were invisibilized and new grievances created. In highlighting the politicizing of tribal identities, the treaty claims process functioned to divide and separate, rather than achieve resolution. Claims seeking the return of family lands were demonstrably ignored, as attested in the Waitangi Tribunal files, and promised benefits to the Ngai Tahu people were embedded in economic policies that reconstructed Maori genealogical and spiritual relationships to the land in economic terms frequently invoked as 'growing an asset'. Fleras and Spoonley note that the proposed fisheries allocation model, which will see Ngai Tahu receive NZ$50 million in fishing quota, and the Ngai Tahu treaty settlement claim, which resulted in a pay-out of approximately NZ$170 million, saw the elevation of Ngai Tahu from 'one of the poorest tribes in New Zealand to the fifth wealthiest South-Island-based corporation'.[71]

The importance of land was a prominent theme throughout the Ngai Tahu claim. Based upon the failure of the Crown to adequately compensate for the loss of lands and the chicanery of the Crown's purchase, the resolution provided for by the Ngai Tahu Settlement Act involved, in addition to the settlement of NZ$170 million, the return of ancestral lands, many of which were important Waitaha sacred sites. As part of the pre-settlement agreement, Crown lands that became available for sale were offered first to Ngai Tahu for inclusion in their 'land bank', so that lands of cultural significance to Ngai Tahu could be bought back by the settlement proceeds. The reconstruction of ancestral lands in economic terms, arguably a principle that is markedly at variance with Maori traditional world views, was evidenced in the return to Ngai Tahu and subsequent sale of land that was culturally significant to Waitaha yet also commercially valuable.[72] The Ngai Tahu development of high quality residential housing on land that has spiritual significance for Waitaha contradicts the traditionally sacred nature of the relationship between indigenous people, in this case Maori, and land.

The wider context in which this discussion sits is that of the hegemonic construction of commodities and the impact of neoliberal ideologies in what might be interpreted as the ultimate colonization of the mind and soul – the commodification of the two fundamentals of Maori being: *whakapapa*, or genealogy, and natural resources. Played out against a background of negotiations and cooptations involving the Crown and indigenous elites, the Ngai Tahu treaty settlement highlights the recolonizing and reinvisibilizing of indigenous groups and the privileging of certain Maori elites that has accompanied Crown dealings with Maori over a period of more than 150 years.

Traditional Values for Alternative Models

Despite the contentious nature of the treaty settlement models discussed here, there are a number of wider implications that come into play. These include the interpretation of sovereignty and self-determination as articulated by indigenous peoples and the restructuring of the state within new global frameworks. While Alfred acknowledges the effectiveness of the concept of indigenous sovereignty in challenging the imposition of state power over indigenous nations, he points out that 'the appropriateness of the concept has gone largely unquestioned'.[73] Contrasting traditional indigenous nationhood, marked by the absence of such features as absolute authority, coercive enforcement of ideas, hierarchical authority and separate ruling entities with dominant understandings of the state, Alfred notes the dichotomy between philosophical principle and politics that sees some indigenous politicians using indigenous nationhood and sovereignty 'as a bargaining chip, a lever for concessions within the constitutional framework'.[74] Consequential to this is the struggle over the construction of indigenous identities.

Cox discusses the 'particular ethnic, nationalistic or gender-based identities' as well as class-based struggles that are evoked in new social movements.[75] Contending that 'there is a material basis to this struggle that is broader than the particular identities that are affirmed in this process', Cox observes that the obscuring of this material basis permits these identities to be manipulated into conflict with each other. There is a salience to this argument that points to the effectiveness of government policies that pit both 'old' and 'new' identity formations against one another in a struggle for self-determination which, in the final analysis, becomes constructed as a struggle over resources. The identification of these problematics around the political construction of contemporary Maori identities should not be taken, however, as implying a lack of existing constructive alternatives. As we saw in Chapter 1, traditional forms of collectivity have been and continue to be integral to indigenous peoples' intellectual, political, social and economic organizing. The important point to be made here is that there are multiple ways in which traditional forms of collectivity have been and continue to be integral to indigenous peoples' struggles for political and legal recognition, for the revival and maintenance of their cultural and spiritual frameworks and in their social, economic and political organization.

New forms of collectively based political and social organizations have arisen at least in part by the positioning of indigenous peoples as 'other' in the context of mainstream constructions across a wide range of arenas. One such alternative model of tribally based collectivity is the tribal confederation model that is based on traditional federalist relationships amongst tribal groups. Another important example is the development of tribal as well as pan-Maori tertiary education initiatives. These models represent successful transformative acts of resistance by indigenous peoples. Graham Smith's model of the states of resistance, conscientization and transformation praxis within which resistance processes are conceptualized, articulates the transformative process within a cyclic model that demonstrates the conscientization and transformation process for many Maori. In the context of the struggle of Maori to develop alternative education models, Smith points out, these conditions do not necessarily follow a linear progression but are engaged in cyclically. As the state responds to Maori initiatives by moving to co-opt Maori aspirations, the cycle of Maori resistance, reconscientization and/or politicization and transformation is propelled forward. In his research into the transformative elements of *kaupapa* Maori as theory and practices,

Smith identifies six key principles as key factors in the conscientization and politicization of Maori. These are relative autonomy (or self-determination), the teachings of the ancestors, culturally preferred pedagogy, mediation of socio-economic factors, the extended family structure and collective vision.[76] The principle on which my argument rests is that of those teachings handed down by our ancestors, one of the most important being the interdependence of all existence. This principle is articulated by indigenous scholars as the key to political and social transformation for indigenous peoples and, by extension, is postulated here as central to a globally transformative framework.

Work by Wilmer and other First Nations scholars has also highlighted the principles of indigenous philosophies as the foundation for new forms of governance that honour diversity and promote harmonious coexistence. As Alfred advocates, in the style of native politics embedded in these principles, the tension between individual and collective rights so contentious within Western-style societies is dissipated within the integrity of a traditionally based indigenous framework.[77] In an indigenous framework, respect for others does not require political or legal uniformity or assimilation to a country but rests on the principle of balance. In her address to Maori graduands in 1993, in which she commented on the emergence of 'rich elites amongst struggling peoples', the outstanding Maori leader and academic Dame Mira Szaszy called for 'a new Maori humanism … a humanism based on ancient values but versed in contemporary idiom'.[78] Maori academic Manuka Henare draws on the symbology of the spiral to articulate these ancient values within a 'spiral of ethics for life' at the centre of which is reverence.[79] He delineates these as follows:

ethic of wholeness, cosmos
ethic of life essences, vitalism, reverence for life
ethic of being and potentiality, the sacred
ethic of power, authority and common good
ethic of spiritual power, of obligatory reciprocal relationships with nature
ethic of the spirit and spirituality
ethic of the right way, of the quest for justice
ethic of care and support, reverence for humanity
ethic of belonging, reverence for the human person
ethic of change and tradition
ethic of solidarity
ethic of guardianship of creation.

The rearticulation of Smith's model as the continuously expanding and upward movement of a spiral provides for the centring of these principles at the core of a model of global order that includes all forms of life within all levels of existence.

The challenge for indigenous peoples who are impelled to coexist within neoliberal state formations is to re-embed these principles at the core of indigenous educational movements, organizational structures and economic aspirations. To do otherwise is to become active participants in the processes of imperialism. It is here that the models articulated by Henare and Smith have particular relevance. The reshaping of world order within a new imperial formation presents what is possibly humankind's greatest historical socio/political crisis. For indigenous peoples, the immediate and urgent question is the nature of our response.

Notes

1 See Hettne, Bjorn (1995). 'Introduction: the international political economy of transformation', in Bjorn Hettne (ed.), *International Political Economy: Understanding Global Disorder*. London: Zed Books, pp. 1–30; Gamble, Andrew and Anthony Payne (1997) 'Introduction: the political economy of regionalism and world order', in Gamble and Payne (eds.), *Regionalism and World Order*. London: Macmillan Press.

2 Mittleman, James H. (2000) *The Globalization Syndrome. Transformation and Resistance*. Princeton, NJ: Princeton University Press, p. 132.

3 Jessop, Bob (1999) 'Globalization and the national state' (draft), published by the Department of Sociology, Lancaster University, accessed 18 July 2001 at http:www.comp.lancaster.ac.uk/sociology/soc012rj.html

4 Smith, G. H. (2002) '*Kaupapa* Maori theory: transformative praxis and new formations of colonization'. Paper presented at 'Cultural Sites, Cultural Theory, Cultural Policy. The Second International Conference on Cultural Policy Research', Te Papa National Museum, Wellington, New Zealand, 23–26 January.

5 Alfred, Taiaiake (1999) *Peace, Power, Righteousness. An Indigenous Manifesto*. Ontario: Oxford University Press.

6 Mittleman (2000).

7 *Ibid.*, p. 226.

8 Cooper, Robert (1998) [1996] *The PostModern State and the World Order*. London: Demos, p. vii.

9 *Ibid.*, p. 42.

10 *Ibid.*, p. 32.

11 *Ibid.*, p. 42.

12 *Ibid.*

13 *Ibid.*, pp. 10–18.

14 *Ibid.*, pp. 19–20.

15 Mack, Andrew and John Ravenhill (1994) *Pacific Cooperation: Building Economic and Security Regimes in the Asia-Pacific Region*. Australia: Allen and Unwin, p. 6.

16 Knopf, cited in Bartlett, R. J. (1948) *The Record of American Diplomacy. Documents and Readings in the History of American Foreign Relations*. New York: A. Knopf, pp. 385–8.

17 See Stubbs, Richard (1994) 'The political economy of the Asia-Pacific region', in Richard Stubbs and Geoffrey R. D. Underhill (eds.), *Political Economy and the Changing Global Order*. Basingstoke: Macmillan.

18 In 1991 ASEAN ministerial meetings widened their focus to include issues of regional security for the first time.

19 See Camilleri, Joseph A. (1994) 'The Asia-Pacific in the post-hegemonic world', in *Pacific Cooperation: Building Economic and Security Regimes in the Asia-Pacific Region*. St Leonards, Australia: Allen and Unwin, pp. 180–208.

20 Palat, Ravi Arvind (1996) 'Pacific century: myth or reality?', *Theory and Society*, 25, p. 303, citing Marx and Engels.

21 Statement of Indigenous Peoples' Caucus, APEC People's Summit: Vancouver, 1997.

22 For a discussion of this, see Kelsey, Jane (1995) *The New Zealand Experiment. A World Model for Structural Adjustment?* Auckland: Auckland University Press with Bridget Williams Books.

23 Discussed in depth in Stewart-Harawira, Makere (2003) '*Te Torino Whakahaere, Whakamuri*. Globalization and the return to empire. An indigenous response'. Unpublished PhD dissertation, School of Education, University of Auckland.

24 Rosenberg, Bill (1999) 'The implications of the APEC agenda.' Paper presented to the Alternatives to the APEC Agenda Conference, University of Auckland, 11 September.

25 'The ratio of the stock of inward foreign direct investment to GDP is a common measure of this. In 1995 (when it was 46.7 per cent in New Zealand), the highest ratios for developed countries were in Australia (30.8 per cent), Belgium and Luxembourg (23.0 per cent) Canada (21.7 per cent), Ireland (20.2 per cent), the Netherlands (28.4 per cent) and the UK (28.5 per cent). Most were less than 20 per cent and many less than 10 per cent. The position is even worse when it is considered that many of these countries had high outward investment to compensate.' (*World Investment Report 1997*, United Nations, Annex Table B6, p. 339 ff., cited *ibid.*).

26 According to Rosenberg, while foreign direct investment stock more than doubled between March 1992 and March 1997 from NZ$22,743 million to NZ$50,775 million (an increase of 123 per cent), employment in overseas companies increased by less than half – only 43 per cent – from 183,021 to 262,110 full-time equivalent jobs. (The data for the stock of foreign direct investment comes from New Zealand's International Investment Position; the employment data are from business activity statistics and labour force data, cited *ibid.*)

27 Foreign Direct Investment Advisory Group, *Inbound Investment: Facts and Figures*, August 1997, *ibid.*

28 See, for instance, the Alliance Report, *The Current State of New Zealand's Public Health System*, 1999. A 1999 study conducted over a four-year period from 1994 to 1997 by the University of Auckland showed tertiary education to be slipping out of the reach of children from low-income families. The number of students from poor schools had dropped by 23 per cent while the numbers of those from wealthy families had increased by almost 25 per cent. In 1997, only 8 per cent of students enrolling in university were from schools ranked in the bottom 3 deciles, with the same trend found in polytechnic institutions. A polytechnic in Auckland found a decline of 17 per cent in students from low-decile schools.

29 Hazeldine, Tim (1998) *Taking New Zealand Seriously*. Auckland: Harper Collins, p. 12.

30 Kelsey, Jane (1993) *Rolling Back the State. Privatization of Power in New Zealand*. Wellington: Bridget Williams.

31 *Ibid.*, p. 30.

32 Kelsey, Jane (1999) *Reclaiming the Future. New Zealand and the Global Economy*.

Wellington: Bridget Williams, p. 78.

33 *New Zealand National Business Review*, 23 July 1999, p. 42.

34 Study by the Auckland School of Medicine, cited *New Zealand Herald*, 8 September 1999.

35 Kelsey (1995).

36 O'Brien, Michael (n.d.) 'To market, to market to buy a ?? Social policy reform in New Zealand', cited in Peters, Michael (2001) *Poststructuralism, Marxism and Neo-liberalism. Between Theory and Politics*. Oxford: Rowan and Littlefield.

37 Kelsey (1999), p. 63.

38 Humphries, Maria (1996) 'The political economy of organization discourse and control in New Zealand's liberalized economy', *Electronic Journal of Radical Organizational Theory (EJROT)*, 2 (1) (June), published by the Waikato Management School, University of Waikato, accessed 3 June 1997 at http://www.mngt.waikato.ac.nz/depts/sml/journal/indexv11/sympos.htm

39 New Zealand *National Business Review*, 23 July 1999, p. 42.

40 Bourdieu, P. (1998) 'Utopia of endless exploitation: the essence of neoliberalism', *Le Monde Diplomatique*, 8 December, cited in Peters (2001), p. 113.

41 Accessed October 1997 at http://www.citizen.org/gtw/factmai.html

42 For a full summary of Maori objections to the MAI, see Harawira, Makere (1997) 'The Multilateral Agreement on Investment: implications for Maori'. Presented at the Public Forum on the Multilateral Agreement on Investment, Wellington, 1 November 1997 published at http://www.hartford-hwp.com/archives/24/066.html

43 Kelsey (1999), pp. 309–10. See also Kelsey's thorough analysis of the MAI, pp. 315–52.

44 See Sharp, Andrew (1997)[1990] *Justice and the Maori. The Philosophy and Practice of Maori Claims in New Zealand since the 1970s*. Auckland: Oxford University Press.

45 Fleras, Augie and Paul Spoonley (1999) *Recalling Aotearoa. Indigenous Politics and Ethnic Relations in New Zealand*. Auckland: Oxford University Press.

46 The problematic of state-constructed forms of political organizations for Maori through which treaty settlements would be directed is also discussed at length in Sharp (1997).

47 Barcham, Manuhuia (2000) '(De)constructing the politics of indigeneity', in Duncan Ivison, Paul Patton and Will Sander (eds.), *Political Theory and the Rights of Indigenous Peoples*. Cambridge: Cambridge University Press, pp. 137–51.

48 *Ibid.*, p. 140.

49 *Ibid.*, p.138.

50 As in the case of Waitaha.

51 Webster, Steven (1996). 'Escaping poststructural tribes', in Michael Peters, Wayne Hope, James Marshall and Steven Webster (eds.), *Critical Theory, Poststructuralism and the Social Context*. Palmerston North: Dunmore Press, p. 238.

52 Clifford, J. (1998) *The Predicament of Culture*. Cambridge, MA: Harvard University Press, cited in *ibid.*, p. 239.

53 Leacock, E. (1983) 'Ethno-historical investigation of egalitarian politics in Eastern North America', cited in Webster (1996), p. 241.

54 Webster (1996), p. 242.

55 Durie, E. (1991) 'The treaty in Maori history', in W. Renwick (ed.), *Sovereignty and Indigenous Rights: the Treaty of Waitangi in International Contexts*, Wellington: Victoria University Press, pp. 156–69, cited in Webster (1996). cited *ibid.*

56 Smith, G. H. (1993). 'The commodification of Maori knowledge and culture: dangerous goods for sale', *Corso Overview*, 49 (November), pp. 6–8.

57 *Ibid.* Cf. Fleras and Spoonley (1999).

58 Alfred (1999), p. 114; also pp. 119–28.
59 *Ibid.*, pp. 128–45.
60 *Ibid.*, p. 144.
61 Tully (2000), p. 44.
62 Ward, Alan (1999) *An Unsettled History. Treaty Claims in New Zealand Today.* Wellington: Bridget Williams Books, p. 58.
63 '*A New Journey: The Nisga'a Treaty*'. Video documentary by Lanyon Phillips, BBDO, British Columbia.
64 Tully (2000), p. 50.
65 Evison, Harry C. (1993) *Te Wai Pounamu. The Greenstone Land.* Christchurch: Aoraki Press.
66 Kymlicka, Will (1989) *Liberalism, Community and Culture.* Oxford: Clarendon Press; New York: Oxford University Press, p. 233.
67 Fleras and Spoonley (1999), p. 138. See also Ward (1999), pp. 58–60.
68 Foucault, Michel (1991) 'Governmentality', in Graham Burchell, Colin Gordon and Peter Miller (eds.), *The Foucault Effect. Studies in Governmentality.* Chicago: The University of Chicago Press, p. 82.
69 For a discussion which draws on interviews with Tipene O'Reagan and other Ngai Tahu negotiators, see Price, Richard T. (2001) *The Politics of Modern History-making: the 1990s Negotiations of the Ngai Tahu Tribe with the Crown to Achieve a Treaty of Waitangi Claims Settlement.* Christchurch: Macmillan Brown Centre for Pacific Studies, pp. 40–2.
70 In regard to Waitaha and the Ngai Tahu claim, the unfounded nature of accusations about the inaccuracy of Waitaha's genealogical claim is evidenced in the 1981 comment of Maori Land Court Judge M. C. Smith who, reporting the Decision of the Maori Land Court South Island District pertaining to Rakiura Maori land, states: 'It is of interest to record that some members of the Waitaha tribe gave evidence on the present application'. Decision of the Maori Land Court South Island District, No. 11, on the application by the Ngai Tahu Trust Board to vest Invercargill Hundred Block I Sec 73D and the lands in 396 other titles situated in Stewart island, Southland and West Otago, in trustees upon certain trusts pursuant to Section 438 of the Maori Affairs Act 1953, delivered in Palmerston North on 29 May 1981, p. 6.
71 Fleras and Spoonley (1999), p. 133.
72 Evidenced in New Zealand Overseas Investment Commission approvals. See the August 1999 approval of the sale by Ngai Tahu of 61 hectares of Te Anau 'land bank' land in New Zealand Overseas Investment Commission, Decisions January to December 1999. Commentary and Index prepared by CAFCA, accessed 27 December 1999 at
http://canterbury.cyberplace.org.nz/community/CAFCA/cafca99/index99.html
73 Alfred (1999), p. 55.
74 *Ibid.*, p. 56.
75 Cox, Robert W. (1996) [1992] 'Global perestroika', in Robert W. Cox (with Timothy J. Sinclair), *Approaches to World Order.* Cambridge: Cambridge University Press, p. 307.
76 Cf. Smith (1997), p. 388.
77 Alfred (1999), p. 140.
78 Szaszy, Mira (1993) 'Seek the seeds for the greatest good of all people'. Address given at the Maori Graduands Capping Ceremony, Victoria University of Wellington, 27 April, pp. 6–7.
79 Henare, Manukau (2001) 'Tapu, Mana, Mauri, Hau, Wairua: a Maori Philosophy of Vitalism and Cosmos', in John A. Grim (ed.), *Indigenous Traditions and Ecology. The Interbeing of Cosmology and Community.* Cambridge, MA: Harvard University Press, pp. 213–14.

CHAPTER 7

＊

Global Governance and
the Return of Empire

The final decades of the twentieth century provided fertile ground for the embedding of a new model of governance that is global in impact. As we have seen, following the onset of the global economic crisis, the ideologies of neoliberalism that dominated the development of world order can be located within a particular historico-philosophical context. A strong universalist socio-politico-economic discourse has accompanied these developments, advancing the notion of inevitability and ontological assumptions of the 'triumph of the Enlightenment, of modernism, and of European civilization'.[1]

In the twenty-first century, notions of crisis and chaos have become the rationale for a new discourse in which empire is the logical outcome of a world no longer secure. Hardt and Negri argue that the notion of international order, as the central constitutive proposal of European modernity, has always been in crisis. Crisis, they assert, has been one of the impelling forces of a continual push towards empire. Discernible in the unravelling of multilateral regimes, in the US rejection of new and violation of existing international agreements to which it is a signatory, in the demonstrated failure of the Bretton Woods system to meet its declared objectives, and in the increasingly broad and globalized resistance to globalization, the crisis of multilateralism is one manifestation of the new formation of empire. Another is the emergence of a strong neoconservative element, epitomized by the return of the once thoroughly discredited doctrine of the pre-emptive strike as a central protectionist strategy in the aggressive militarism of American empire.

I begin this chapter with an analysis of key aspects of the global economic order that emerged out of the completed Uruguay Round of GATT negotiations. Within the new global economic architecture of the WTO, the expansion of trade, removal of tariffs and the privatization and commodification of the commons are integral to the expansion of the open society. The hollowing out of the state has seen state sovereignty reconceptualized in ways that support the needs of the market, and new ways have been found to elevate rights that attach to property over all forms of human rights, including collective rights. In the process, civil society has been reordered, with the construction of new categories of knowledge and difference. The construction of the global framework and the reconstruction of knowledge and difference, particularly in the realm of education, are important connective themes in this chapter. In both accounts, biological determinations of difference have given way to sociological and cultural determination. The events of 11 September 2001 opened the door to new racially based categorizations of difference, underscored by the self-righteous morality of Western-conceived freedom and justice. One of the most striking features of this situation, Bacevich and others note, is the continuity of policy across successive Republican and Democratic governments, in which neoliberalism and neoconservativism represent the two ideological poles of twenty-first century American empire. Leaving aside the extreme right or left, Bacevich writes, these ideological poles share a broad consensus.

Two quite distinct yet similar conceptualizations provide the basis from which I explore the concept of new formations of empire in the final section. Cooper's new voluntary imperialism, centred within the EU model of postmodernism, allocates difference according to a market-based model. In this Manichean construct of inside/outside, civil order and the global economy are within and the disorder of the natural world without.[2] In Hardt and Negri's conceptualization, the dialectic between the civil and natural orders has given way to a new 'non-place' in which there is no longer an outside and power is both 'everywhere and nowhere'.[3]

Arrighi explains the hegemonic breakdowns that occur as hegemonic systems disintegrate and systemic chaos ensues as the moment when new hegemonies are forged.[4] There are at least two different ways in which this could be understood, both of which are to do with the twin forces of disintegration and reintegration. One is the disintegration of the liberal international hegemonic world order and the reintegration of a neoconservative global dominance that weds economic openness and military force in a new imperialist formation. The other is an approaching disintegration of unilateralism and the reintegration of the world within new formations yet to be determined. Cox's penetrating analysis of militarist and economic interventionism as key coercive strategies in the construction of the global order informs my examination of the return of the doctrine of the 'just war', the once thoroughly discredited notion of preemptive war and the discourse on terrorism as key strategies in the construction of global order. The final section of this chapter takes us back to the question of ontology. Against the background of events of this century, the need for a revisoned ontology of world order becomes more urgent than ever before.

The Economic Architecture of Global Governance

The paradigmatic shift from a multilateral system of regimes to a framework of global governance was given expression in the words of Renato Ruggerio, the first Secretary-General of the World Trade Organization (WTO), when he declared 'We are establishing the framework for a new global order'.[5] The transformation of the GATT into a new multilateral structure charged with overseeing, administering and enforcing a set of global trade rules – the result of the protracted Uruguay Round of GATT negotiations in December 1993 and the signing of the Marrakech Agreement in April 1994 – represented the cementing in place of the architecture for a new global system of governance.

Together with the Bretton Woods institutions, the newly formed World Trade Organization constituted the framework of what Ruggerio described as 'a single global economy'.[6] The new trading rules established in the Uruguay Round represented a profound shift in the nature and definition of trade and commodities, in the management of inter-state disputes and in the nature and inter-pretation of state sovereignty. As the arbiter of disputes over trade and investment and the enforcer of the rules of the global economy, the WTO is a powerful instrument for the assertion of the new global economic order, in which market rights take precedence over state sovereignty, human rights and environmental concerns. As the body established to oversee and administer the processes of inter-national trade liberalization by states and to resolve inter-state conflicts in all matters relating to trade, an enormous amount of legal authority has accrued to the WTO. The regime of trade liberalization, open markets and tariff reductions administered under the auspices of the WTO has been described by the UN Sub-Commission on the Promotion and Protection of Human Rights as the basic foundation for most contemporary developments associated with globalization.[7]

The most important signifiers of this new structure are its ideological roots. In Foucauldian terms, the shift towards new forms of neoliberal governance can be understood either as a return to the classic liberalism of the sixteenth to eighteenth centuries, or as the emergence of a new form of liberalism variously referred to as neo- or hyperliberalism. Characteristic of the re-embedding of the social within the economic is the reconstruction and broadening of the category of 'the poor' and the reframing and redisciplining of the categories and roles of 'population' and 'citizenship' within the global economic order. Parallels can be drawn between the establishment and expansion of the Lockean state system and the shift towards global systems of governance. Critical strategies have included the dismantling of central banks within contender states, the removal of state controls over finance and capital, the denationalization and privatization of public commodities, goods and services and the recommodification of land, water and other natural resources, including those designated as the global commons. Allied to these is a restructuring of the concept of development in ways that promote deepening social inequality, and the emergence of new forms of social darwinism associated with universalist notions of an enterprise culture, the knowledge economy and, at the level of government-mentality, the internationalization of the state. Accompanying this shift is an alarming expansion in the development of new forms of social control.

The Internationalization of Trade: Implications for State Sovereignty

The incremental development of international trade law that occurred within the framework of seven years of negotiations among countries provided new impetus to debates regarding state sovereignty and its meaning and relevance to the contemporary global economic order. As the previous chapter demonstrated, the notion of the state as self-limiting as opposed to having limitations imposed externally continues to be located at the centre of ongoing debates and consideration of the form and process of global governance.

McCrae provides an international law perspective of the implications for state sovereignty of the WTO.[8] From some viewpoints, he states, the very idea of international law contradicts any claim to absolute state sovereignty. The other side of this debate is whether, in fact, international law is law at all. He emphasizes that the basis of international trade is no longer the mercantilist model whereby each state seeks to enhance its own economic well-being through competing against and at the expense of others. The globalization of manufacturing has eroded the concept of domestic manufacturing. National firms now relocate to where they can produce more efficiently in terms of labour costs and economies of scale. In the process, trade has been transformed from a purely national process into one in which neither national boundaries nor the state of nationality of any of the participants in the process have particular relevance. McCrae's analysis provides a useful insight into processes that are central to the workings of the WTO. Fundamental to the world trading regime is the principle of comparative advantage in which the notions of specialization and exchange are applied to exchanges across borders. His explanation of what lies behind this principle is worth quoting in full here. He states,

> Specialization in the production of goods and services at which you are most efficient results in the production of more goods and services. If you then purchase what you need from others who are producing what they are most efficient at … you will have saved yourself the greater expense of producing those goods yourself. Thus … production has been enhanced and savings have been made from the avoidance of inefficient production, hence, contributing to greater demand and investment and maximizing global welfare.[9]

According to this economic rationale, the principle of economic advantage only works in an environment of non-distorted production costs. In addition to the elimination of tariffs and the prohibition of quantitative restrictions, subsidies are also prohibited, thus representing a significant change in the ability of states to define what are legitimate policies concerning national social and economic well-being. In this context, the dispute resolution mechanisms of the WTO have critical importance not only for developing countries but also between the major industrialized nations.

Decision Making and Dispute Resolution

The complete reform of the GATT dispute settlement system (DSU) through the appointment of a dispute settlement panel whose decisions are binding and whose processes are carried out behind closed doors had important ramifications for state sovereignty. Article 23 of the DSU requires member states seeking to resolve disputes within the jurisdiction of the covered agreements to follow the rules and procedures of the DSU. In particular, it prohibits members from making unilateral determinations that a violation has taken place, or that benefits and concessions have been nullified. Unilateral retaliatory action is also prohibited. The fact that this directly impedes, at least in principle if not in fact, the exercising of Section 301 of the US Trade Act of 1974 (Section 301) by the US is a source of ongoing contention. Under US domestic law, Section 301 provides authority for the US to 'take retaliatory action', including import restrictions, 'to enforce US rights against violations of trade agreements by foreign countries and unjustifiable, unreasonable or discriminatory foreign trade practices that hinder or restrict US commerce'. Continued efforts by the US to exercise the right to unilateral retaliatory measures, as in the case of the US–EU beef hormone dispute, not only test the strength and authority of an economic system of which the US was one of the chief architects, but, more importantly, signify the contested and contradictory nature of the decision-making processes that underlie the world trading system.[10]

As the first and only set of rules covering international trade in services, decisions within the WTO are officially reached through consensus or by voting. In point of fact, however, voting in the WTO is on a weighted basis, with an 85 per cent vote required to make change in any of the processes. The fact that the US holds 17 per cent of the vote means, of course, that no change can take place without the agreement of the US. In the US-dominated environment of the annual Ministerial Meetings of the WTO major decisions are negotiated behind closed doors among the four major member states, known as the 'QUAD countries'. The lack of transparency, exclusionary policies and practices regarding WTO trade rules and their ability to be manipulated by the central group of so-called QUADs – the US, Canada, Japan and the European Union – came to public attention during the November 1999 meeting of the WTO in Seattle. The processes of 'green room' negotiations saw the representatives of the majority of nations excluded and their governments offered the choice of signing to the completed deal or being left out of the world trading system. The extraordinary influence of industry in the shaping of WTO rules also became a focus of public attention. Leaked minutes of the Liberalization of Trade in Services (LOTIS) committee recorded 14 secret meetings between Britain's chief service negotiators, the Bank of England, and leading financiers, including the Goldman Sachs International Chairman, Peter Sutherland, and former Chair of the European Union and Vice-Chairman of UBS Warburg Dillon Read, Leon Brittan, refuelling concerns about a lack of transparency and the manipulation of the trading system.[11]

Arguably, the most important change brought about by the new economic regime concerns the nature of trade itself. In the realm of trade in goods, the expansion of tradeable goods to include agriculture, traditionally considered a legitimate domestic policy area, signalled the opening up of all aspects of domestic production to the rules of international trade. The rules of the new trade regime also saw the definition of tradeable goods extended to include services, 'trade-related' investment measures, and 'trade-related' intellectual property rights. The conclusion of the Uruguay Round of GATT negotiations in 1994 ushered in the first of a new set of trade rules that includes trade-related intellectual property rights (TRIPS), trade-related investment measures (TRIMS) and the General Agreement on Trade in Services (GATS). To be further negotiated over time, the inclusion of these disciplines within the compulsory rules of the WTO has wide-ranging implications.

Trading in Services

The architecture of the GATS entered into force on January 1, 1995 is significantly different from that of the GATT. Its two specific commitments of national treatment and market access apply to four 'modes of supply': cross-border supply of a service (not requiring the physical movement of supplier or consumer), provision implying movement of the consumer to the location of the supplier, services sold in the territory of a member by legal entities that have established a presence there but originate in the territory of another member, and provision of services requiring the temporary movement of natural persons. While these commitments apply only to those service sectors that are listed by governments and are subject to 'most favoured nation' exemptions (limited to a ten-year period and required to be renegotiated in subsequent rounds), the subjection of the positive list approach to continuous expansion of sectoral commitments is a fundamental principle of GATS. Examples of its implications are contained in the list of 160 subsectors and activities submitted in the European Union's *Schedule of Specific Commitments, European Communities and their Member States* as an outcome of the Uruguay Round.[12] Specific commitments to tradeable services include financial services, research and development, communications, postal services, information technologies, environmental services including the construction and maintenance of roads, rubbish collection, sewage disposal, water delivery, protection of the landscape and urban planning, transportation, human and animal health and all levels of education.

Despite a lack of true assessment of macro-economic factors or the social and environmental implications of services liberalization on developing countries, embedded in the GATS Agreement is a presupposition regarding the benefits of service and sectoral liberalization. The terms of GATS provide for the imposition of punitive measures on countries that wish to renegotiate their commitments following their first signing of the Agreement. The inequalities manifest in the negotiating process that allows countries such as the US, in particular, to wield excessive influence in forcing demands on smaller developing countries are most evident in the shaping of the negotiations agenda. Rather than increasing competitiveness, services liberalization has facilitated the growth of global oligopolies representing new forms of domination by foreign capital and accompanied by significant job losses.

Commitments to tradeable services have implications in the limiting of access to services to the increasing number of impoverished people. Among the most significant of these are the privatization of health, education, and the basic requirements for life, such as water. As was the case with the trade in seeds, the privatization of and trade in services enables the monopolizing of water provision by transnational giants such as Monsanto. In reference to the increasing pressure on natural resource markets, this company's reported standpoint is: 'These pressures and the world's desire to prevent the consequences of these pressures will create a vast economic opportunity.' Looking at the world through 'the lens of sustainability', they have declared that 'we are in a position to see current and foresee impending resource market trends and imbalances that create market needs. We have further focused this lens on the resource market of water and land.'[13]

It has become an accepted fact that in this century wars will be fought over water. Moves to commodify and privatize the elements of life arguably comprise the worst kind of exploitation. In the process, the poor, the indigenous and minorities are exposed even further.

Trading in Knowledge and Property Rights

The transformation in the nature of knowledge is one of the most significant aspects of the global economic structure. The Trade-Related Intellectual Property Rights (TRIPS) Agreement annexed to the Marrakech Agreement constitutes one of the main pillars of the WTO. Recent developments in biotechnology have been a compelling force in the development of a strong intellectual property rights (IPRs) regime, particularly on the part of industrialized countries. Making IPRs subject to a binding disputes procedure by placing them within the jurisdiction of the WTO, rather than the World Intellectual Property Organization (created in 1967 for the promotion of IPRs), enabled trade sanctions in any area to be placed on non-compliant WTO members.

One of the most controversial elements of TRIPS is the requirement for WTO members to make patents available for all inventions. This includes processes as well as products. Further polarizing the debate regarding the TRIPS Agreement is the inclusion of rules on domestic enforcement procedures and remedies for the first time in international law. The object of controversy in developed as well as developing countries, and of enormous concern to indigenous peoples because of its wide-ranging implications for life forms and the ownership of knowledge, Article 27.3(b) of the TRIPS Agreement provides for the exclusion from patentability of plants and animals, although not micro-organisms. It requires the provision of protection for new plant varieties using patents, an effective *suis generis* system, or a mixture of both. Article 28.1(a) concerning patents confers the right to prevent third parties from 'making, offering for sale or importing for those purposes the product without the patentee's consent'.[14] The use of the process as well as the commercialization of a product 'obtained directly by that process' is prevented for patents relating to processes. As Tansey points out in a discussion paper for Quaker Peace and Services, the patenting of a process to produce a plant thus confers exclusive rights with respect to plants obtained by that process, the burden of proof to show that the product is not being produced by that process being placed on the producer.[15]

The transformation of knowledge from a public good to a private good allows the owners of intellectual property to recoup their expenditure in creating new knowledge. Underpinning this is a mixture of Hegelian utilitarian rationalism that allocates ownership by viewing ideas as an extension of their creator and Lockean ideologies that allocate ownership on the basis of the transformation of an object through the action of labour upon it. Thomas Cottier's exploration of international law and world trade law in relation to the protection of genetic resources and traditional knowledge illuminates some of the underlying assumptions of debates in this area.[16] Summarizing the historical development of resource allocation and property rights, he notes that in the latter part of the twentieth century debates concerning resource allocation and property rights have centred around the oil, gas and mineral resources of the seas.

The process of allocation of the sea's resources, Cottier states, was impelled by scientific and technological innovations such as the invention of the combustion engine and other uses for oil, gas and minerals, as well as by large-scale factory fishing. The current directional shift is thus an extension of the historical process that, since the 1970s, has seen natural genetic resources recontextualized as commercially important assets, owing to both an intensification of technological innovation and an increasing scarcity of genetic resources.[17] Placed alongside the predicted doubling of the world's population by the year 2050, the issue of increasingly scarce genetic resources is underscored in much of the emerging consensus discourse regarding biotechnology, genetic engineering and property rights.

As in the case of East Timor, access to and control over these resources drives many of the territorial disputes concerning sovereignty over various islands. In New Zealand, government legislation passed in the face of vociferous opposition by Maori[18] removed Maori customary rights over their foreshore and seabed (other than some minor limited specific rights to be vested in Maori who can prove continuous use since 1840) and reinvested ownership in the Crown, opening up possibilities for seabed exploitation through mining and mineral exploration.[19] Given that New Zealand assets held in Crown ownership have been incrementally traded or sold off since 1984, this legislation fuelled Maori protest to a level unprecedented since the historic walk to Parliament in 1975 to protest ongoing confiscation of Maori lands.

Indigenous Peoples and the Intellectual Property Rights Regime

In the new political economy of knowledge, the search for profit is intimately connected to the production of new knowledge, to which rapid advances in biotechnology make an important contribution. Stimulated by these advances, the importance of traditional knowledge to innovations in new product development sits at the centre of debates concerning the relationship between indigenous and traditional knowledge and intellectual property rights. Tensions between advocates of intellectual property rights and communities of traditional and indigenous peoples reflect broadly diametrically oppositional positions. John Mugabe has summarized these debates for the World Intellectual Property Organization.[20] Proponents of extending IPRs to include traditional knowledge, potentially including patenting indigenous knowledge, argue that to do this will promote technological innovation by the dissemination and development of knowledge in the economic arena. Further, some argue that recognition of indigenous IPRs will provide incentives for conservation of the environment and management of diversity by local and indigenous peoples, and that industrialized countries have a moral obligation to ensure that fair and equitable benefit sharing takes place. Those who oppose this view argue that the extension of intellectual property rights would function to destroy the social basis for generating and management of knowledge. Nabhan voices this view in the following way:

> It is crucial to remember that the underlying purpose of IPR is to turn knowledge into a marketable commodity, not to conserve such knowledge in its most fitting cultural context. This goal necessarily translates into a focus on segregating and isolating information into identifiable and manageable pieces that can be protected by law as intellectual property. In contrast, ethnobiological knowledge by its very nature is integrative, holistic and synergistic. It is most meaningful *in situ*, where plants are understood in relation to the ecological and cultural environments in which they are grown, managed and used by local residents. IPR departs from such traditions by valuing the discrete properties of plants that can most easily be taken out of their natural and cultural context and replicated through artificial

selection in a laboratory or greenhouse. Given the legal premises upon which IPR are based, it is unlikely that IPR will ever be a useful model for protecting ethnobotanical knowledge.[21]

Human Rights versus the Rights of Property

The UN Commission on Human Rights highlighted the conflict between human rights and intellectual property rights in a series of resolutions calling on the cooperation of governments in the realization of the International Covenant on Economic, Social and Cultural Rights.[22] Its appointment in December 2000 of two Special Rapporteurs,[23] charged with studying and reporting on the issue of globalization and its impact on the full enjoyment of all human rights, reflected the rapidly growing level of concern and involvement on the part of the UNCHR regarding the impact of economic globalization. Following their preliminary report, the Sub-Commission noted circumstances identified within the Human Development Reports 1999 and 2000 that are 'attributable to the implementation of the TRIPS Agreement' and that 'constitute contraventions of international human rights law'.[24] The Report highlighted actual and potential conflicts between the realization of economic, social and cultural rights and the implementation of the TRIPS Agreement, including (amongst others) 'impediments to the transfer of technology to developing countries, the consequences for the enjoyment of the right to food of plant varieties and the patenting of genetically modified organisms, and control over their own genetic and natural resources and cultural values'.[25]

The Sub-Commission commended efforts being made within the Conference on the Parties to the Convention on Biodiversity to assess the relationship between biodiversity concerns and IPR. Nevertheless, it noted, fundamental differences remain between the holistic, 'values-based' knowledge systems of indigenous peoples and the notion of private economic rights embedded within the property rights regime.[26] Mugabe suggests that the problem lies in the nature of intellectual property law regimes, which, being conceptualized within Western capitalist frameworks, are inimical to the protection of indigenous knowledge. Despite the advances made within international law regarding the acknowledgement and protection of indigenous knowledge, to date none of the international measures being negotiated within the CBD or within the WTO Council on

TRIPS provide an appropriate framework for the protection of indigenous and local knowledge from appropriation and exploitation whilst simultaneously protecting the collective nature of the ownership of such knowledge.

Critical issues that arise for indigenous and local peoples within the IPR framework are biopiracy, our right to control over our own natural resources, and gene transfer. Four years after the launch of the Human Genome Organization (HUGO), a multi-billion dollar research project whose objective is to map the human genome, the Rural Advancement Foundation (RAFI) reported on the emergence of companies engaged in the identification and commercialization of human genes. Sanda Awang draws attention to the work of Nobel Prize winner H. J. Muller, the founder of molecular biology and an early advocate of a critical shift in the reconceptualization of biological science: the relocation of the essence of life in the gene and the redefining of life as a series of 'instructions', 'codes', 'puzzles' or 'cryptograms'.[27] Emerging from this shift, the central question for biology in the future was seen as managing the evolutionary process. According to Muller, one of the opportunities that would emerge for those working along 'classical genetic lines' was that of 'creating in their chosen organisms a series of artificial races for use in the study of genetic … phenomena…. The time is not ripe to discuss here such possibilities with reference to the human species.'[28]

Critics such as the executive editor of the *New England Journal of Medicine*, Dr Marcia Engell, have pointed to the racialization of the genomic industry, citing experiments on pregnant women in Africa, Thailand and the Dominican Republic, as a result of which 'over 1,000 infants who could have been saved will contract the AIDS virus needlessly'.[29] In the context of HUGO, whose aims included to collect 'blood, skin and hair samples from more than 700 ethnic groups in the world and use new techniques to preserve genetic information indefinitely, either by isolating cell lines or by isolating and storing DNA segments using PCR (polymerase chain reaction)',[30] applications such as those to patent the T-cell line of a member of the Hagahai by the National Institutes of Health[31] and the US Department of Health and Human Services, and that lodged by the US Department of Health in 1990 to patent the HTVL-infected T-cell of a Guaymi woman[32] are viewed by many indigenous peoples as the ultimate commodification of their lifeworld.

Such examples demonstrate the tensions between human rights and property rights that underpin IPR debates within the WTO. In the latter instance, the T-cell line belonged to one of three Guaymi women found to have an unusual capacity to resist adult T-cell leukaemia (lymphoma). A number of organizations and indigenous writers have acknowledged the particular health benefits that may derive from gene therapy, particularly in combating diabetes and other similar diseases to which, it must be acknowledged, indigenous peoples have become increasingly prey. In November 2000 the Indigenous Peoples' Secretariat (Canada) on the Convention on Biological Diversity reported the acquisition of the right to research the genetic make-up of the population of Tonga. Iceland has similarly given access to the medical and genealogical records of the island to a medical research company. As these examples demonstrate, the complex nature of the issues is a catalyst for debates that seek to identify more appropriate methods of protection for indigenous and traditional IPRs.

In New Zealand the already polarized debate – between proponents of genetic engineering as an important and highly profitable advance in biotechnology and those for whom the high level of uncertainty attached to genetic manipulation demands an extremely cautious approach[33] – was propelled to a new level in 2001, with the appointment of the Royal Commission on Genetic Modification charged with examining issues surrounding genetic modification and its potential contribution towards New Zealand's economy. These differences emerge most strongly at the interface of transgenic science and the commodification and marketization of knowledge, and were visible in Maori submissions to the Royal Commission. Most notable was the emergence of new interpretations of traditional knowledge and a reconstructed genealogy of hierarchically organized knowledge.

In marked contrast to submissions that drew on traditional interpretations of oral genealogies and the sanctity of species to argue for either a more cautious approach or the complete cessation of all experiments involving transgenic processes, a submission prepared by two Maori academics and made on behalf of the Life Sciences Network argued that traditional genealogies evidence Maori manipulation of the natural world 'for the betterment of people within a pragmatic framework'.[34] The potential for enormous economic gain as well as the possibility for medical breakthroughs in Maori health is the driving force behind their advocacy of Maori involvement in biotechnology. Traditional concepts and practices such as *karakia* or sacred chants that traditionally under certain conditions could be employed to minimize any adverse consequences that might accrue from the manipulation of the natural world, were advocated somewhat tongue-in-cheek as a means of appeasing any misgivings held by certain groups.

Reconstructing Difference

Increasingly, the production of knowledge has taken a central role in the advancement of global capitalism. Represented by new forms of 'distributed governance', the diffusion of power underpinning the global politico-economic framework is identifiable within the articulation of particular forms of knowledge and subjectivities as desirable objectives within the global economy. It is here that the radical restructuring of state education since the 1980s has played a key role. For Martin Carnoy, the oppositional forces of the intensification of the transmission of world culture through information networks and a corresponding increasing contestation by global movements constitute a new kind of struggle over the meaning and value of knowledge.[35] Peters identifies three accounts of the way in which the production and classification of knowledge have become central ingredients in knowledge capitalism, two of which are in the realm of world policy. In the 1996 OECD report *The Knowledge-Based Economy*,[36] the codification and transmission of knowledge and its relationship to traditional economy, an important aspect of 'new growth theory', has become an important area of analysis. The knowledge economy and its relationship to development have similarly become a focus of study by the World Bank. In its 1998/9 *World Development Report*,[37] knowledge and development were linked to the concept of universities as leading service industries of the future, and research and development that builds upon indigenous knowledge was seen as crucial to local knowledge creation. The third account of the globalization of knowledge considered by Peters comes from Alan Burton-Jones, who contends that 'knowledge is fast becoming the most important form of global capital – hence knowledge capitalism'.[38] As probably the least understood and most undervalued of all economic activities, Burton-Jones argues, knowledge is 'fundamentally altering the basis of economic activity'.[39]

James Marshall denounces the new instrumental emphasis on the concept of information as knowledge: he sees it as an impoverished view of knowledge that treats information as neutral and is implicitly bound up with empirical conceptions of knowledge as data. He cites the New Zealand Curriculum Framework 1994 as an example: 'in

the new mode of information associated with electronic communication ... knowing has been replaced with knowing how,
content has been replaced with form, and product by process'.[40] The
reshaping of education policy within the framework of the global
economy has seen the entry of market-oriented discourses of
flexibility and cutting-edge innovation into the lexicon of
education.[41] Outcomes include the re-aligning of education with the
need for a ready supply of skilled labour to attract foreign investment,
the internationalization and standardization of curriculum and
assessment, and the application of information technology as a means
of low-cost dissemination.[42] In New Zealand, the 'knowledge
economy' has become the determinant for the content and delivery
of curricula and, importantly, for the categorizing of knowledge.
Among the subjectivities and identities this has produced are new
forms of class relations within discourses of power that are related to
the development of the 'competitive state'. Underpinning these new
social divisions is the commodification of knowledge and the construction of new hierarchies determined by who can afford these
commodities. Thus educational discourses based on new technologies
and the knowledge economy operate as new forms of exclusion/
inclusion, amplifying existing discourses of deficit.

Popkewitz's Foucauldian approach to the power/knowledge configuration is useful here. Popkewitz sees the 'functional ordering of
knowledge' that emerged by the end of the eighteenth century as
having enabled a revision of the principles of governance within a
rationality that included the inner as well as the outer attributes of the
individual.[43] Parallel to the colonization of the inner person was a
colonization of time and space within an empiricist configuration
that constructed both time and space as controllable, stabilized and
rational measurements constituting 'a regulating effect of power'.[44]
One of the effects of power is the 'construction of distinctions that
are made legitimate and reasonable'. Popkewitz suggests that the
debates about the ordering of knowledge have implications for the
governing of the self. This has particular relevance in terms of
changes in patterns of inclusion/exclusion that 'inscribe an unequal
playing field' within a globalized society. Norman Fairclough under-
scores this point, writing that, rather than homogenizing, the
neoliberal order entails 'a specific restructuring of difference'.[45] At
issue is a new structuring of identity within a 'narrative of progress'
that contributes to 'actualizing forms of identity, new values and
subjectivities within new formations of power'.[46] Occurring within

particular historical conjunctures, the legitimating of sets of ideas is, Popkewitz declares, allied to 'changes in international institutions, social movements and technology and the knowledge economy'.[47] As he argues, this reordering of knowledge is closely allied to the construction of forms of imperialist governance. Accompanying this formation are new disciplinary methodologies and technologies of control.

Societies of Control

One of the embedded contradictions of globalization that has accompanied the privatization of goods and services and the liberalization of trade is that between the discourse of freedom and the tightening of individual liberties. Foucault's discussion of panopticism as a system of surveillance that operates by permitting the relentless and continual observation of inmates at the periphery by officials at the centre speaks to the re-emergence of new forms of surveillance that have accompanied market liberalism and the domination of the local by the global. These technologies of power operate in relation to the emergence of new forms of knowledge and discourses. The construction of new subjectivities within new forms of deficit in relation to particular forms of knowledge and technology captures the global spread of telecommunications and electronic networks within particular and specific constructions of the subject. Together these constitute new biopower technologies of power and domination.

Deleuze's concept of societies of control encapsulates the multi-layered technologies of control that have accompanied the transformation of the Keynesian Fordist state to a transmission belt for global capital, and provides a useful framework within which to examine the shift in the extension of power over individuals and populations through multilayered networks of electronic technologies, legislation and discursive shifts in the concept of democracy. Discussing his conceptualization of three kinds of power, Deleuze contends that the shift from 'disciplinary societies' in which confinement was the main technology towards 'control societies that ... no longer operate by confining people but through continuous control and instant communication'[48] is reflected in a shift in technologies of control. The escalation of control that accompanied the shift towards a competitive state and a market-based global order raises urgent questions about privacy, transparency and civil rights. The September 2001 attack on the World Trade Centre opened the door to a significant removal of civil rights including privacy rights, intellectual freedom and citizenship rights in many countries around the globe. Officially entitled 'Uniting and Strengthening America by Providing Appropriate Tools Required to Intercept and Obstruct Terrorism (USA PATRIOT ACT) Act of 2001', the USA Patriot Act is far-reaching in its impact. Ostensibly designed 'To deter and punish terrorist acts in the United States and around the world, to enhance law enforcement investigatory tools, and for other purposes', the Act removed wide-ranging freedoms previously protected under the US constitution.

The unconstitutional nature of the Patriot Act is evidenced in the finding by a US federal judge that parts of the Act are in violation of the First and Fifth Amendments to the US constitution. In a ruling handed down in January 2004, US District Judge Audrey Collins said the ban on providing 'expert advice or assistance' is impermissibly vague, in violation of the First and Fifth Amendments. As written, the ruling stated, the law does not differentiate between impermissible advice on violence and encouraging the use of peaceful, non-violent means to achieve goals. By thus placing no limitation on the type of expert advice and assistance that is prohibited and banning the provision of all expert advice and assistance regardless of its nature, the judge declared, that section of the US Patriot Act is unconstitutional.[49]

Nonetheless, the US Patriot Act continues to have global reverberations, not the least of which is the normalization of escalating levels of monitoring and control. In the US this includes extending the use of 'registers that record numbers dialled, and trap-and-trace devices such as email'[50] for the use of which warrants are not required because they are 'not considered searches under the Fourth Amendment'. Biometric technologies for the recording of fingerprint and iris patterns for border controls have become an acceptable level of monitoring not only in the US, but also in countries such as Canada and New Zealand.[51] Advances in satellite and computer technology have largely rendered existing systems of agreement and participation between countries redundant, further leveraging US control over the coerciveness of covert technical surveillance.

This is exampled in the US Homelands Security Act, otherwise known as legislation for 'Securing the Homeland, Strengthening the Nation'. Among other things, this provides for the access and transfer of all EU passenger records, not restricted to US passengers, from the databases of EU carriers into the US Department of

Homeland Security database. According to a preliminary report released by Privacy International in February 2004, while this in itself creates enormous issues for individual privacy, it has also propelled the EU into planning for a centralized database that would not only facilitate data transfer to the EU but would also be utilized by the EU for law enforcement purposes. Thus, they say, the European Commission is 'transformed from a protector of privacy rights into an opportunistic institution seeking to reduce privacy in its own interests'.[52] In the US, the sweeping US reforms in response to the terrorist attack on the World Trade Centre in September 2001 prompted a past Inspector-General of the CIA, Brian J. Weiss, to comment:

> The challenges ahead to civil liberties are significant. New technologies for data search and pattern recognition, combined with greater investigative freedom, have enormous potential for abuse. Even if used within the law, the capability of the government to search and correlate large amounts of data on its citizens ... frightens most Americans.[53]

Similar comments might be made about New Zealanders in 2004. A proposal contained in the Counter-Terrorism Bill before the New Zealand parliament for its first reading in April 2004 significantly expanded the powers of the Terrorism Act of 2002. Included in these expanded powers are (subject to judicial approval) the widened application of hidden installation of tracking devices in undefined 'things' which may include anything from cars to homes to luggage. In sweeping new powers awarded to the New Zealand Security Intelligence Service and the Government Communications Security Bureau, similar legislation previously requiring judicial approval has undergone amendments that removes such limitations. The Counter-Terrorism Bill also provides for wide-ranging amendments to other Acts, including the Crimes Act, the Misuse of Drugs Act and the Summary Proceedings Act. Concerns raised in submissions include broad and ambiguous definitions of terrorist, classified security information, and the right to designate persons or groups as terrorists without trial or the right to see any evidence against them, and a lack of reasonable safeguards. Operating in conjunction with established forms of disciplinary techniques and new discursive technologies of coercion, new surveillance strategies comprise key components in the framework of a multi-layered network of global power and control.

The Return of the 'Just War' and the Pre-emptive Strike

One of the characteristics of Empire, Hardt and Negri suggest, is that it resides within a context – in this case, a world context – that 'continually calls it into being'.[54] The Gulf War provided the conditions in which US initiative saw hegemony reorganized in preparation for a new imperial project of network power.[55] In the words of Secretary of Defence Rumsfeld, the Gulf War provided a great strategic opportunity, 'the kind of opportunity that World War Two offered – to refashion the world'.[56] The ending of the Gulf War signalled the assumption by the US of the role of global defender of freedom and dispenser of justice in a new variant of both the 'just war' and 'pre-emptive first strike' doctrines. It also signalled the beginning of a new and overt geopolitical strategy that had as its objective the establishment of US dominance over such wealthy oil- and energy-rich regions as remained outside its dominion. Demonstrated in a series of military attacks legitimated through a carefully crafted discourse of terrorism, the decade of the 1990s saw a return to the doctrine of the 'just war' as a justification for excursions into energy-rich regions, the militaristic overthrow of elected governments and the installation of US-friendly administrations. Dominating the redefined relationships were discourses of security underpinned by a shift from the common road of universal civilization to global apartheid.

Brzezinski, Co-Chairman of the Bush National Security Advisory Task Force on Foreign Relations, echoes the popular view that the 'defeat and collapse' of the Soviet Union was the 'final step in the rapid ascendance of a Western Hemisphere power, the US, as a sole, and, indeed, the first truly global superpower'.[57] In his carefully constructed analysis of the global politics of the twenty-first century, Brzezinski outlines a definitive geostrategy in which America's chief political prize, and one upon which America's global primacy is utterly dependent, is control over the Caspian/Central Asian region. Undertaken without a UN mandate and therefore in flagrant disregard of international law, the 2003 war on Afghanistan by a US-led coalition of countries was the first of what promises to be a strategic series of wars and invasions in the oil-rich Central Asia and Middle East. Here, as with Robert Cooper's analysis of the post-modern state, discourses of chaos and terror provide the supreme legitimation for a new imperial domination.

Bacevich argues that, through globalization, war was rapidly becoming obsolete, until the events of 11 September. Since then, he contends, globalization is making war 'an inescapable part of life in the twenty-first century'.[58] In fact, the idea of war as an inescapable fact of life in this century has long been viewed as part of the strategy to preserve and advance the strategy of openness. Certainly the events of 9/11 provided what Harvey calls the 'critical moment on which to construct patriotic fervour and solidarity'. It was also, he notes, the opportunity to co-opt US citizens into sacrificing civil liberties. Like the conditions that made possible the Truman Doctrine of 1947, September 11 was a blank check for interventionism at a global level. While it has been widely regarded as the rationale for American militarism and the war against terror, global military domination, as we have seen, was planned long before. In an early statement as the US Assistant Secretary of Defence for Democracy and Peacekeeping, CFR Fellow Morton Halperin declared that during the 1990s the US would 'take the lead around the world' not only in assisting but also in 'guaranteeing' the results of 'free elections' and in defending what he termed constitutional democracies 'through military action when necessary'.[59] Ballistic missile defence that was advertised as early as 2001, but planned long before, was not intended to protect America, Lawrence F. Kaplan writes in the *New Republic*. Rather, it was a 'tool for total domination'.[60]

Regime change was to become a core objective of this strategy. This doctrine for foreign policy was elaborated in the report of a new neoconservative think tank, the Project for a New American Century, initiated in 1997. Composed to a large extent of members of the Bush Cabinet such as Cheney, Armitage, Wolfowitz and Rumsfeld, all of whom became key figures in the defence and foreign policy team, the PNAC projected a set of key principles for American foreign policy, many of which became transplanted into the first National Security Strategy released by the Bush government in 2001. One of the most controversial doctrines in the document is the expansion of 'pre-emption' to 'first strike'. Section V of the National Security Strategy definitely states this shift:

> The United States has long maintained the option of pre-emptive actions to counter a sufficient threat to our national security. The greater the threat, the greater is the risk of inaction and the more compelling the case for taking anticipatory action to defend ourselves, even if uncertainty remains as to the time and place of the enemy's attack. To forestall or prevent such hostile attacks by our adversaries, the United States will, if necessary, act pre-emptively.

As the Centre for Defence Information (CDI) notes in its analysis, both strategies rely on knowledge that an attack is imminent as their justification.[61] Historically, they point out, such assessments have been questionable. The important question that fails to be addressed, however, is that of the possible boomerang effect. What, they ask, will be the implications of China, Russia or Iraq doing likewise? The mismatch between rhetoric and reality, the CDI pointedly comments, is most notable in the declaration that pre-emptive options will be supported by close coordination with allies 'to form a common assessment of the most dangerous threats'.

With millions of people worldwide declaring their opposition to the 2003 attack on Iraq, and the concerns voiced by many allies of the US regarding the accuracy of the supposed threats, the subsequent attack on Iraq demonstrated unilateralism at its 'full potency'. Perhaps most alarming of all is the reported signing of a document that specifically delineated plans for a war on Afghanistan as part of the Administration's 'war against terrorism' only six days after the attack on the World Trade Centre.

The introductory letter to the 2001 National Defence Strategy states the intention behind the policy. 'The United States', Bush declares, 'will use this moment of opportunity to extend the benefits of freedom across the globe. We will actively work to bring the hope of democracy, development, free markets, and free trade to every corner of the world'. The link between free markets and the war on Iraq was succinctly spelled out by Defence Secretary Rumsfield in the *Wall Street Journal*, when he stated that the Bush Administration is committed to a post-Saddam regime in Iraq that is headed by 'those who favour market systems'. Writing in the *New York Times* in 1999, Thomas Friedman articulated the relationship between militarism and the market even more openly:

> The hidden hand of the market will never work without a hidden fist – McDonald's cannot flourish without McDonnell Douglas, the builder of the F-15. And the hidden fist that keeps the world safe for Silicon Valley's technologies is called the United States Army, Air Force, Navy and Marine Corps.[62]

Full Spectrum Dominance: Space, the Global Frontier

The last remaining neutral arena of the global commons, outer space, has become the final frontier to be targeted for US expansion and domination. Cecil Rhodes, possibly the world's greatest imperialist, envisaged expansion into space as an imperial project to be a logical, if then impossible, step following the conquest and division of the world. According to his friend and biographer W. T. Stead, Rhodes, whom Spengler once described as 'the first precursor of a Western type of Caesar' made the following statement,

> The world is nearly all parcelled out, and what there is left of it is being divided up, conquered and colonized. To think of the stars that you see overhead at night, these vast worlds which we can never reach. I would annex the planets if I could; I often think of that. It makes me sad to see them so clear and yet so far away.[63]

The neoconservative position regarding annexation of space is elucidated in the statement of the Commander-in-Chief of the United States Airforce, General Howell Estes III. Citing Alvin Toffler's[64] statement that, 'the way a nation makes its wealth is the way it makes war', Howell Estes III declared galactic space to be 'critical to both military and economic instruments of power – the main source of national strength'.[65] In this way the US military-industrial complex sets its sights on the 'vast worlds' that, a century earlier, had saddened Rhodes by eluding his grasp. The justification for this violation of international agreements to maintain space as a friendly zone and part of the global commons is that, in the words of the Joint Vision 2020 policy document that superseded the 2001 document, dependence of the US on space capabilities 'rivals its dependence upon electricity and oil'. The two principal themes in the document are domination of the space medium and 'integrating space power through military operations'. Together these themes comprise the foundation for maintaining the pre-eminence of US military space power. Referred to as 'the fourth medium of warfare', space and the development of space power are described in the Joint Vision 2010 of the US Armed Forces as vital in 'moving towards the Joint Vision goal of being persuasive in peace, decisive in war, and pre-eminent in any form of conflict'.[66] In the words of the Vision document, 'Air and space superiority is a fundamental requirement for all operational concepts in *JV 2010* and is a prerequisite to achieving Full Spectrum Dominance'.

Four operational concepts comprise the conceptual framework for realizing Vision 2010 capabilities: the control of space, defined as 'the ability to assure access to space, freedom of operations within the space medium, and an ability to deny others the use of space, if required'; global engagement, defined as 'the application of precision force from, to, and through space'; full force integration, defined as 'the integration of space forces and space-derived information with land, sea and air forces and their information'; and global partnerships involving the augmentation of military space capabilities 'through the leveraging of civil, commercial, and international space systems'.[67] Writing in *The Progressive*, Karl Grossman of the Commission on Disarmament Education notes the importance of nuclear power in this scenario. The 1996 US Air Force Board report, *New World Vistas: Air and Space Power for the Twenty-First Century*, states:

> In the next two decades, new technologies will allow the fielding of space-based weapons of devastating effectiveness to be used to deliver energy and mass as force projection in tactical and strategic conflict.... These advances will enable lasers with reasonable mass and cost to effect very many kills.... Setting the emotional issues of nuclear power aside, this technology offers a viable alternative for large amounts of nuclear power in space.[68]

Seen in the context of US unilateral action across a range of multilateral arenas,[69] the linking of space with military and economic dominance as the mainstay of national interest demonstrates a retreat to forms of protectionism that contradict the fundamental premises of the global economic architecture and exacerbates the unravelling of multilateralism. To borrow a phrase from Harvey, the militarization of space comprises the final act in an inexorable strategy of 'accumulation by dispossession'. The commons, understood as the waters, forests, land, air, and space, no longer belong to the peoples of the world. They have become the sole domain of the holders of power and of the military, and the latter functions solely on behalf of the former.

The Return to Empire: Two Perspectives

As we have seen, the opening years of the twenty-first century saw the zero-sum politics and liberal internationalist ideologies upon which the post-World War Two order was presaged give way to a new ideology of imperialist power. Cooper's neoconservative account and the Marxist perspective offered by Hardt and Negri enable a useful comparison of current conceptualizations of empire. For Cooper, empire is the solution to the crisis of the global order.[70] In contrast to the 'postmodern state' that he advocates for the EU, 'modern' and 'premodern' states constitute threats to the members of the postmodern world. A return to imperialism, albeit a postmodern imperialism, is thus necessary for the establishment and maintenance of global order and the defence of the postmodern state. Interventionism and double standards function as key signifiers in Cooper's imperialism. He draws a parallel between empire in the ancient world and in the present one. In the ancient world, he declares, the condition of empire was 'order, culture and civilization' whereas outside the empire, all was 'barbarians, chaos and disorder'. Similarly, the security and order of the postmodern world is threatened by the modern and premodern zones. The threat of the classical modern state lies in the persistence of nationalist tendencies in an era that calls for a more highly evolved ethical and political state. The risk constituted by the premodern world of chaos and instability is that, having lost the monopoly or legitimacy of the use of force, the 'collapsed' premodern state provides a base for non-state actors involved in illegitimate activities.

Under these conditions, Cooper insists, the rebirth of empire is essential to the maintenance of global order and the defence of the postmodern state. Here he advances the notion of a 'double standard' as necessary and legitimate in the defence of the new, voluntary, postmodern imperialism. Inside empire, the conditions of inter-dependence and openness are safeguarded by mutual surveillance and mutual interference. There is no room here for mutual trust. In the case of the 'more old-fashioned kinds of states' the behaviour of earlier imperial forces is deemed appropriate. Deception and the pre-emptive attack are legitimate and necessary behaviours for the maintenance and defence of empire. As in the past, the function of today's empire is to protect the needs of capital and investment. To be a member of this new empire requires the relinquishment of state sovereignty over investment to the dictum of international finance. To remain outside empire risks being denoted a threat and thus vulnerable to deception and pre-emption. Openness and internal surveillance within, deception and external surveillance without. In this coercive model of contemporary imperialism, the 'just war' is a legitimate use of force upon those who remain outside the walls. Harvey notes that the same sort of classification was used to 'justify keeping India in tutelage and exacting tribute from abroad while praising the principles of representative government in "civilized" countries'.[71]

In Hardt and Negri's account of the development of US sovereignty and imperialism, the notion of the immanence of power as the defining characteristic of US sovereignty is contrasted to the transcendent power of European sovereignty. US sovereignty, they state, 'relies heavily on the exercise of control'.[72] Where European sovereignty is bounded, US sovereignty is expansive, opening itself to the outside 'with extra-ordinary force', directing its energies towards an 'open expansive project on an unbounded terrain'.[73] This immanent notion of sovereignty expands to include the powers it faces within its own network. Thus sovereignty in this form is conceived as 'an expansive power in networks',[74] its foundational characteristic being the notion that space is always open. In this circumstance, Hardt and Negri note, the struggle between the principle of expansion and the forces of limitation and control is always resolved in favour of expansion.[75]

Historically, the principle of the 'utopia of open spaces'[76] invisibilized the subordination and genocide of the indigenous peoples of the Americas, regarded as a subhuman species. As Hardt and Negri note, acknowledgement of the Native American peoples as fully human would have meant there was no expansiveness possible, no empty space to be filled. In fact, they state, 'their exclusion and domination were essential conditions of the functioning of the Constitution itself'.[77] Unlike black Americans the exploitation of whose labour was essential and who, on that basis, were given recognition in the US Constitution as being equal to three-fifths of a free person,[78] the indigenous peoples were cast as a problem of nature to be eliminated. In a very important sense, then, they suggest, imperial sovereignty can be traced back to earliest origins of the United States of America – to wars of genocide against Native Americans and black slavery.

Whereas Wilson's later response to the closure of space was to extend the US constitutional project to the production of peace through a world network of powers, Roosevelt used the 'civilizing mission' to justify the imperialist conquest and domination of the Philippines, so that 'people living in barbarism' could be freed from their chains. At the basis of the development and expansion of empire, Hardt and Negri declare, is an 'idea of peace'. In marked contrast to the founding image of an 'Empire of Liberty', the Cold War period and its Manichean extremes brought forth a new image of US constitutionalism, an overt demonstration of brutality reminiscent of the covert brutality upon which the US constitution of freedom and democracy was established. During this period, they argue, the shift in the locus of hegemony from the US to transnational capital prepared the way for the current project of empire. Importantly, despite what they see as the 'privileged position' of the US within the global constitution, in their account Hardt and Negri do not see 'the coming empire' as American, nor the US its centre.[79] Rather, the elaborate network of regimes, agreements and coordinating institutions through which global power is distributed constitute central aspects of the 'first phase of the transformation of the global frontier into an open space of imperial sovereignty'.[80]

In both Cooper's vision and Hardt and Negri's analysis, the heart of imperial power is capitalism, mediated through the mechanisms of the market. In both cases, the multiple networks of the global economy are the mechanisms through which imperial power is distributed. In Cooper's postmodern vision, the boundedness of European empire is reborn in the inside/outside of the postmodern empire. In Hardt and Negri's empire, the distributive and expansive nature of the posmodern empire subsumes and dissolves boundaries, and empire becomes a 'non-place'. The disciplinary modalities of the modern state have been replaced by the modalities of biopolitical control. Within the new empire, the capacity for the total extinction of life, exercised through a state monopoly of physical force and represented by the ever-present threat of thermonuclear weapons, has become the ultimate form of biopower. In the political economy of the new global order, sovereignty has been transformed, hegemony has been relocated from the local to the global, and 'freedom' and 'democracy' have become tools for the assertion of global domination. Overarching the modalities of the global financial markets and globalized production, deterritorialization of communicative space and the exercise of surveillance and control, as Hardt and Negri note, is the permanent threat of terror.

Globalization from Below: Resistance and Transformation

Hardt and Negri remind us that the issue of decline as one of the defining characteristics of empire opens up new spaces for transformation. In 'the elements of crisis', they state, exist 'the margins of possible reaction and the alternatives of destiny'.[81] As we saw in the previous chapter, there are discernible signs of opposing regionalized movements, the full impact of which has yet to be seen. The planned integration of European countries under the umbrella of the proposed European Constitution constitutes one possible challenge to American economic and political dominance. Another can be discerned in East Asia and in the emergence of China onto the world's economic stage. What may yet pose the greatest challenge to the unipolar order of twenty-first-century European imperialism, however, is the 'clash of civilizations' predicted by Huntington, a clash that is being daily fanned by funded chaos and both civil and state-sponsored forms of terrorism. In this context, there are urgent questions to be addressed about the shape of the new global order and the role of international law. Underlying these questions are much bigger questions about meaning and purpose. It is those questions that require our urgent attention.

Drawing a parallel between Polanyi's double movement of the nineteenth century and the 'powerful globalizing economic trend' of the late twentieth century, Cox posited the protective response of society in 1992 as 'less sure, less coherent' than that which occurred in the nineteenth century.[82] Largely ignored by media orthodoxy and initially fragmentary, the response of civil society groups since then has developed in strength and coherence. Emerging in strength alongside the WTO meeting in Seattle in November 1999, the resistance strategies of civil society groups and social movements have focused on the inequalities inherent within the global economic framework of commodification, trade and the 'free' market. By 2002, the hesitancy that Cox identified had been transformed into a powerfully globalized movement of resistance and opposition. Included in the demands for social and economic transformation are the reshaping of the global economic architecture, a redirection of the globalization process, and a reconceptualization of the notion of development. Exacerbated by biospheric crises, the social crises that accrue from the increasing racialization of poverty and the manipulation of group differentiation by the forces of global economic politics, the new social movement of opposition has broadened rapidly to include increasingly diverse groupings and individual identities. Responding to the increase in militarist interventionism within the world's largest oil and mineral producing region of Eurasia, voices of opposition have gained strength amongst members of the US Congress and the ruling Labour Party in Britain. Arguably, however, the greatest crisis facing the synthesized new social movements, labour unions, democratization movements, ecological movements and indigenous peoples is that of ontology.

For Hardt and Negri, the solution lies in a new form of militancy, a new resistance by the multitude, a response that demands the right to global citizenship with all workers being given this right in full – a reappropriation, indeed, by the multitude of control over space and a reassertion of the cooperative. This multitude, they carefully point out in *Multitude,War and Democracy in the Age of Empire,* published in 2004, does not imply any form of homogeneity.[83] St Francis of Assisi is offered as a model of the kind of militancy that such a response demands:

> Consider his work. To denounce the poverty of the multitude he adopted that common condition and discovered there the ontological power of a new society.... Francis in opposition to nascent capitalism refused every instrumental discipline, and in opposition to the mortification of the flesh (in poverty and in the constituted order) he posed a joyous life, the birds of the field, the poor and exploited humans, together against the will of power and corruption. Once again in post-modernity we find ourselves in Francis's situation, posing against the misery of power the joy of being. This is a revolution that no power will control – because biopower and communism, cooperation and revolution remain together in love, simplicity, and also innocence.[84]

'This', Hardt and Negri declare, 'is the irrepressible lightness and joy of being communist'. I would argue that this is the 'irrepressible lightness and joy' of participatory transformation. Understood as centred on collective well-being as opposed to the reification of capital and finance, and on the interdependence of existence instead of separation, St Francis's call to the unity of the world provides one metaphor for the search for a new political ontology of being. It is at precisely this point, I contend, that indigenous ontologies are profoundly relevant.

Notes

1 Cox, Robert W. (1995) 'Critical political economy', in Bjorn Hettne (ed.), *International Political Economy. Understanding Global Disorder.* Halifax, Nova Scotia: Fernwood Publishing, p. 36.
2 Cooper, Robert (2002) 'The postmodern state', in Mark Leonard (ed.), *Re-ordering the World: the Long-term Implications of September 11th.* London: Foreign Policy Centre, published in the *Observer,* 7 April 2002 as 'The new liberal imperialism', accessed 3 October 2002 at
http://www.observer.co.uk/Print/0,3858,4388912,00.html
3 Hardt, Michael and Negri, Antonio (2000) *Empire.* Cambridge, MA: Harvard University Press, p. 190.
4 Arrighi, Giovanni and Silver, Beverly J. (1999) *Chaos and Governance in the Modern World System.* Minneapolis and London: University of Minnesota Press.
5 Ruggerio, Renato (1996) Opening Address, World Trade Organization Conference, Singapore.

6 Ruggerio, cited *Agence France Presse*, Rome, 17 December 1998.
7 UN E/CN4/Sub 2/2000/13.
8 McCrae, Donald (1996) 'From sovereignty to jurisdiction: the implications for states of the WTO', in Mark Buchanan (ed.), *The Asia-Pacific Region and the Expanding Borders of the WTO: Implications, Challenges and Opportunities*. Victoria, British Columbia: Centre for Asia-Pacific Initiatives, University of Victoria.
9 *Ibid.*, p. 44. In a note to this explanation McCrae points out that comparative advantage is not about the distribution of benefits (other than the degree to which the principle of efficiency has distributional benefits) and notes the argument that the liberalization of capital means that some states will benefit from specialization much more than others. The principle of comparative advantage, then, assumes that capital will be relatively immobile.
10 Iwasawa usefully discusses the legalities of unilateralism in the context of the WTO dispute settlement rules, drawing on specific examples. See Iwasawa, Yuji (1996) 'Lawfulness of unilateral economic retaliation under international law', in Buchanan (1996), pp. 75–94.
11 LOTIS meeting minutes accessed 3 December 2001 at
   http://www.corpwatch.org/issues/wto/background/2001/lotis.html
   See also WTO confidential memo, 19 March 2001, accessed 3 December 2001 at
   http://www.corpwatch.org/issues/wto/background/2001/gatsdocs.html
12 GATS/SC31.
13 Monsanto strategy paper, cited Shiva, Vandana (1999) 'Monsanto's expanding monopolies. From seeds to water'. ZedNet Commentaries, 17 July 1999, online at
   http://www.zmag.org/sustainers/content/1999-07/17shiva.htm
14 Tansey, Geoff (1999) 'Trade, intellectual property, food and biodiversity. A discussion paper'. London: Quaker Peace and Service, p. 3.
15 *Ibid.*, p. 6.
16 Cottier, Thomas (1998) 'The protection of genetic resources and traditional knowledge: towards more specific rights and obligations in world trade law', *Journal of International Economic Law*, 1 (4), pp. 555–84.
17 *Ibid.*
18 For full discussion of this, see the website of te Ope Mana a Tai,
   http://www.teope.co.nz/hui/background.htm
19 New Zealand Government, Foreshore and Seabed Act, 2004.093.
20 Mugabe, John (1998) 'Intellectual property protection and traditional knowledge. An exploration in international policy discourses'. Paper prepared for the World Indigenous Peoples Organization (WIPO), Geneva, Switzerland, December 1998, African Centre for Technology Studies, accessed 17 September 2000 at
   http://www.acts.or.ke/paper%20-@20intellectual%20property.htm
21 Nabhan, G. R. *et. al.* (1996) in Stephen B. Brush and Doreen Stabinsky (eds.), *Valuing Local Knowledge, Indigenous People and Intellectual Property Rights*. Washington, DC and Covelo, CA: Island Press, p. 193, cited in Mugabe (1998), p. 8.
22 In 1998, the first of this series of resolutions called for a review from a human rights perspective of the draft text of the MAI Agreement by member states of the OECD and for the development of appropriate expertise to address 'the human rights implications of international and regional trade, investment and financial policies'.
23 Oloka-Onyango, J. and Udagama, Deepa (2000) *The Realization of Economic, Social and Cultural Rights: Globalization and Its Impact on the Full Enjoyment of Human Rights*. Preliminary Report submitted in accordance with Sub-Commission Resolution 1999/8. E/CN.4/Sub.2/2000/13.
24 UN Sub-Commission on the Protection and Promotion of Human Rights, Fifty-second Session. *Intellectual Property Rights and Human Rights*. E/CN.4/Sub.2/2000/7, 17 August 2000.

25 *Ibid*. It is noteworthy that in 2000, as reported by a representative of UNESCO at a meeting organized by UNCTAD, approximately 95 per cent of the patents in the world were held by developed countries. Capdevila, Gustavo (2000) *Indigenous Peoples Defend Traditional Knowledge*. BIO-IPR, GRAIN, 14 11/2000.

26 Indigenous peoples have articulated this position within multiple international and local forums, including the negotiations within the Conference of the Parties to the Convention on Biodiversity. See, for instance, UNCTAD reports as well as those by RAFI, a non-indigenous NGO that works closely with indigenous and traditional communities to preserve and maintain biodiversity.

27 Awang, Sandra S. (2000) 'The Human Genome Diversity Project', in George J. Sefa Dei, Budd L. Hall and Dorothy Goldin Rosenberg (eds.), *Indigenous Knowledges in Global Contexts. Multiple Readings of Our World*. Toronto, Buffalo and London: University of Toronto Press.

28 Muller, H. J. (1927), 'Artificial transmutation of the gene', *Science*, 66 (1699), pp. 84–7, cited in *ibid*., p. 125.

29 Awang (2000), p. 127.

30 Posey, D. A. and G. Dutfield (1996) 'Human genes for whose humanity', in *Beyond Intellectual Property: Towards Traditional Resource Rights for Indigenous Peoples and Local Communities*. Ottawa: International Development Research Centre, cited in Mead, Aroha Te Pareake (1997) 'Human genetic research and *whakapapa*', in Pania Te Whaite, Marie McCarthy, and Arohia Durie, (eds.), *Mai I Rangiatea. Maori Wellbeing and Development*. Auckland: Auckland University Press and Bridget Williams Books, p. 132.

31 RAFI reported in 1994 that to date no attempt had been made by the US government to gain consent for the patenting of this T-cell line, nor has any attempt since been made by the US government to acknowledge this violation of human rights.

32 Dutfield (1996), cited in Mead (1997).

33 See, in particular, Office of the Parliamentary Commissioner for the Environment (2001), *Key Lessons from the History of Science and Technology: Knowns and Unknowns, Breakthroughs and Cautions*. Wellington, March.

34 Ammunson, Paora and Tamati Cairns. Witness Brief on behalf of New Zealand Life Sciences Network, Submission No. IP 24, Royal Commission on Genetic Modification, 2001.

35 Carnoy, Martin (2000) *Globalization and Educational Restructuring*. Paris: International Institute of Educational Planning, cited in Peters, M. (2002) 'Education policy in the age of knowledge capitalism'. Keynote Address to the World Comparative Education Forum, Beijing Normal University, 14–16 October 2002.

36 OECD (1996) *The Knowledge-Based Economy*. Paris: Organization for Economic Cooperation and Development.

37 World Bank (1998/9) *Knowledge for Development. World Development Report*, Washington, DC, online at http://www.worldbank.org/wdr/wdr98/ index.htm

38 Burton-Jones, Alan (1999) *Knowledge Capitalism: Business, Work and Learning in the New Economy*. Oxford: Oxford University Press, cited in Peters (2002).

39 *Ibid*.

40 Marshall, James (1999) 'The mode of information and education: insights on critical theory from Michel Foucault', in Thomas S. Popkewitz and Lynn Fendler (eds.), *Critical Theories in Education. Changing Terrains of Knowledge and Politics*. New York and London: Routledge, p. 162.

41 Blackmore, Jill (2000) 'Globalization: a useful concept for feminists rethinking theory and strategies in education?' in Nicholas C. Burbules and Carlos Alberto Torres (eds.), *Globalization and Education. Critical Perspectives*. London; New York: Routledge, pp. 133–56.

42 Carnoy, cited in Peters (2002).
43 Popkewitz, Thomas S. (1999) 'A social epistemology of educational research', in Popkewitz and Fendler (1999), p. 20.
44 *Ibid.*, p. 23.
45 Fairclough, Norman (1999) 'Neoliberalism as a focus for critical research on language'. Programmatic text, *Globalization Research Network,* October 1999, accessed 7 June 2001 at http://bank.rug.ac.be/global/programme2.html
46 *Ibid.*
47 Popkewitz (1999), p. 36.
48 Deleuze, Gilles (1995) 'A Portrait of Foucault', in *Negotiations, 1972–1990* (trans. M. Joughin) New York: Columbia University Press, pp. 177–82 cited in Peters, M. (2001) *Poststructuralism, Marxism and Neoliberalism. Between Theory and Politics.* Oxford: Rowan and Littlefield, p. 98.
49 CNN Law Centre, at http://www.cnn.com/2004/LAW/01/26/patriot.act.ap/
50 Pub. L. No.107–56 Stat 272 (2001), cited in Hitz, Frederick P. and Brian J. Weiss (2004) 'Helping the CIA and the FBI connect the dots in the war against terror', *International Journal of Intelligence and Counter-Intelligence,* 17(1) (Spring), p. 17.
51 New Zealand Customs Service (2003) *Contraband. New Zealand Customs Service Magazine* (September), Wellington, pp. 8–12.
52 Privacy International. *Transferring Privacy. The Transfer of Passenger Records and the Abdication of Privacy Protection.* February 2004, online at http://www.privacyinternational.org/issues/terrorism/rpt/transferringprivacy.pdf
53 Hitz and Weiss (2004).
54 Hardt and Negri (2000), p. 181.
55 *Ibid.* pp. 179–80.
56 Bacevich, Andrew J. (2002) *American Empire. The Realities and Consequences of US Diplomacy.* Cambridge, MA and London: Harvard University Press, p. 227.
57 Brzezinski, Zbigniew (1997) *The Grand Chessboard. American Primacy and Its Geostrategic Imperatives.* New York: Basic Books, p. xiii.
58 Bacevich, (2002), p. 225.
59 Cited Robinson, William I. (1996) *Promoting Polyarchy. Globalization, US Intervention, and Hegemony.* Cambridge: Cambridge University Press, p. 100.
60 Cited Bacevich (2002), p. 223.
61 Centre for Defence Information (2002) *The Bush National Security Strategy. A First Step.* 26 September, online at http://www.cdi.org/index.cfm
62 Friedman, Thomas L. (1999) 'A manifesto for the fast world', *New York Times Magazine,* 28 March, p. 42.
63 Stead, W. T. (1902) *The Last Will and Testament of Cecil John Rhodes.* Cited at http://www.cecilrhodes.net/sword.html
64 Author of *Future Shock,* published New York: Random House, 1970.
65 Estes, Howell M. III (1998) 'Foreword', *US Space Command Long Range Plan Executive Summary.* http://www.spacecom.af/mil/usspace
66 United States Space Command (1996) *Vision for 2020,* online at http://www.spacecom.af/mil/usspace
67 *Ibid.*
68 Grossman, Karl (2000). 'Master of space', in *The Progressive,* 6 January 2000. It should be noted that HR 3616, the Space Preservation Act of 2002, reintroduced by Representative Dennis Kucinich (Democrat, Ohio) in January 2001, calls on the US to ban all research, development, testing, and deployment of space-based weapons, and if passed would require the US to enter negotiations toward a World Treaty to Ban Weapons in Space.
69 Specific instances include withdrawal by the US from the Kyoto Agreement, the imposition of tariffs as high as 30 per cent on most steel imports from Asia and

Europe, and the recent refusal of the US to recognize the International Court of Justice unless full exemption of US citizens is guaranteed. In his comprehensive summation of instances in which US practice breaches international human rights agreements, Chomsky identifies these strategies as the behaviour of a 'rogue state'. Chomsky, Noam (2000) *Rogue States. The Rule of Force in World Affairs*. Cambridge, MA: South End Press.

70 Cooper, Robert (2002) 'The new liberal imperialism', accessed 3 October 2002 at http://www.observer.co.uk/Print/0,3858,4388912,00.html

71 Harvey, David (2003) *The New Imperialism*. Oxford: Oxford University Press, p. 210.

72 Cooper (2002).

73 Hardt and Negri (2000), p. 165.

74 *Ibid.*

75 *Ibid.*, p. 166.

76 *Ibid.*, p. 169.

77 *Ibid.*, p. 170.

78 An important point made by Hardt and Negri is that the one of the contradictions that had to be overcome in the US Constitution was the ideological contradiction between black and slavery, and free and white. Indigenous peoples, on the other hand, were simply excluded. They existed outside of the constitution.

79 *Ibid.*, p. 384.

80 *Ibid.*, p. 182.

81 *Ibid.*, p. 376.

82 Cox, R. W. (1996) [1992] 'Towards a posthegemonic conceptualization of world order: reflections on the relevancy of Ibn Khaldun', in Robert W. Cox (with Timothy J. Sinclair), *Approaches to World Order*. Cambridge: Cambridge University Press, p. 155.

83 Hardt, Michael and Negri, Antonio (2004) *Multitude. War and Democracy in the Age of Empire*. New York: Penguin Press, p. 355.

84 Hardt and Negri (2000), p. 413.

✳

The Spiral Turns

Global Crisis and Transformation:
An Indigenous Response

In the beginning, Io Mata Ngaro, God of the Gods, Father and Mother of the Unborn Creator of All, called the Universe into being. And all those born of the stars were brothers and sister, kin within one family.[1]

In these pages, I have endeavoured to trace the development of world order, the impact on indigenous peoples and the reciprocal relationship of indigenous peoples to and within the world system. I have sought to show that the dialectic nature of this relationship has been mutually transforming through the twin logics of economic expansionism and exploitation, and international human rights law. Against the practice of accumulation by dispossession, indigenous peoples' praxis has effected some important transformations in international law. In the twenty-first century, indigenous peoples have finally won the right to a Permanent Forum at the United Nations. Indigenous rights to self-determination are still fiercely debated; many of the world's 370 million indigenous peoples continue to be dispossessed, marginalized and disenfranchised; but the indigenous voice can no longer be silenced. Aspirations to sovereignty and self-determination remain the politicizing impetus for many groups of indigenous peoples, including Maori, even if definitions of these concepts are strongly contested. In the international arena, the sovereignty of states and the principle of non-intervention are key determinants for the ordering of inter-state relationships and provide the terrain within which indigenous rights and other human rights are contested. International law remains an arena of critical importance for the advancement of human rights and the reassertion of indigenous self-determination. However, in the context of legal norms and political enforcement, the twin principles of state sovereignty and non-intervention continue to mitigate against these aspirations.

As at the international level, so local political engagement by indigenous people has involved the development of counter-hegemonic discourses and the assertion of indigenous sovereignty across multiple arenas. The recognition of indigenous peoples' customary rights in international law, combined with local and international activities, has led to the renegotiation of relationships with states. In some instances, the successful negotiation of treaty settlements has enabled enhanced decision making authority and the opportunity to exercise limited forms of self-determination within the boundaries of state sovereignty. This has sometimes involved the extinguishment of customary rights in return for financial settlements and citizenship rights. In other cases, partial recognition of customary rights has remained, providing a right of consultation over the treatment of natural resources – required, for instance, under New Zealand's Resource Management Act (1991). Notably however, this requirement does not extend to giving effect to the outcome of such consultation. More recently, these remaining limited rights have been the subject of renewed contention as the New Zealand government has sought to vest the ownership of the foreshore and seabed in the Crown, further limiting Maori customary rights in the process.

At the same time, the ideological strategies of divide and rule that underpin the contested politics of the settlement process function to ensure divisiveness and frequently the further marginalization of groups or nations such as Waitaha. The reformulation of indigenous self-determination within the economic framework of treaty settlements, the commodification of resources and the allied commodification of indigenous identities within corporate distributive frameworks have facilitated the emergence of new hierarchies of power, the limiting of significant benefit sharing to the few, and the marginalizing of traditional forms of knowledge. This has raised questions about the origin and interpretation of the concept of sovereignty, the reconstruction of traditional political structures and, most importantly, the determination of new collective frameworks.

Tracing the development of international law and the processes that initially recognized indigenous peoples as sovereign peoples within their own territories, and then divested them of that same sovereignty, I argued that underpinning these strategies were sets of ideologies that operated at the conjunction of particular formations of power and knowledge. The vigorous propagation of these ideologies by transatlantic networks of elites, although contested, has succeeded in dominating intellectual and political visions of world order sufficiently to have shaped the structural and ideological framework from the sixteenth century through to the beginning of the twenty-first. I have sought to demonstrate that the international world order of the twentieth century was constructed around two opposing mandates – those of human rights (with the protection of minorities) and the economic imperative of expansion.

During the early part of the second half of the twentieth century, a critical neoliberal project involved carving out consensus for limited forms of democracy, for new forms of political and militarist interventionism within resource-rich and strategically located countries, and for the reshaping of their social, political and economic structures in ways that would support the interests of the industrial countries. In the latter part of the twentieth century, human rights discourses accompanied by polyarchic forms of limited democracy legitimated US-led military interventions in developing countries, which also sought to reform their frequently authoritative regimes. These interventions frequently saw democratically elected governments who sought autonomy from the US replaced with what were often more dictatorial regimes that, for various reasons, supported the US agenda for economic expansionism and political control. The key objective underpinning these processes has been access to and control over resources, a project that was mapped during the years of the Second World War and that marked the vast majority of the world's resources within the territories of the Middle East. On this account, the sustained undermining of the mandate and legitimacy of the United Nations can be understood as part of a wider strategic effort to assert US military power as the leading principle of an expansive global order that encompasses all spheres.

The Crisis of Global Order

Writing in 1993, Cox suggested that the conflict situation in the Middle East could become characteristic of the transition from globalization to a 'postglobalization' world order. The central features of territorial confrontation, he argued, would perhaps obscure the far more profound implications that lie in the transformation of societies. Contributing factors to this transformation were 'the spread of new production relations, the unleashing of an affirmation of suppressed ethnic, religious and gender identities and the attendant challenges to existing forms of states'.[2] This challenge that was visible in parts of the Third World and in the disintegration of the Soviet Empire would, he predicted, eventually become visible in 'the most powerful centres of the world economy'.[3] The opening events of the twenty-first century, beginning with the spectacle of what commentator Greg Palast described as 'the theft of the presidency',[4] the war on Afghanistan, rapidly followed by the launching of a 'first strike' attack on Iraq in defiance of UN Security resolutions are some of the signs that Cox's prediction has been overtaken. The legitimators for these events are coercive Manichean discourses in which words such as freedom and democracy, peace and prosperity, technology and war, have taken on new meaning. They have become the legitimating discourse for a 'war on terrorism' that has its origins in centuries of European terrorism, violence, exploitation and dispossession.

Schell draws parallels between the events of August 1914 and 11 September 2001. On both occasions, a period of political liberalization, economic globalization and peace – albeit confined to the privileged areas of the planet – was brought to an abrupt halt with a sudden, violent eruption. Schell could have added that, then as now, prosperity and peace for the privileged was founded on the oppression and exploitation of the non-privileged. On both occasions, he also notes, an unpredictable chain of events was set in motion, with the world heading, in many cases unknowingly, to the edge of a precipice. The Bush administration's unilateral response to the September 11 attack and its declaration – ignoring voices calling for a cooperative strategy – of a 'war' on international terrorism wherever it might reside, galvanized the might of the American military machine. This was rapidly followed by a strategy of 'regime change' designed to legitimate the overthrow of governments and leaders such as Saddam Hussein who had outlived their usefulness and no longer danced to America's tune.

From there the war was expanded to include weapons of mass destruction. An 'axis of evil' representing the most apparently dangerous challenges to peace in the twenty-first century legitimated the once-abhorred course of pre-emptive action – including the right to use nuclear weapons from anywhere in the world, or even from space. No country was to be permitted to challenge US global dominance. No international treaties were to impede US sovereignty at home and global dominance abroad. This intent was unequivocally stated in the National Security Strategy document issued in 2002. Throughout the entire world, it declares, only one economic and political system remained viable, the American model of liberal democracy and free enterprise. And it would henceforth be promoted and defended through the unilateral use of force, pre-emptively if necessary. Wars for self-determination would no longer be viable. Violent struggles against oppression and exploitation would no longer be tolerated. Empire had emerged in full glory. Schell calls it an 'imperial delusion' which, if carried to its logical end, may see 'the destiny of the American republic ... flare out in a blaze of pointless mass destruction'.[5]

There is an identifiable relationship between the development of modernity – within which a radical transformation occurred in the nature of knowledge and the meaning of being, one that directly shaped the politico-economic structural framework of the liberal international order – and the current crisis of globalization. Hardt and Negri draw attention to two distinctive aspects of the period between the thirteenth and sixteenth centuries. First, knowledge is brought from the plane of transcendence to that of immanence: 'the occult secrets of nature', in Francis Bacon's words, became the objective of 'a more powerful technique of the mind and intellect'.[6] At the same time, power and authority were reformulated and the concept of liberation was reconceptualized. By the time of Spinoza's declaration of the oneness of nature and humanity in the seventeenth century, the horizons of immanence and the democratic political order coincided. It was at this point, they declare, that the historical, technical and political construction of the new humanity was determined, the point at which 'the singular is recast as the multitude'.[7]

In their account, the Thirty Year War that was born of the struggle between the revolutionary and counter-revolutionary processes of the Renaissance saw the emergence of a new strategy of power that played on the fears and anxieties of the multitude, fuelling the desire to reduce the uncertainty of life and to increase security. In the ensuing demand for peace, Hardt and Negri postulate, peace itself was transformed from the humanist connotations that endowed it with its transformative power, to '[T]he miserable condition of sur-vival, the extreme urgency of escaping death'.[8] The subsequent counter-revolution sought to 'dominate and expropriate the force of the emerging movements and dynamics' by attempting to 'relativize the scientific capabilities of transformation' and to oppose the reappropriation of power by the multitude.[9] Above all, the objective was to establish an overarching structure of domination.

Foucault's analysis of the relationship between power, right and truth speaks to the current production of new discourses of truth and right that permeate the 'war on terrorism'.[10] In this racialized discourse of terrorism, the power to determine truth and right rests with today's Emperor, the imperial power that almost single-handedly has undermined the regime of multilateral agreements and treaties that protected the global commons, the environment, and the human rights of groups and individuals. In this case, the use of 'terrorist' as the defining signifier for the 'Other' is legitimated by the supporting discourses of 'freedom' and 'democracy': on that basis others are determined to be 'either for us, or against us'. The construction of the terrorist 'Other' as non-White and non-Christian, and by definition non-civilized and barbaric, is produced through a form of power that creates its own truth and, in Foucault's words, 'institutionalizes, professionalizes, and rewards its pursuit'.[11] In today's hierarchization of difference, the discourse of terrorism functions to 'efface the domination intrinsic to power in order to present the latter at the level of appearance under two different aspects: on the one hand, as the legitimate rights of sovereignty, and on the other, as the legal obligation to obey it'.[12] Faced with the imminent prospect of a Third Gulf War under the rubric of 'the war on terrorism' and the potential for increased terrorism in repercussion, it might well be argued that, once again, peace has been transformed from 'its humanist connotations', with the potential for social transformation, to '[T]he miserable condition of survival, the extreme urgency of escaping death'.

The crucial difference between 1914 and now, to which Schell draws our attention, is that in the former case, once the armies were 'hurled across the borders, it was too late to withdraw'.[13] In this instance, the moment that Schell describes as one of exceptional fluidity and unpredictability, the moment that Wallerstein calls 'trans-formational timespace', is upon us – and may be about to run out. Schell articulates the plea of many for a different kind of choice; the choice to build a 'cooperative non-violent world'. As he poignantly argues, the imperative is to 'secure not only peace, but our own survival'.[14] The question Hardt and Negri pose is, 'given that empire is defined by crisis and that its decline has already begun ... is it possible in this dark night to theorize positively and define a practice of the event?'[15]

Alternatives to Empire

Of the multiple discourses of globalization that proliferated during the last three decades of the twentieth century, the most pervasive is the neoliberal notion of inevitability or 'there is no alternative', generally interpreted as no alternative to the redrawing of the global political landscape, to the hollowing-out of the nation state and to the establishment of a neoliberalist, market-based global economy and political order.

Global social and political transformation is certainly inevitable. But contrary to neoliberal and neoconservative doctrine, there is nothing inevitable about either the processes by which this may occur or the form that this may take. The transformation of the global political and economic framework has been accompanied by the emergence of an increasingly broad social movement of resistance that is global in membership and, more importantly, in impact. This new global movement represents one opportunity for intervention. Hardt and Negri's joyous multitude, 'a global biopolitical subject of absolute democracy' has, as Schell also asserts, unlimited power for the bringing about of change and may yet, by its refusal to count-enance the horrors of an unjust unilateralism, be the downfall of globalized domination. Other possibilities are envisaged in the deve-lopment of new political formations whose form is yet to be determined. Regionalized economic and political structures such as the European Union – fifteen European heads of states condemned the unjust war on Iraq and asserted the leadership of the UN in the international order – represent another possibility for change. Federal models that celebrate and endorse multiplicity are another.

The concept of nested forms of democratic governance within and across nations and states is an important approach to addressing the multiple and diverse claims of cultural identity and self-deter-mination. Political theorists working in this arena acknowledge the inherent shortcomings in the existing system of political governance that assumes the nation state as the primary international actor. The notion of overlapping identities and structures in a variation of the American model of 'nations within' is one such model. Kymlicka highlights the trend towards self-governing minorities through emer-ging forms of federalism, often in the form of 'nations within': however, this liberal model has a number of issues that require resolution. Kymlicka is at pains to point out that the influence of American liberalism has the inevitable effect of further marginalizing minority rights on the basis that 'the solution to ethnic conflict is individual rights, not group rights'.[16] This attitude, Kymlicka acknowledges, completely fails to resolve the issues involved in minority nationalism – and, I would add, those involved in indigenous claims to either sovereignty or self-determination. For those who point to the US model of nations within, Kymlicka reminds us that the US has not differed in its treatment of minorities from any other Western democracy. Strategies of oppression were followed by attempts at accommodation within some form of political status that provides limited forms of self-determination. Tully, as we saw, calls this extinction by accommodation.

Liberal nationalism holds that nations have the right to self-determination but that all nations, whether majority or minority nations, should consist of post-ethnic models in which residence and participation rather than blood quantum and community recognition are the determinants, a view that Kymlicka says is often mistakenly seen as inherently incompatible with minority nationalism. In Kymlicka's account, 'minority nationalism and cosmopolitan multiculturalism operate at different levels.'[17] In his view, democratic federalism or quasi-federalizing power-sharing arrangements provide 'a means for domesticating and pacifying nationalism while at the same time respecting individual rights and freedoms'.[18] Carens provides a helpful discussion of some of the problematics of Kymlicka's model.[19] Of these the most salient and problematic is Kymlicka's advocacy of 'the diffusion by the state of a common culture in the name of equality'. The administration of George W. Bush adopts the same argument when it declares the US model of liberal democracy to be the single acceptable political and economic model for the world. At its worst, this not only gives rise to extremisms such as those demonstrated by Friedman but, more dangerously, ascribes to itself a right of preemptive enforcement which, when disputed, calls forth accusations of terrorism.

Schell also argues for a federal model, although a more expansive version that that offered by Kymlicka. For Schell, the critical ingredients for a new political framework are the 'delaminating' or sharing of sovereignty, collective rights and federalism. Following Gottlieb, Schell proposes a model in which individuals would each hold two internationally recognized statuses, one as a member of a nation, the other as a citizen of a state. Conceived along similar lines to Kymlicka's layers of minority nationalism and multicultural cosmopolitanism, the ability to claim multiple identities would resolve the problem of overlapping boundaries between nations and states and provide for certain cultural and other collective rights such as the right to one's language, to control schooling and to practise one's culture or religion. Thus the single boundaries of state, people and territory would be dissolved and, with them, absolute state sovereignty. In Schell's model, the right to self-determination would give way to self-determinations, and collective interventions in cases of human rights abuses and crimes against humanity would be mandatory. Collective rights would increasingly be protected within international law and the negative right of peoples not to be extinguished by physical or legislative means would be protected.

Like Hardt and Negri, Schell's response to the crisis of our time is to call for a revolution. His revolution, however, is one against violence in the world and is based on the power of collective action based on common goals and principles. Among some of the key components or plans that such action might include are disarmament, human rights, democratization, reform of the UN, social and ecological programmes, the advancement of international law, a programme of international intervention; enforcement of a prohibition against crimes against humanity; and a democratic league. The vehicle for such collective action is ultimately new structures of cooperative power. Structures of cooperative power in which sovereignty is shared, he points out, have flourished. In this regard the European Union model is offered as a model of the possible, of the 'incremental pursuit of revolutionary ends by peaceful, reformist means'.[20] In Schell's account, the EU model of divided power is made possible by the voluntary decisions of states to 'throw in their lot together'.[21] However, as Young points out, this model is itself highly problematic. She argues that its very size and structure render it undemocratic and that many of its policies and practices are determined by 'a relatively small group of state-based elites' without little or no input from ordinary citizens. Its two-tiered nature also means that power is unevenly distributed.

Young's global federation model also involves the notion of shared sovereignty.[22] Like Schell, Young questions the morality of a state sovereignty that is based on the principle of non-intervention or that claims sole rights to natural resources and internalizes its environmental practices. Drawing on Homi Babha's notion of postcolonial hybridity, Young offers a model that she calls 'decentred diverse democratic federalism'. Babha's concept of hybridity calls for a reinterpretation of modern history as hybrid rather than as a linear progression in which national identities are both objects of and influenced by the strategies of subversion that emanate from the Other. This notion provides a context for considering the debates concerning the degree to which the Iroquois model of federalism and its Great Law of Peace influenced the development of the US constitution. For Young, the importance of this debate lies in the way it hybridizes the idea of democracy, rather than viewing it as a purely Western concept. Hybridity also informs the concept of 'deep diversity' that Young, like both Tully and Taylor, places at the centre of a federated polity in which open dialogue and diverse discourses are the fabric of interrelationships.

In so far as they offer alternative political frameworks for addressing the multiplicities of cultures and identities that comprise the world of nation states, these discussions offer possibilities for the development of sound alternative political frameworks in which justice and equality can be mediated for all. Pluralistic models involving shared sovereignty provide useful frameworks within which to address some of the issues raised in questions of self-determination and collective rights. Where many of these discussions fall short is in failing to acknowledge the inseparable link between political frameworks and economic ideologies and the ideologies of consumption and exploitation upon which the dichotomies of 'them and us' are predicated. Without interrogating the ontologies upon which political and economic frameworks are predicated, any alternative structure is ultimately bound to repeat the same power relations of dominance and subordination, of expansion and exploitation. Schell's model of cooperative power attempts to address this issue. For Schell, the starting point for a world politics based on cooperative power would be the power of collective action, a power referred to variously by Havel as 'living in the truth', by Gandhi as *satyagraha* and by Arendt as 'non-coercive power'.[23] It would require the act of choosing and fostering cooperative power at every level of political life. Such action, he declares, would be based on common goals and common principles. Rather than the monopoly of any one group of interests, the process he envisages 'would develop as the common creation of all and any comers acting across every political level on the basis of common principles'.

Young suggests that the Iroquois model of federalism contained many key characteristics shared by other indigenous nations, including Waitaha: deliberation and consultation, collective approaches to problem solving and local self-governance, often situated within the larger context of loosely organized federalism. In Young's view, these models have much to offer to the 'project of rethinking democracy in a post-colonial age'. She is not alone in this view. Influenced in no small measure by the crisis of the biosphere, some Western academics have made the investigation of indigenous belief systems and social practices a significant aspect of their endeavours to develop alternative social structures as well as environmental practices. Indigenous author Barriero cites a senior official at the Canadian Development Agency as saying 'we all know something is terribly amiss ... and there is a feeling that indigenous peoples are closer to a better idea of how to correct the problems'.[24]

Indigenous Ontologies and Global Order

Indigenous writers argue that the revival and maintenance of indigenous knowledge systems is not only a cultural imperative but an imperative also for the continuing viability of human occupation of the planet within a paradigm of peaceful coexistence. In this vein, Leopold Sédar Senghor's offering draws on Cesaire to develop the notion of negritude as both an instrument of liberation and as a 'humanism of the twentieth century'. For Senghor, negritude is,

> the sum of the cultural values of the black world; that is, a certain active presence in the world, or better, in the universe... it is essentially relations with others, an opening out to the world, contact and participation with others. Because of what it is, negritude is necessary in the world today: it is a humanism of the twentieth century.[25]

The circumstances that led to the undermining, devaluing and mythologizing of indigenous ontologies within the dominant Western scientific paradigm have readied us for a return movement of the double spiral. The transformational timespace of the present moment parallels that of the sixteenth century point of decision in which the understanding of the unity of 'One' was relinquished in favour of division and separation and a reconstruction of the nature of 'science'. Parallels can be drawn between the Baconian shift from a spiritually based awareness of the interconnectedness of life to a positivist mode in which humankind was elevated to a position of domination over the rest of creation. Then, as now, issues of power underpinned the transition from a unifying ontology based on an understanding of Oneness, to an ontology based on division and separation. As Hardt and Negri insightfully declare:

No metaphysics, except a delirious one, can pretend to define humanity as isolated and powerless. No ontology, except a transcendent one, can relegate humanity to individuality. No anthropology, except a pathological one, can define humanity as a negative power. Generation, that first fact of metaphysics, ontology and anthropology, is a collective mechanism or apparatus of desire. Biopolitical becoming celebrates this 'first' dimension in absolute terms.[26]

Indigenous political and educational initiatives have been critical strategies for the insurrection of indigenous cultural and spiritual values, ontologies and epistemologies. In New Zealand, Maori educational institutions are a pivotal focus of Maori transformative strategies involving the assertion and legitimation of Maori ontologies and epistemologies. As Graham Smith has explained, the development of these transformative pedagogical initiatives has been underpinned by a model of engagement that is embedded in *kaupapa* Maori as praxis – the theory and practice of 'being Maori'. In the context of a new ontology for global order, the most pressing challenge for indigenous leaders and educationalists is to recentre the relevance of traditional indigenous ontologies and epistemologies in the construction of inclusive, sustainable and pluralistic forms of governance. The manner by which this recognition and understanding will become firmly rooted has to do with moving beyond resistance to the study and application of traditional ontologies of being within multicivilizational frameworks. The contribution and impact of indigenous educational strategies in this process has yet to be fully explored.

Full engagement in the spiral of transformation that is centred in indigenous ontologies and cosmologies requires the re-embedding of traditional spiritually based cultural values at the centre of indigenous socio-politico-economic and educational endeavours. It requires dismantling hierarchically driven political frameworks of exclusion and the development of genuinely cooperative and inclusive frameworks that promote 'the greatest good for all people'.[27] Fundamentally, it requires recognition of the paucity of economically constructed frameworks for governance and a return to the traditional spiritual values of our *tupuna*, of our ancestors. Alfred calls this 'self-conscious traditionalism'.

The timespace of today's moment, as Wallerstein and many others have emphasized, is one of choice. Like the rest of humanity, indigenous peoples stand poised within this moment. In the context of politico-economic models of self-determination that are predicated on the commodification of the lifeworld, indigenous peoples are confronted with critical choices. Should we relinquish the traditional cosmologies and ontologies grounded in oneness and interconnectedness, the subjugated knowledges that defined us as peoples, in favour of economic freedom? Or should we re-examine the notion of sovereignty in the context of those ancient values and traditional ontologies that have been posited as an alternative model for global order – a new humanism embedded in the principles of social justice, the sacredness of existence and the oneness of being?

For Waitaha, our responses to these choices for the future will surely be shaped by the lifestream of our own past, in which Waitaha were known as the people of peace and welcomed all within their ranks. These questions also have an impact at a professional and personal level. Scholars and academics cannot afford the luxury of being unconscious of the impact of our own discourses and practice. Neither can we afford to be oblivious to the consequences of continuing to legitimate the dominant ontologies that are embedded in the global order. A critical question that arises for me is that of the most effective response to what I perceive as a new crisis for indigenous knowledge, that of its expropriation and subsumption within new formations of capital and globalized orders of production. Another concerns my personal response to the crisis of this transformational moment.

The Transformative Spiral

Throughout this book, while endeavouring to avoid the pitfalls of essentialism, I have argued that the principles identified within traditional indigenous ontologies, some of which have been articulated in *kaupapa* Maori and other indigenous models, illumine an alternative cooperative model for global order. My central objective has been to argue that traditional indigenous ontological principles provide a framework and context for the development of a socio–politico–economic ontology of the possible. This ontological framework is grounded in a new eco–humanism, at the root of which is awareness of the spiritual reality of existence. A corollary of this is the need for economic principles to be grounded in spiritual values that express the fundamental interconnectedness of all realms of being.

A deep understanding of the interconnectedness of all existence is not only fundamental to indigenous ontologies but has been empirically demonstrated in the studies of leading quantum physicists such as David Bohm. In common with indigenous peoples, the ancient Stoics and many other groups, Bohm understood that existence was to be seen as 'undivided wholeness'.[28] Hannah Arendt also understood this concept of oneness; however, for her, cooperation without boundaries leads to unity based on sameness, a model that she rightly rejected. Hardt and Negri's model of cooperation is based on the hybridity and flexibility of a multitude joined together in a joyous movement of constituent power that Passavant and Dean refer to as 'self-organized democracy'.[29] Neither of these models fully expresses the knowledge of interconnectedness that lies at the heart of indigenous ontologies. Deleuze's expression of immanence, as recounted by Passavant, perhaps comes closest of all when he writes of 'Being as multiple multiplicities', of 'members of an infinite number of sets of attributes', of 'multiple voices raised in a clamour' in which 'Being is in common' and in which 'this multiplicity is joined together in common through this clamour'.[30]

There can be no doubt that to secure survival for ourselves as well as the rapidly diminishing lifeforms on this planet we require an urgent revisioning of the way in which we understand the past, present and future, of the way in which we view relationships, and, in particular, of the form and shape of a new global order. In the first chapter, I offered the double spiral as a metaphor for transformation. This metaphor is grounded in a Waitaha perspective of the meaning of being and yet is common to many other ancient traditions. The double spiral motif of ancient peoples represents a deep understanding of chaos as potentiality and of coming into being. It represents the minute shift at the centre that transforms the whole. Skolimowski calls this 'participatory reality'.[31] The double spiral is an expanding dialectic spiral, a spiral of transformation that encapsulates the past as constitutive of the present and future and that encompasses the totality of our shared human experience and relationships across all levels of existence. It represents the dialectic between the material and spiritual spheres; the bringing forth from the past that which will transform the future. In that sense, it is a metaphor also for the way in which I have approached this work.

For me as for Szaszy, the 'new humanism' required today and in the future is one that brings forth into the future the ancient values of our traditional past and rearticulates them in a contemporary context. The nature and urgency of this project for a new humanism is what I have endeavoured to demonstrate. Schell suggests that transformation through the power of collective action grounded in the principles of love and freedom need not be a spiritual project, although he acknowledges that it can be. It originates, he writes, in 'the heart and mind of each ordinary person'.

I follow Schell in advocating revolution in the hearts and minds of the ordinary person. I contend also, however, that without a fuller understanding of the interrelationships between the material and spiritual worlds and between the human and ecological spheres, and without an embedding of these understandings at the heart of our socio-politico-economic structures, efforts at just models of governance are doomed to failure. The development of a just political and economic framework for global well-being involves matching the outward exploration of existence with an inward exploration of the meaning of being, of the nature of being human and of the purpose of existence. It requires the reframing of scientific capacities for creation and recreation within a paradigm of the interconnectedness of the material and spiritual worlds, of pre-existence, emergence and the fulfilment of potential. It involves coming to terms with the spiritual reality of our collective existence. It requires the embedding of these principles as the cornerstone of a pluralistic social, political, economic and educational framework for global justice and well-being.

The transformation of hearts and minds that is called for in this critical timespace is surely one of spirit. The development of a just global order requires nothing less.

Notes

1   Song of Waitaha. *The Histories of a Nation.* Christchurch: Wharaiki Publishing, p. 15.
2   Cox Robert W. (1996) [1993] 'Production and security' in Robert W. Cox (with Timothy J. Sinclair), *Approaches to World Order.* Cambridge: Cambridge University Press, p. 293.
3   *Ibid.*
4   Palast, Greg (2001) 'The theft of the Presidency', on BBC-TV Newsnight, 15 February 2001, accessed 28 February 2001 at http://www.gregpalast.com/detail.cfm?artid=29&row=1
5   Schell, Jonathan (2003) *The Unconquerable World: Power, Nonviolence, and the Will of the People.* New York: Metropolitan, p. 345.
6   Bacon, Francis. *Works* (1857). James Spalding, Robert Ellis, and Donald Heath (eds). London: Longman and Co., Vol. 1: pp. 129–30, cited in Hardt, Michael and Antonio Negri (2000) *Empire.* Cambridge, MA: Harvard University Press, p. 72 (see note 7, p. 429).
7   *Ibid.*, p. 73.

8 *Ibid.*, p. 75.
9 *Ibid.*, p. 74.
10 Foucault, Michel (1980) 'Two lectures', in C. Gordon (ed.), *Power/Knowledge. Selected Interviews and Other Writings 1972–1977.* New York and London: Harvester Wheatsheaf, pp. 78–108.
11 *Ibid.*, p. 93
12 *Ibid.*, p. 95.
13 Schell (2003), p. 332.
14 *Ibid.*, p. 354.
15 Hardt and Negri (2000) p. 386.
16 Kymlicka, W. (2000) 'American Multiculturalism and the "nations within"', in Duncan Ivison, Paul Patton and Will Sanders (eds.), *Political Theory and the Rights of Indigenous Peoples.* Cambridge: Cambridge University Press, p. 234.
17 *Ibid.*, p. 231.
18 *Ibid.*, p. 227.
19 Carens, Joseph H. (2000) *Culture, Citizenship, and Community. A Contextual Exploration of Justice as Evenhandedness.* Oxford and New York: Oxford University Press.
20 Schell (2003), p. 349.
21 *Ibid.*, p. 366.
22 Young, Iris Marion (2000) 'Hybrid democracy: Iroquois federalism and postcolonial project', in Ivison *et al.*, p. 237.
23 Schell (2003), pp. 350–1.
24 Cited Wilmer, Franke (1993) *The Indigenous Voice in World Politics. Since Time Immemorial.* London and New Delhi: Sage, p. 205.
25 Senghor, Leopold Sédar (1970) 'Negritude: a humanism of the twentieth century', in *The Africa Reader: Independent Africa.* London: Vintage, Random Century, reprinted in Laura Chrisman and Patrick Williams (eds.) (1993), *Colonial Discourse and Post-Colonial Theory.* London and New York: Harvester Wheatsheaf, pp. 27–35.
26 Hardt and Negri (2000), p. 388.
27 Szaszy, Mira (1993) 'Seek the seeds for the greatest good of all people'. Address given at the Maori Graduands Capping Ceremony, Victoria University of Wellington, 27 April.
28 Bohm, David (1980) *Wholeness and the Implicate Order.* London and Boston: Routledge and Kegan Paul, p. 11.
29 Passavant, Paul A. (2004) 'Introduction: postmodern republicanism', in Paul Pssavant and Jodi Dean (eds.), *Empire's New Clothes. Reading Hardt and Negri.* New York and London: Routledge, p. 11.
30 Deleuze, Gilles (2001) 'Immanence: A Life', in *Pure Immanence: Essays on a Life* [trans. Anne Boyman] New York: Zone Books, p. 27., cited in *ibid.*
31 Skolimowski, Henryk (1994) *The Participatory Mind. A New Theory of Knowledge and of the Universe.* London: Arkana.
32 Schell (2003), p. 387.

EPILOGUE

❀

Writing as Politics

The struggle of Maori during the twenty-first century repeatedly intersects with and contests the agenda of global capitalism. It has become an integral part of Maori social, political, cultural and economic life. For this reason, it is impossible for Maori academics endeavouring to articulate these issues in a theoretically and politically meaningful way to stand apart from or outside of these struggles. The struggle of some is the struggle of us all. This meant that it was impossible to write the results of my research without at the same time 'writing' myself.

Linda Smith comments that the challenge to place 'our' own histories, understandings, and experiences at the centre of our writing is one that is frequently articulated not only by Maori but also by other writers within the categories of 'indigenous', 'Third World', 'of colour' and otherwise marginal.[1] One of the dilemmas faced by Maori women writers and academics is the fact that, as T. Minh-ha Trinh points out, 'imputing race or sex to the creative act has long been a means by which the literary establishment cheapens and discredits the achievements of non-mainstream writers'.[2] Writing about the 'growing ethnic–feminist consciousness', which has not only made it more difficult for woman writers of colour to 'turn a blind eye to the specification of the writer as historical subject' but also problematized 'writing itself as a practice located at the intersection of subject and history', Trinh refers to the 'triple bind' of women writers of colour, which is that, no matter what position she takes, she will eventually be 'made to feel she must choose from among three conflicting loyalties. Writer of colour? Woman writer? Or woman of colour?'[3]

254

This issue sits at the heart of the dilemma with which Maori academic women writers are faced.[4] As whom do we write, and for whom? Do we write as an academic, as woman, as Maori – or as all three? In the contemporary climate of tensions concerning issues of national and ethnic identity, Maori writers are often attacked on the grounds of being either 'too Maori', and therefore somehow not sufficiently 'academic' or 'not Maori enough', and therefore not really qualified to speak, act or write from a Maori perspective. In this sense, the political act of writing as Maori leaves one exposed to attack from both sides, regardless of the position within which one chooses to locate oneself. Yet for Maori, as for other indigenous peoples and marginalized groups, the act of 'writing back' is a critical act that goes beyond resisting the continued marginalization of *kaupapa* Maori as a vital, dynamic and legitimate knowledge base, to the reclaiming of Maori ways of being and knowing as vitally meaningful and relevant in today's world. Thus, as Linda Smith states, for many Maori women, writing as 'Maori woman academic' becomes simultaneously an act of resistance and reclamation. For myself, the decision to write as Maori despite the fact of also being half-Scots reflects my commitment to a value system that is deeply embedded in the land in which I grew up, a value system that has been undermined by both the divide-and-rule tactics of a state-imposed treaty settlement process and the imposition of a set of norms that measures success in terms of the free market and knowledge by its monetary value.

Of Existence and Being

The research for this work was driven by an accelerating sense of crisis in the world, in the political, economic and social structures that support our various societies, in the fragility of the biosphere and loss of biodiversity, and in the nature of the ideologies that maintain our policies and practices. Many of the choices that we continue to make at multiple levels exacerbate that crisis. There are many reasons behind these choices - one that predominates in the discourse is that of inevitability. It is this sense of inevitability as well as its ontological underpinnings that I have sought to challenge.

Conceptualizations of the future are inextricably bound up with particular ways of knowing and being. In this sense, conceptualizations of the future are integral to any analysis of current frameworks and to the development of alternative models for a future global order. I have argued that the ideologies that gave impetus to Western capitalist expansion represent a radical departure from the belief systems evidenced in the earliest forms of Western philosophy.[5] More importantly, in terms of the focus of this work, I maintain that the dominant ideologies of global capitalism are antithetical to the traditional epistemologies and ontologies of Maori as well as those of many other traditional peoples. Such fundamental differences are reflected in the tensions and contestations that epitomize the relationship between the structures of global capitalism and indigenous peoples today. They are demonstrated in the disjuncture between indigenous peoples' social, cultural and political aspirations and the emerging global system of the twenty-first century.

The mounting volume of evidence recounted in a multitude of reports strengthened my conviction that the critical issue for indigenous peoples is that of our contribution towards a saner, truly sustainable, inclusive, socially just and spiritually informed framework for our collective global existence. In this sense, the most important function of this book is to argue for a recovery of the sacred, of the awareness of the interconnectedness of all the parts within the whole, and the recognition that this interconnectedness includes *all* beings. And to argue that at least part of the solution to the crisis of our coexistence is to incorporate these understandings into the cosmo-political world.

It is my belief that the retrieval of ancient wisdoms is a responsibility that is shared by all indigenous women, perhaps by all women everywhere. During a conference of the Women's International League of Peace and Freedom in Tokyo in 1999, I commented:

> As a race of beings, we have lost touch with the sacred. We have lost touch with the deep spiritual essence of our 'being'ness. We need to reclaim our own histories; we need to reclaim our true reality. As more and more women are doing. More and more women are remembering that there was a time when the societies of human beings that lived on this planet, our home, were much more matriarchal in nature, when the values by which existence was ordered were based on a spirituality that connected us to Mother Earth, to each other and to the universe. Those histories are today being rediscovered, being brought forth. Indigenous women, Celtic women, the healers and the gatherers in whom the genetic memory is stored, all women everywhere are re-membering, re-envisioning, re-weaving, re-turning the ancient knowledge, the ancient epistemologies towards the re-construction of a different political and economic paradigm for coexistence.[6]

This work represents a minute attempt in this direction. Speaking at the University of Alberta, Nobel Peace Prize Laureate Shirin Ebadi, the first Muslim woman to win the Nobel Prize (2003), a truly inspiring and courageous woman who was imprisoned in Iran for her beliefs and her passion for justice, stated: 'It is not *who* governs that is important, what is important is *how* we govern'.[7] There is, indeed, nothing that requires our urgent attention more.

Notes

1   Smith, Linda Tuhiwai (1999) *Decolonizing Methodologies: Research and Indigenous Peoples*. London and New York: Zed Books; Dunedin: Otago University Press, p. 19.
2   Minh-ha Trinh, T. (1989) *Woman, Native, Other: Writing Postcoloniality and Feminism*. Bloomington: Indiana University Press, p. 3.
3   *Ibid.*
4   See, for instance, Smith, Linda Tuhiwai (1992) 'Maori women: discourses, projects and *mana wahine*', in Sue Middleton and Alison Jones (eds.), *Women and Education in Aotearoa 2*. Wellington: Bridget Williams Books; Johnston, Patricia and Leonie Pihama (1994) 'The marginalization of Maori women', *Hecate*, 20 (2), pp. 83–97.
5   See discussion in Chapter 2, pp. 78–81.
6   Harawira, Makere (1999) 'Women and economic globalization in New Zealand'. Presentation at the Consultation of the Women's International League for Peace and Freedom, 'Women Meeting the Challenge of Economic Globalisation'. Tokyo, 18–22 October.
7   Ebadi, Shirin (2004) Visiting Lecture on Human Rights, University of Alberta, Canada, 21 October. In 1975, Dr Shirin Ebadi became the first woman to be President of the Teheran City Court in Iran. As a consequence of her work and her commitment to justice, she routinely faces threats to her life.

INDEX

Aboriginal people (Australia) 127-8, 131, 137
Académie des Sciences 45, 64
accountability 102, 145, 169
Afghanistan 135, 158, 223, 238
Africa 39, 41, 74-6, 106-7, 148, 216 ; Scramble for 74-5
Agreement Governing Activities of States on the Moon (1979) 161
agriculture 64, 102, 124, 210
aid 105, 167-8, 179, 183-4
AIDS 216
Algiers, Treaty of (1913) 75
American Convention on Human Rights 136
Americas 1, 58-60, 66-7, 115, 218; Central America 59, 170; North America 165, 178, 192; South America 59, 106
Amoco 164
Annan, Kofi 18, 168-9
Anti-Ballistic Missile Agreement 3
anti-globalization movement 172
apartheid, global 170, 222
Aquinas, Thomas 44
Arbitration Treaty (1911) 91
Arendt, Hannah 244, 248
Aristotle 44, 59
Armitage, Richard 223
Asia 7, 18, 105, 148, 164, 171, 178-84, 223, 229; Central 5, 223; East 171, 178, 182, 184, 229; South-east 164, 178, 183

Asian tigers 184
Asia-Pacific Economic Cooperation (APEC) 165, 179, 184-6, 189-90
Asia-Pacific region 13, 179-84
Association of South-East Asian Nations (ASEAN) 184
Atlantic Charter 95, 99
Australia 17, 61, 78, 96, 99, 110n, 127-8, 179, 185
Austria 103
Austro-Hungarian Empire 73, 120

Bacon, Francis 25, 44, 64, 100, 239
Balfour, Lord 75
Bandung Conference (1955) 148
Banks, Joseph 64
Basel, Treaty of (1795) 2
Berger, Samuel 4
Berlin Wall 90
Berlin, Treaty of (1885) 75
Bilbo 128
biodiversity 17, 36, 162, 214-15, 253; Convention on Biodiversity (CBD) 162, 215, 217
Biological and Toxins Weapons Convention 3
biopiracy 216
biopolitics 229, 231
biopower 27, 80, 220-1, 229, 231
biotechnology 58, 212-14
black Americans 228